DATE DUE

3-22-02			

Demco, Inc. 38-293

THE 1960s
CULTURAL
REVOLUTION

**Other Titles in the Greenwood Press Guides
to Historic Events of the Twentieth Century**
Randall M. Miller, Series Editor

The Persian Gulf Crisis
Steve A. Yetiv

World War I
Neil M. Heyman

The Civil Rights Movement
Peter B. Levy

The Breakup of Yugoslavia and the
War in Bosnia
Carole Rogel

Islamic Fundamentalism
Lawrence Davidson

Frontiers in Space Exploration
Roger D. Launius

The Collapse of Communism in the
Soviet Union
William E. Watson

Origins and Development of the
Arab-Israeli Conflict
Ann M. Lesch and Dan Tschirgi

The Rise of Fascism in Europe
George P. Blum

The Cold War
Katherine A. S. Sibley

The War in Vietnam
Anthony O. Edmonds

World War II
Loyd E. Lee

The Unification of Germany,
1989–1990
Richard A. Leiby

The Environmental Crisis
Miguel A. Santos

Castro and the Cuban Revolution
Thomas M. Leonard

The End of Apartheid in South Africa
Lindsay Michie Eades

The Korean Conflict
Burton I. Kaufman

The Watergate Crisis
Michael A. Genovese

The Chinese Revolution
Edward J. Lazzerini

The Women's Liberation Movement
in America
Kathleen Berkeley

THE 1960s CULTURAL REVOLUTION

John C. McWilliams

Greenwood Press Guides to
Historic Events of the Twentieth Century
Randall M. Miller, Series Editor

Greenwood Press
Westport, Connecticut • London

Library of Congress Cataloging-in-Publication Data

McWilliams, John C., 1949–
    The 1960s cultural revolution / John C. McWilliams.
        p.   cm.—(Greenwood Press Guides to historic events of the twentieth century,
    ISSN 1092–177X)
    Includes bibliographical references (p.   ) and index.
    ISBN 0–313–29913–7 (alk. paper)
    1. United States—History—1961–1969.   2. United States—Civilization—1945–
3. Nineteen sixties.   4. United States—Social conditions—1960–1980.
5. Subculture—United States—History—20th century.   I. Title.   II. Series.
E841.M37   2000
973.92—dc21   99–058963

British Library Cataloguing in Publication Data is available.

Library of Congress Catalog Card Number: 99–058963
ISBN: 0–313–29913–7
ISSN: 1092–177X

First published in 2000

Greenwood Press, 88 Post Road West, Westport, CT 06881
An imprint of Greenwood Publishing Group, Inc.
www.greenwood.com

Printed in the United States of America

The paper used in this book complies with the
Permanent Paper Standard issued by the National
Information Standards Organization (Z39.48–1984).

10 9 8 7 6 5 4 3 2 1

Copyright Acknowledgments

The author and publisher gratefully acknowledge permission for use of the following material:

From Mary O. Bradley, "Stories of the Century," *The Harrisburg (Pennsylvania) Patriot-News*.

From *Takin' It to the Streets* by Alexander Bloom and Wini Breines, eds. (Oxford University Press, 1995).

From *From Camelot to Kent State* by Joan Morrison and Robert K. Morrison. Copyright © 1987 by Joan Morrison and Robert K. Morrison. Reprinted by permission of Random House, Inc.

Except where noted the photographs in this book are reprinted by permission from AP/Wide World Photos.

Every reasonable effort has been made to trace the owners of copyright materials in this book, but in some cases this has proven impossible. The author and publisher will be glad to receive information leading to more complete acknowledgments in subsequent printings of the book and in the meantime extend their apologies for any omissions.

Contents

A photo essay follows page 82

Series Foreword

As the twenty-first century opens, it is time to take stock of the political, social, economic, intellectual, and cultural forces and factors that made the twentieth century the most dramatic period of change in history. To that end, the Greenwood Press Guides to Historic Events of the Twentieth Century presents interpretive histories of the most significant events of the century. Each book in the series combines narrative history and analysis with primary documents and biographical sketches, with an eye to providing both a reference guide to the principal persons, ideas, and experiences defining each historic event, and a reliable, readable overview of that event. Each book provides analyses and discussions, grounded in both primary and secondary sources, of the causes and consequences, in thought and action, that give meaning to the historic event under review. By assuming a historical perspective, drawing on the latest and best writing on each subject, and offering fresh insights, each book promises to explain how and why a particular event defined the twentieth century. No consensus about the meaning of the twentieth century emerges from the series, but, collectively, the books identify the most salient concerns of the century. In so doing, the series reminds us of the many ways those historic events continue to affect our lives.

Each book follows a similar format designed to encourage readers to consult it as both a reference and a history in its own right. Each volume opens with a chronology of the historic event, followed by a narrative overview, which also serves to introduce and examine briefly the main themes and issues related to that event. The next set of chapters is composed of topical essays, each analyzing closely an issue or problem of interpretation introduced in the opening chapter. A concluding chapter suggesting the long-term implications and meanings of the historic event brings the strands of the preceding chapters together while placing the event in the larger historical context. Each book also includes a section of short biographies of the principal persons related to the event, followed by a section introducing and reprinting key historical documents illustrative of and pertinent to the event. A glossary of selected terms adds to the utility of each book. An annotated bibliography—of significant books, films, and CD-ROMs—and an index conclude each volume.

The editors made no attempt to impose any theoretical model or historical perspective on the individual authors. Rather, in developing the series, an advisory board of noted historians and informed high school history teachers and public and school librarians identified the topics needful of exploration and the scholars eminently qualified to examine those events with intelligence and sensitivity. The common commitment throughout the series is to provide accurate, informative, and readable books, free of jargon and up to date in evidence and analysis.

Each book stands as a complete historical analysis and reference guide to a particular historic event. Each book also has many uses, from understanding contemporary perspectives on critical historical issues, to providing biographical treatments of key figures related to each event, to offering excerpts and complete texts of essential documents about the event, to suggesting and describing books and media materials for further study and presentation of the event, and more. The combination of historical narrative and individual topical chapters addressing significant issues and problems encourages students and teachers to approach each historic event from multiple perspectives and with a critical eye. The arrangement and content of each book thus invite students and teachers, through classroom discussions and position papers, to debate the character and significance of great historic events and to discover for themselves how and why history matters.

The series emphasizes the main currents that have shaped the modern world. Much of that focus necessarily looks at the West, especially Europe and the United States. The political, commercial, and cultural expansion of the West wrought largely, though not wholly, the most fundamental changes of the century. Taken together, however, books in the series reveal the interactions between Western and non-Western peoples and society, and also the tensions between modern and traditional cultures. They also point to the ways in which non-Western peoples have adapted Western ideas and technology and, in turn, influenced Western life and thought. Several books examine such increasingly powerful global forces as the rise of Islamic fundamentalism, the emergence of modern Japan, the Communist revolution in China, and the collapse of communism in eastern Europe and the former Soviet Union. American interests and experiences receive special attention in the series, not only in deference to the primary readership of the books but also in recognition that the United States emerged as the dominant political economic, social, and cultural force during the twentieth century. By looking at the century through the lens of American events and experiences, it is possible to see why the age has come to be known as "The American Century."

Assessing the history of the twentieth century is a formidable prospect. It has been a period of remarkable transformation. The world broadened and narrowed at the same time. Frontiers shifted from the interiors of Africa and Latin America to the moon and beyond; communication spread from mass circulation newspapers and magazines to radio, television, and now the Internet; skyscrapers reached upward and suburbs stretched outward; energy switched from steam, to electric, to atomic power. Many changes did not lead to a complete abandonment of established patterns and practices so much as a synthesis of old and new, as, for example, the increased use of (even reliance on) the telephone in the age of the computer. The automobile and the truck, the airplane, and telecommunications closed distances, and people in unprecedented numbers migrated from rural to urban, industrial, and ever more ethnically diverse areas. Tractors and chemical fertilizers made it possible for fewer people to grow more, but the environmental and demographic costs of an exploding global population threatened to outstrip natural resources and human innovation. Disparities in wealth increased, with developed nations prospering and underdeveloped nations starving. Amid the crumbling of former European colonial empires, Western technology, goods, and culture increasingly enveloped the globe, seeping into, and undermining, non-Western cultures—a process that contributed to a surge of religious fundamentalism and ethno-nationalism in the Middle East, Asia, and Africa. As people became more alike, they also became more aware of their differences. Ethnic and religious rivalries grew in intensity everywhere as the century closed.

The political changes during the twentieth century have been no less profound than the social, economic, and cultural ones. Many of the books in the series focus on political events, broadly defined, but no books are confined to politics alone. Political ideas and events have social effects, just as they spring from a complex interplay of non-political forces in culture, society, and economy. Thus, for example, the modern civil rights and woman's rights movements were at once social and political events in cause and consequence. Likewise, the Cold War created the geopolitical framework for dealing with competing ideologies and nations abroad and served as the touchstone for political and cultural identities at home. The books treating political events do so within their social, cultural, and economic contexts.

Several books in the series examine particular wars in depth. Wars are defining moments for people and eras. During the twentieth century war became more widespread and terrible than ever before, encouraging new efforts to end war through strategies and organizations of international cooperation and disarmament while also fueling new ideologies and instruments of mass persuasion that fostered distrust and festered old national rivalries. Two world wars during the century redrew the political map, slaughtered or uprooted two generations of people, and introduced and hastened the development of new technologies and weapons of mass destruction. The First World War spelled the end of the old European order and spurred communist revolution in Russia and fascism in Italy, Germany, and elsewhere. The Second World War killed fascism and inspired the final push for freedom from European colonial rule in Asia and Africa. It also led to the Cold War that suffocated much of the world for almost half a century. Large wars begat small ones, and brutal totalitarian regimes cropped up across the globe. After (and in some ways because of) the fall of communism in eastern Europe and the former Soviet Union, wars of competing cultures, national interests, and political systems persisted in the struggle to make a new world order. Continuing, too, has been the belief that military technology can achieve political ends, whether in the superior American firepower that failed to "win" in Vietnam or in the American "smart bombs" and other military wizardry that "won" in the Persian Gulf.

Another theme evident in the series is that throughout the century nationalism has continued to drive events. Whether in the Balkans in 1914 triggering World War I or in the Balkans in the 1990s threatening the post–Cold War peace—or in many other places—nationalist ambitions and forces would not die. The persistence of nationalism is yet another reminder of the many ways that the past becomes prologue.

We thus offer the series as a modern guide to and interpretation of the historic events of the twentieth century and as an invitation to consider how and why those events have defined not only the past and present but also charted the political, social, intellectual, cultural, and economic routes into this century.

Randall M. Miller
Saint Joseph's University, Philadelphia

Preface

The sixties. Few eras in American history evoke such diverse and conflicting images of the human experience. The sixties rarely fail to conjure up recollections of outrageous behavior, rebellion, anti-authoritarianism, and social and sexual experimentation—in short, a world turned upside down. Freedom Riders, Free Speech, and Freedom Summer. Teach-ins, "be-ins," and "love-ins." March to Selma or March on the Pentagon. We could drop out or sit in. Little wonder that our knowledge and comprehension of the "real" sixties are so muddled. Sometimes when I think about how anguish and anxiety coexisted with "peace and love" in the 1960s, I wonder if history was winking at us. Not that the sixties were all ballyhoo years. Surely much of what happened was very serious, as were the people and events who shaped the era, but certain events nearly defied credibility.

We are now because of what we were then. That is, an individual is the sum product of cumulative experiences. As one of the original baby boomers (born between 1945 and 1950), I am a product of the 1960s. My coming of age occurred during one of the most eventful, volatile, and sometimes terrifying eras in American history. And I missed it. At least it feels that way. I lived through it, but I—like most of my fellow boomers, I suspect—was not attuned to the day's headlines and certainly not actively involved in the day's events. I was mostly oblivious to the "Negro problem" in Mississippi, the discriminatory inconsistencies of the draft, and the three days of "peace and music" at Woodstock. Growing up in a small town in north-central Pennsylvania, I lived in a quasi-cultural vacuum, safely tucked away and insulated from real-world problems. I could identify Roger Maris, Mickey

Mantle, and Yogi Berra by the way they approached home plate, but I would not have recognized Tom Hayden, Stokely Carmichael, or Robert S. McNamara on a bet. I could sing along with almost every Top Forty hit, but I was ignorant about Hayden's *Port Huron Statement*, Martin Luther King, Jr.'s "I Have a Dream" speech, or President Lyndon B. Johnson's nationally televised address in March 1968, announcing he would not run for reelection. Four months after LBJ conceded that Vietnam had gotten out of hand, I was called for a pre-induction physical examination. I came this close to being drafted and likely doing a tour of duty in Vietnam. My future hung in the balance, and I was indifferent to the possibility. The war was there; I was here. Life was simple. I share this cathartic revelation with readers because my experiences—or lack of them—were more representative of my generation than the sex, drugs, rock 'n' roll label often applied to boomers in the 1960s.

More than any other event, the tragic American experience in Vietnam is how most people remember the sixties, and it is the singular event that most people use to define the decade, probably because it was one of the most tragic American experiences ever. Each time I have visited the Vietnam Memorial, at the foot of a sitting Abraham Lincoln at the end of the Mall in Washington, D.C., I am nearly mesmerized by the seemingly endless list of names emblazoned in the black marble wall. All the while I gaze over those 58,000 names, the same nagging question runs through my mind: "Why?" No matter how noble or how ignominious the rationale for American involvement in Southeast Asia, the Vietnam War polarized the nation more than any other event since the Civil War and left us with so little to show for so great a sacrifice.

Perhaps because it was such a chaotic time, the 1960s have been overstated and underrated. They have been glorified and debunked. However we might view the 1960s, there is little question that the decade left an indelible cultural imprint not yet expunged. The sixties were a kaleidoscope of events—contentious and complicated, occasionally ordinary, but rarely mundane.

Three distinct movements—the New Left, the antiwar movement, and the counterculture—which are the focus of this book, define and, I hope, dramatize the cultural revolution that was the 1960s for readers unfamiliar with the decade as well as those who recognize passages as part of their past. The purpose of this study is to provide a balanced, objective account of events and the people who shaped the sixties.

Seldom has an era been simultaneously exaggerated and oversimplified, reviled and revered. The sixties. History in motion. At warp speed. We may never be the same.

Acknowledgments

Many people contributed in different ways and varying degrees to the completion of this book. The Penn State University–DuBois Campus library staff accommodated my research needs and processed hundreds of interlibrary loan requests for books and journal articles. In Terri Frutiger, I was blessed with the most capable work-study student one could hope for. She not only completed the aforementioned forms, she demonstrated uncommon resourcefulness and initiative locating sources and organizing material. She also saved me a small fortune in library fines. Mike Tharon helped tie up loose ends in the copyediting phase, and Chris Klinger transformed the primary documents into manuscript style. The campus administration facilitated my research and writing by permitting me some flexibility in my teaching schedule. Via numerous e-mail exchanges, Gary Largo, a fellow historian who teaches a 1960s course at Scottsbluff High School in Nebraska, offered insightful suggestions. Barbara Rader, my Acquisitions Editor at Greenwood Press, provided critical input along the way. And she was patient. A special thanks to Maureen Melino for her valuable assistance in securing permission to reprint documents and photographs. Few authors complete a quality book-length manuscript without a talented, accomplished editor. I am not one of them. I cannot imagine working with a more discerning, skillful, and empathetic editor than Randall M. Miller. His input enabled me to produce a better, smoother work. I thank him for inviting me to be a series contributor. Polly understood my preoccupation with the 1960s, especially as it related to our early history. Others will recognize their influence on the content. Callan always provided welcomed, unconditional support.

Chronology of Events

1946–1950

1946   The number of births in the United States is 3,411,000, an increase of nearly 600,000 from 1945 and the highest number recorded in the nation's history

1959

July 8   Two American soldiers, killed by the Vietcong at Bienhoa, are the first Americans to die in Vietnam during this era; by the end of the year, there will be 760 U.S. military personnel in Vietnam

1960

January 24   "Running Bear," by Johnny Preston tops song pop chart

February 16   Four black students at North Carolina A&T College in Greensboro stage first lunch counter sit-in at local Woolworth's store

February 28   "Theme from *A Summer Place*" replaces "Teen Angel" as number-one hit song

March 20   Paul Anka's "Puppy Love" number-one hit

                  The U.S. Army discharges Elvis Presley

May 9   Food and Drug Administration approves first public sale of birth control pills

May 13   San Francisco police battle student protesters outside House Un-American Activities Committee hearings

May 29	Everly Brothers have number-one hit song with "Cathy's Clown"
August 14	"Itsy Bitsy Teeny-Weeny Yellow Polkadot Bikini" number-one hit song
October 3	*The Andy Griffith Show* makes its television debut
November 8	John F. Kennedy and Lyndon B. Johnson defeat Richard M. Nixon and Henry Cabot Lodge in the closest presidential election since 1884
November 25	Last radio soap opera leaves the air

1961

January 3	United States breaks diplomatic relations with Cuba
January 20	President John F. Kennedy challenges the nation in his inaugural speech to "ask not what your country can do for you, ask what you can do for your country."
January 30	The Shirelles are the first female rock 'n' roll group to have a number-one song hit, "Will You Still Love Me Tomorrow?"
February 19	Lawrence Welk's "Calcutta" is the number-one hit song
March 1	Mattel introduces a boyfriend named "Ken" as a companion for its doll "Barbie"
March 1	President Kennedy creates the Peace Corps with an executive order; 13,000 young Americans apply as volunteers over the next six months
March 29	The Twenty-third Amendment to the Constitution, giving Washington, D.C., three electoral votes, is ratified
April 17	About 1,500 CIA-trained Cuban rebels make a disastrous attempt to invade Cuba at the Bay of Pigs
April 29	President Kennedy sends another 100 American military advisers and 400 Special Forces troops to South Vietnam
April 30	Del Shannon has number-one hit song with "Runaway"
May 4	Two busloads of Freedom Riders leave Washington, D.C., for New Orleans to protest segregated bus facilities; in Anniston, Alabama, a bomb hospitalizes twelve passengers
May 5	Alan B. Shepard makes a successful fifteen-minute flight in the *Mercury* capsule, reaching an altitude of 116.5 miles in a 302-mile suborbital arc; said he had "about 30 seconds to look out the window"
May 9	Federal Communications Commission chairman Newton Minow describes television programming as a "vast wasteland"

July 16	Number one-hit song is Bobby Freeman's "Tossin' and Turnin' "
August 13	The Soviet Union and East Germany begin erecting a wooden and barbed-wire fence along the 25-mile border between East and West Berlin; within three days they will build the Berlin Wall, sealing off access from East Berlin to West Berlin
September 24	"Take Good Care of My Baby," by Bobby Vee is number-one hit song
	The Rocky and Bullwinkle Show makes its television premiere
October 1	Roger Maris hits a record-breaking sixty-first home run
	Mr. Ed premiers on television
October 2	*The Dick Van Dyke Show* makes its television debut
October 29	Dion's "Runaround Sue" is number-one hit song
November 3	Advisers recommend that President Kennedy increase military aid and commit 6,000 to 8,000 troops to South Vietnam
December 11	President Kennedy sends 400 helicopter crewmen, the first military personnel, to South Vietnam
December 14	President Kennedy establishes the President's Commission on the Status of Women, headed by Eleanor Roosevelt
December 24	The Tokens have the number-one hit song with "The Lion Sleeps Tonight"
	The postwar baby boom crests with a record 4.27 million births
	Coca-Cola introduces the no-return glass bottle

1962

January 1	Chubby Checker sparks new dance craze with "The Twist"
January 11	President Kennedy announces that American noncombat troops in Vietnam have orders to fire if fired upon
February 17	"Duke of Earl," by Gene Chandler is the number-one hit song
February 20	John H. Glenn, Jr., is the first American astronaut to orbit the earth, circling it three times
March 9	Pentagon verifies reports that American pilots are flying combat missions in Vietnam
March 15	Secretary of Defense Robert J. McNamara confirms that American soldiers are exchanging fire with the Vietcong

April 7   "Johnny Angel," by Shelley Fabares takes over the
                   number-one chart spot

May 23   *Cosmopolitan* editor Helen Gurley Brown publishes *Sex
                   and the Single Girl*

June 2   Ray Charles has number-one hit song with "I Can't Stop
                   Loving You"

June 11–15   Students for a Democratic Society hold national convention
                   at Port Huron, Michigan

June 25   In *Engel v. Vitale* Supreme Court decides, 6–1, that prayer
                   in public schools is unconstitutional

August 5   Actress Marilyn Monroe dies from an alleged massive
                   overdose of sleeping pills

August 11   Neil Sedaka's "Breaking Up Is Hard to Do" is number-one
                   hit song

September 15   Four Seasons debut with number-one hit song "Sherry"

September 26   *Beverly Hillbillies* makes television premiere

September 30   Cesar Chávez founds United Farm Workers union

October 1   After riots that resulted in two deaths and hundreds of
                   injuries, James Meredith is the first black student to attend
                   the University of Mississippi under federal guard

October 2   *The Tonight Show Starring Johnny Carson* premieres

October 15   American pilots in Vietnam shoot first despite orders to fire
                   only in defense

October 20   "Monster Mash," by Bobby Boris Pickett and the
                   Crypt-Kickers is number-one hit song

October 28   Soviets back down from U.S. blockade of Cuba to end the
                   missile crisis

November 3   "He's a Rebel" by the Crystals is the number-one hit song

November 5   Rachel Carson's *Silent Spring*, alerting the nation to the
                   dangers of pesticides, heads the nonfiction list

November 7   After losing the California gubernatorial race, Richard
                   Nixon tells reporters, "You won't have Dick Nixon to kick
                   around anymore"

November 17   Dulles Airport in Washington, D.C., the first airport
                   designed for jets in the United States, opens

December 23–24 The last of the Bay of Pigs survivors are ransomed from Castro

December 31   Reports confirm 11,000 American advisers and technicians
                   are aiding South Vietnam

December 31	The Volkswagen Beetle accounts for 192,570 of the 339,160 cars imported into the United States
	Royal Crown Cola sells the first sugar-free cola; *Coca-Cola* introduces *Sprite*

1963

January 2	United Press International reports that thirty Americans have been killed in Vietnam combat
January 7	A first-class stamp costs five cents
January 11	Whiskey-a-Go-Go in Los Angeles is the nation's first discotheque
February 9	"Hey Paula" by Paul and Paula is number-one hit song
February 19	Betty Friedan publishes *The Feminine Mystique*, a critique of the cultural, social, and economic limits imposed on middle-class women
March 1	Civil rights groups conduct Mississippi voter-registration drive
March 18	Supreme Court rules that indigents are entitled to free counsel in *Clarence v. Gideon*
March 30	Chiffons have the number-one hit song with "He's So Fine"
April 12	Martin Luther King, Jr., is arrested after leading assault against segregation in Alabama, where he writes "Letter from a Birmingham Jail"
April 27	Little Peggy March has number-one song hit, "I Will Follow Him"
April–September	Demonstrations against discrimination in schools, employment, and housing are held throughout the country; nearly 14,000 persons are arrested in seventy-five southern cities
May 4	The Beach Boys' "Surfin' U.S.A." enters chart
May 27	Harvard University fires research psychologists Richard Alpert and Timothy Leary for experimenting with LSD
May 29	*Dr. No*, the first James Bond film, debuts
June 1	Leslie Gore has the number-one hit song, "It's My Party"
June 11	Buddhist monk dies from self-immolation protesting religious persecution in South Vietnam
	During his swearing-in ceremony, Alabama Governor George Wallace pledges "segregation now, segregation tomorrow, segregation forever"

June 12	Medgar Evers, field secretary for the National Association for the Advancement of Colored People in Mississippi, is murdered entering his home in Jackson; two trials end in hung juries
June 29	Peter, Paul, and Mary record Bob Dylan's antiwar anthem, "Blowin' in the Wind"
July 1	Five-digit postal zip code goes into effect
July 20	Jan and Dean's "Surf City" leads pop chart
August 28	Martin Luther King, Jr., delivers "I Have a Dream" speech before a crowd of 200,000 to conclude the March on Washington
August 30	Hot-line between Soviet Union and the United States is installed
August 31	The Angels' "My Boyfriend's Back" is the number-one hit song
September 15	Four young girls killed when the 16th Street Baptist Church is bombed in Birmingham, Alabama; the bomber has never been apprehended
September 17	*The Fugitive* makes its television premiere
September 27	CBS televises mafiosi Joe Valachi's testimony about mob activities before Senator John McClellan's Permanent Investigations Subcommittee
October 12	Jimmy Gilmore and the Fireballs have the number-one hit song, "Sugar Shack"
November 2	With the CIA's knowledge, South Vietnamese President Ngo Dinh Diem and his brother are killed in a coup
November 20	American military personnel in Vietnam number 16,800
November 22	President Kennedy is assassinated in Dallas, Texas; Lee Harvey Oswald is charged
November 24	Jack Ruby kills Oswald
November 29	Newly sworn-in President Lyndon B. Johnson appoints commission headed by Chief Justice Earl Warren to investigate Kennedy's assassination
December 7	The Kingsmen's "Louie, Louie" is the number-one hit song
December 30	*Let's Make a Deal* makes its television debut

1964

January 11	The U.S. Surgeon General's special committee report, *Smoking and Health*, links cigarette smoking with cancer and calls for federal regulation of cigarettes

February 4	The Twenty-fourth Amendment to the Constitution, forbidding poll or other taxes used to qualify voters in federal elections, takes effect
February 9	With "I Want to Hold Your Hand," the Beatles dominate the record charts
April 25	President Johnson appoints Lieutenant General William C. Westmoreland to replace General Paul Harkins as head of the United States Military Assistance Command in South Vietnam
	Unveiled this month at the World's Fair, the Ford Mustang breaks the sales record of 1 million during the next twelve months
June 10	After invoking a cloture to end a seventy-five-day filibuster, the Senate passes the Civil Rights Act of 1964 to ban discrimination in education, employment, and public places; President Johnson signs the bill July 2
June 21	Three civil rights workers participating in the Student Non-Violent Coordinating Committee's movement to encourage voter registration are arrested for speeding in Mississippi, held for six hours, and are not seen again; their bodies are found buried in a dam on August 4
June 24	The Federal Trade Commission announces that cigarette packages must carry a health warning label beginning in 1965
July 3	Lester Maddox, later elected governor of Georgia in January 1967 on a segregationist platform, encourages the use of axe handles against black persons entering his restaurant
July 8	Since December, American casualties in Vietnam have totaled 1,387
July 16	Rioting begins in New York City after a police officer shoots and kills a fifteen-year-old black male during a disturbance, touching off riots in many northern cities; this would be the first of several "long, hot summers"
July 27	The United States increases its troop commitment in Vietnam to 21,000
August 4	President Johnson announces on national television that the North Vietnamese have attacked two U.S. destroyers in international waters in the Gulf of Tonkin

August 7	The House of Representatives approves by a vote of 416–0 the Gulf of Tonkin Resolution, approving "all necessary measures by the president to repel any armed attack against U.S. forces"; only two members of the Senate, Wayne Morse (R–OR) and Ernest Gruening (D–AK) oppose the resolution
September 5	The Supremes have their first number-one hit song, "Where Did Our Love Go?"
September 16	Television network ABC introduces *Shindig* in response to surveys indicating that adult listeners make up a fair percentage of the "hard rock" radio audience
September 17	*Bewitched* makes its television premiere
September 26	*Gilligan's Island* makes its television debut
September 27	A special seven-member commission, headed by Chief Justice Earl Warren, unanimously concludes that Lee Harvey Oswald acted alone when he assassinated President Kennedy
October 14	At age thirty-five, Martin Luther King, Jr., is the youngest recipient of the Nobel Peace Prize for the "furtherance of brotherhood among men"
November 3	With 43.13 million votes to Republican candidate Barry Goldwater's 27.8 million votes, President Johnson wins the election by the greatest popular vote landslide in American history
December 3	The Free Speech Movement at the University of California at Berkeley ends when police arrest 796 student demonstrators
December 4	The FBI arrests twenty-one white men on conspiracy charges related to the deaths of the three civil rights workers; a week later the charges are dismissed on a technicality
	The movies *Dr. Strangelove or How I Learned to Stop Worrying and Love the Bomb* and *A Hard Day's Night* (starring the Beatles) are released

1965

January 4	In his State of the Union address, President Johnson promises a "Great Society" that will improve the quality of life for all Americans; his budget is the greatest expansion of domestic welfare programs since Franklin D. Roosevelt's New Deal

February 7	President Johnson orders the first air strike against North Vietnam in response to a Vietcong attack against the U.S. military barracks at Pleiku, which killed thirty-two Americans; two weeks later American planes begin dropping napalm, an incendiary chemical
February 21	Thirty-nine-year-old black nationalist Malcolm X is shot to death during a rally in Harlem
March 7	In Selma, Alabama, a confrontation between 200 Alabama state troopers using tear gas, whips, and nightsticks, and 525 blacks marching to protest the denial of voting rights, temporarily stops the demonstration; on March 21, after President Johnson mobilizes 4,000 troops, 25,000 people complete the march to Montgomery
March 8	The Supreme Court unanimously decides that conscientious objector status must be granted for those who believe that registering for the draft is contrary to their religious beliefs
	President Johnson sends the first American combat troops to South Vietnam; total troop count is 27,000
March 24	The first antiwar "teach-in" takes place at the University of Michigan
April 1	U.S. military personnel in Vietnam increase by 20,000
April 17	Students for a Democratic Society organize 15,000 students and others to demonstrate at the White House against American involvement in Vietnam
April 24	Wayne Fontana and the Mindbenders' "Game of Love" is the number-one song
May 4	President Johnson asks Congress to approve $700 million in addition to the $1.5 billion annual costs already appropriated for the war effort in Vietnam
May 15	Antiwar protests mark Armed Forces Day
June 19	The number-one hit song is "Wooly Bully," by Sam the Sham and the Pharaohs
July 10	The Rolling Stones have the number-one hit song, "I Can't Get No Satisfaction"
July 21	The Department of Defense reports that 503 Americans have been killed in Vietnam
July 28	President Johnson announces an increase in military personnel in Vietnam from 75,000 to 125,000, and that he will double the monthly draft quota

July 30	President Johnson signs the long-awaited Medicare bill that provides medical assistance financed through social security for persons over the age of sixty-five
August 6	President Johnson signs the Voting Rights Act of 1965
August 14	Sonny and Cher have their first hit song, "I Got You Babe"
August 11–17	During a heat wave, riots break out when police arrest a black drunken driver in the predominantly black Watts area of Los Angeles; six days of violence results in four thousand arrests, $40 million in damage, and thirty-five deaths
August 31	Congress passes a law making it a crime to burn draft cards
	The Department of Housing and Urban Development is established
September 15	*Hogan's Heroes* is a new prime-time television comedy
September 17	NBC television airs first episode of *I Spy*
September 25	The number-one hit song is Barry McGuire's "Eve of Destruction"; some radio stations ban it
October 9	The Beatles' "Yesterday" is the number-one hit song
October 15–16	Approximately 70,000 to 100,000 persons participate in weekend antiwar protests in forty cities throughout the nation
October 17	Antiwar protesters numbering 20,000 march in Washington, D.C.
November 2	A Quaker, protesting the Vietnam War, burns himself to death in front of the Pentagon
	American forces—about half of them combat troops—have increased from 20,000 to 185,000; General Westmoreland asks for more men
December 4	American troops in Vietnam total 170,000
	The post–World War II baby boom, producing over 4 million births a year since 1954, ends as the birthrate falls below 20 per 1,000
December 31	On the final day of a Christmas truce in Vietnam, President Johnson announces that since peace efforts over the past thirty-seven days have failed, the United States will resume bombing raids on North Vietnam
	By the end of this year, American casualties in Vietnam are 1,340 dead, 5,300 wounded, and approximately 150 missing or captured

December 31	First approved by the Food and Drug Administration in 1960 as an oral contraceptive, "the Pill" has become a popular adopted phrase

1966

January 1	"The Sounds of Silence" by Simon and Garfunkel is the number-one hit song
January 11	Controversy arises over the draft when student demonstrators are reclassified as 1-A, placing them at the top of the draft
February 1	LSD, a hallucinogenic drug, comes under federal regulation
February 10	The first person to burn his draft card is convicted
March 5	Barry Sadler's "The Green Beret" is the number-one hit song
March 24	The Selective Service System announces that college deferments will now be based on academic performance
April 14	About 350 persons buy ad space in the *Washington Post* declaring their refusal to pay taxes to support the Vietnam War
April 21	The U.S. combat toll in Vietnam reaches 3,047
May 1	U.S. forces fire on targets in Cambodia for the first time
	President Johnson characterizes those who oppose the war in Vietnam as "nervous Nellies," as 10,000 persons picket the White House and 63,000 have pledged not to vote for any pro–Vietnam War candidate
May 14	Black Power advocate Stokely Carmichael is elected head of the Student Non-Violent Coordinating Committee, a radical civil rights organization
June 6	A sniper shoots James Meredith, the first black student to attend the University of Mississippi in 1962, during a "pilgrimage" to Jackson, Mississippi, to show the state's black population it has nothing to fear; the Student Non-Violent Coordinating Committee, Congress of Racial Equality (CORE), and Martin Luther King's Southern Christian Leadership Conference continue the march
June 11	Secretary of Defense Robert McNamara announces that military strength in Vietnam will increase to 285,000

June 25	By a 5–4 margin in its *Miranda v. Arizona* decision, the Supreme Court decides an accused person has the right to remain silent, that an attorney can be present during police interrogation, and that an attorney will be appointed if the defendant cannot afford one
June 30	The House of Representatives' Armed Services Committee recommends lowering the draft age from twenty-two to nineteen or twenty
	Led by Betty Friedan, disillusioned delegates from the President's Commission on the Status of Women form the National Organization for Women (NOW); by fall NOW's membership will reach 300; by the end of the decade, NOW will claim 8,000 members
July	Black-white violence erupts in the slum areas of sixteen cities
August 5	After five hours of near-rioting by 4,000 whites, Martin Luther King, Jr., says he has "never seen such hate—not in Mississippi or Alabama—as I see here in Chicago"
August 13	The Lovin' Spoonful have the number-one hit song with "Summer in the City"
September 8	*That Girl* and *Star Trek* debut as prime-time television shows
September 12	*The Monkees* makes its television premiere
September 17	*Mission: Impossible* debuts on television
September 19	Timothy Leary proclaims LSD as the sacrament of his new religion
September 21	The Treasury Department reports that the Vietnam War is costing $4.2 billion a month
October 13	Congress establishes the Department of Transportation
October 15	At 320,000, American troops outnumber regular South Vietnamese troops
November 29	The mental standard for U.S. military inductees is lowered from a score of 16 to a score of 10 out of a possible score of 100
December 22	American fatalities in Vietnam number 6,407

1967

January 14	Approximately 25,000 hippies pour into Golden Gate Park to conduct the first "be-in"
	By the end of the month, 380,000 U.S. troops are in Vietnam

February 10	The Twenty-fifth Amendment to the Constitution is ratified, defining presidential succession
March 25	The Turtles' "Happy Together" is the number-one hit song
April 15	Sponsored by the Spring Mobilization Committee, the largest antiwar protests to date are held in New York (100,000–125,000) and San Francisco (75,000)
April 16	Riots break out in the black ghetto area of Cleveland, the first of 159 riots that will occur this summer
April 24	General Westmoreland criticizes the antiwar factions as "unpatriotic"
April 28	Muhammad Ali loses his heavyweight boxing title for refusing army induction
May 11	One Jackson State University student dies during rioting
May 13	In New York City 70,000 persons demonstrate in support of American military involvement in Vietnam
May 20	The Rascals' "Groovin' " is the number-one hit song
June 20	Congress gives the president the power to cancel the draft deferments of most graduate students
June 27	Critics claim that sixteen of the top forty popular songs make a positive reference to drugs or drug use
	Some New Left activists launch Vietnam Summer—modeled after the Freedom Summer program to register black voters in Mississippi—to stop the war in Vietnam
July 1	The Beatles' *Sgt. Pepper's Lonely Hearts Club Band* becomes the number-one album
July 11	Twenty-six persons are killed during a riot in Newark, New Jersey
July 23	The worst riot of this century breaks out in Detroit, where blacks, who comprise one-third of the city's population, are unemployed at double the national average; 2,000 persons are injured, almost 500 buildings are damaged or destroyed, and 43 people are killed
July 27	President Johnson appoints the Special Advisory Commission on Civil Disorders to investigate the riots in Detroit and 120 other cities
	A *Seventeen* magazine survey of 1,567 teenage girls shows that fewer than 5 percent of the respondents approve of premarital sex for couples with no intention of marrying

September 7	The United States has 464,000 troops in Vietnam
September 11	*The Carol Burnett Show* makes its television debut
September 30	President Johnson approves $20 billion for military actions in Vietnam during fiscal year 1968
October 21	In Washington, D.C., an estimated 100,000 people gather at the Lincoln Memorial to protest the war in Vietnam; about 50,000 of the demonstrators then march two miles to the Pentagon to hold a vigil
	Thousands of New Yorkers show support of American troops serving in Vietnam by driving with their headlights on
October 26	Following the draft protests, General Lewis B. Hershey, head of the Selective Service System, instructs local draft boards to cancel deferments of persons who have participated in the demonstrations
December 4–8	In response to General Hershey's directive, a coalition of some forty antiwar groups disrupt registration centers nationwide
December 15	The Federal Bureau of Narcotics reports that the number of known drug addicts has increased to almost 60,000, with about half of them between the ages of twenty-one and thirty
December 20	The number of American troops in Vietnam has increased by over 100,000 to a total of 486,000, exceeding the total number of American troops involved in the Korean War; the tonnage of bombs dropped in Vietnam exceeds the total tonnage that the United States dropped in Germany during World War II
December 31	The terms *acid rock* and *psychedelic* become part of the American vocabulary
	The death toll in Vietnam this year was 9,353, nearly 3,000 more than the previous six years combined
	The films *The Graduate, Guess Who's Coming to Dinner?* and *Bonnie and Clyde* are released

1968

January 5	Since January 1, 1961, the American death toll in Vietnam has risen to 15,997
January 22	*Rowan and Martin's Laugh-In* makes its television debut

January 30	Vietcong troops launch a surprise massive offensive during the Tet truce in South Vietnam, costing 1,110 American lives
February 8	State police fire at South Carolina State College students attempting to desegregate a local bowling alley; three persons are killed and thirty-seven wounded
February 16	Draft deferments are abolished for most graduate students
February 29	The President's National Advisory Commission on Civil Disorders (Kerner Commission) warns that massive black unemployment, unfulfilled civil rights promises, and the government's reluctance to enforce civil rights laws are pushing the country toward two "separate and unequal" societies
March 10	A Gallup poll finds that 49 percent of the respondents feel that committing American troops to Vietnam was a mistake
	General Westmoreland requests an additional 206,000 troops for Vietnam
March 12	Senator Eugene McCarthy of Minnesota wins a surprising 42 percent of the vote in the New Hampshire Democratic primary; President Johnson wins 48 percent
March 14	The number of U.S. combat deaths in Vietnam reaches 19,670
March 31	In a nationally televised speech, President Johnson, with his Gallup poll approval at a record low of 36 percent, announces that he will not seek or accept nomination for another term and that he is unilaterally ordering a halt of the bombing in North Vietnam
April 4	While supporting a strike of black garbage collectors in Memphis, Martin Luther King, Jr., is shot to death; 46 persons are killed in race riots in Washington, D.C., New York City, Chicago, Detroit, and 100 other cities
April 11	President Johnson signs the Civil Rights Act of 1968, also known as the Fair Housing Act, prohibiting racial discrimination in the sale and rental of houses and apartments
April 23	At Columbia University in New York City, 800 to 1,000 students occupy several campus buildings to protest Columbia's ties to Pentagon-funded research and the university's plans to erect a gymnasium in a low-cost housing area
April 29	The counterculture musical *Hair* opens on Broadway

May 13   The United States and North Vietnam open peace talks in Paris

May 17   Nine antiwar protesters, led by the Revs. Philip and Daniel Berrigan, burn four hundred draft records at the Selective Service headquarters in Catonsville, Maryland

June 6   Shortly after his win in the California Democratic primary, Robert F. Kennedy is assassinated in Los Angeles

June 10   General Creighton W. Abrams takes over the command of U.S. troops in Vietnam from General Westmoreland

August 1   American troops in Vietnam total 541,000

August 8   Richard M. Nixon wins the Republican presidential nomination in Miami Beach; Spiro T. Agnew is his running mate

August 26   The FBI reports 61,843 state marijuana arrests, a 98 percent increase from 1966

August 28   Against a backdrop of violence in Chicago's streets during the Democratic convention, Vice President Hubert H. Humphrey wins the presidential nomination; his running mate is Senator Edmund S. Muskie

September 24   The CBS television news magazine *60 Minutes* airs for the first time

                  An estimated 30 percent of the population attend elementary and secondary schools; 950 colleges register 1.6 million students, a 50 percent increase since 1963

September 28   The Beatles' "Hey Jude" is the number-one hit song

October 31   President Johnson announces the end of all bombing in North Vietnam, and Hanoi agrees to include the South Vietnamese government and the National Liberation Front, or Vietcong, in the negotiations in Paris

November 5   In one of the closest elections in American history, Richard M. Nixon wins the presidency with 43.4 percent of the popular vote, beating Democratic candidate Hubert Humphrey and American party candidate George Wallace

December 12   The number of American combat fatalities in Vietnam reaches 30,057, as troop levels increase to 540,000 during the year.

                  Between June 1963 and May 1968, some 15,000 persons were arrested during 369 major civil rights demonstrations

                  McDonald's introduces the "Big Mac" hamburger sandwich

1969

January 16	After ten weeks of deliberations, American and North Vietnamese delegates agree on the shape of the table to be used when the South Vietnamese and National Liberation Front representatives join the talks
April 3	The American combat death toll in Vietnam—33,641—has surpassed the 33,629 lives lost during the Korean War; by the end of the month, U.S. troops will peak at 543,482
April 4	CBS network executives censor *The Smothers Brothers Show* because of its antiwar skits
May 15	Governor Ronald Reagan orders the National Guard to spray antiwar protesters with the same skin-stinging powder used against the Vietcong in Vietnam at the University of California–Berkeley campus
June 8	President Nixon announces the withdrawal of 25,000 troops from Vietnam
June 17	The play *Oh, Calcutta!* begins the first of 1,314 performances on Broadway
June 22	A radical splinter group of Students for a Democratic Society called Weathermen carry out violent demonstrations in Chicago
June 29	Several days of rioting and marches follow a police raid on Stonewall Inn, a gay bar in New York City's Greenwich Village
July 20	Astronaut Neil Armstrong is the first person to land on the moon
July 22	H. Rap Brown resumes his leadership of the Student Non-Violent Coordinating Committee
August 15–17	More than 400,000 people attend a three-day rock festival at Woodstock in upstate New York
August 24	The antiwar movie *Alice's Restaurant*, starring Arlo Guthrie, is released
September 13	The *New York Times* reports that the United States is "torn by dissent" over the issue of sex education in public schools
September 20	The Archies have the number-one hit song with "Sugar, Sugar"
September 26	*The Brady Bunch* makes its television premiere

October 15   The First National Moratorium Day observance draws thousands of people to protest the Vietnam War, including many members of the middle class; Coretta King, widow of Dr. Martin Luther King, Jr., leads 45,000 in a candlelight parade past the White House

October 19   Vice President Spiro Agnew labels the antiwar demonstrators as "an effete corps of impudent snobs who characterize themselves as intellectuals"; a poll shows that 55 percent of Americans responding sympathize with the protesters

November 12   Lieutenant William Calley, Jr., is charged with the murders of unarmed South Vietnamese men, women, and children at the village of My Lai

November 13–15   In the largest antiwar demonstration to date, the New Mobilization Committee to End the War attracts 800,000 mostly white, middle-class people to protest in Washington, D.C.

December 1   The Selective Service System conducts the first draft lottery since 1942

December 15   President Nixon announces the third American troop withdrawal from South Vietnam, bringing the total withdrawal to 115,000

1970

January 1   The number-one hit song is B. J. Thomas's "Raindrops Keep Falling on My Head"

April 22   An estimated 30 million Americans protest the pollution of the environment in the largest demonstration in history

May 4   An American offensive into Cambodia triggers a wave of protests around the country; at Kent State University in Ohio, National Guardsmen kill four students and wound nine others in 15 seconds of gunfire

                    President Nixon calls college radicals "bums" and soldiers in Vietnam "the greatest"

                    The number-one hit song is the Jackson Five's "ABC"

May 9   Between 60,000 and 100,000 demonstrators peacefully gather in Washington, D.C., to protest the Cambodian incursion

May 10   A noontime rally in New York City draws an estimated 60,000 to 150,000 construction workers, longshoremen, and others who support the White House policy in Vietnam

May 14	Police fire into a crowd of students at Jackson State College in Mississippi, killing two students and wounding twelve; a federal grand jury fails to return any indictments
September 17	*The Flip Wilson Show* debuts on television
September 19	*The Mary Tyler Moore Show* makes its television premiere
September 24	The television show *The Odd Couple* premieres
September 26	The United States Commission on Campus Unrest reports that the crisis on American college campuses could threaten "the very survival of the nation"
December 31	Approximately 9,200 drug violations were recorded among American soldiers in Vietnam
	The film *Woodstock* is released
	Since January 1, 1961, 44,241 Americans have been killed in Vietnam

1971

January 2	Beginning today, cigarette advertising is banned from television
January 12	CBS television introduces *All in the Family*
April 7	The number of American troops in Vietnam drops to 184,000
May 3–5	Antiwar demonstrations climax in Washington, D.C., as thousands try to close down the government by disrupting city traffic
May 13	Peace negotiations over Vietnam begin their fourth year
June 30	The Twenty-sixth Amendment to the Constitution, giving eighteen-year-olds the right to vote, is ratified in a record two months and seven days
	The Supreme Court, by a 6–1 margin, upholds the right of the *New York Times* and the *Washington Post* to publish the *Pentagon Papers*
	The movie *Shaft* is released

1972

January 14	*Sanford and Son* makes its television debut
January 19	The National Commission on Marijuana and Drug Abuse reveals that 24 million Americans—40 percent of the eighteen- to twenty-five-year-old group—have smoked marijuana at least once

June 17 A security guard finds burglars in the Democratic party headquarters at the Watergate Hotel complex

June 29 In its 5–4 *Furman v. Georgia* decision, the Supreme Court declares the death penalty unconstitutional

July 13 Actress Jane Fonda makes an antiwar speech in North Vietnam, earning her the nickname "Hanoi Jane"

September 14 *The Waltons* debuts on television

September 17 *M*A*S*H* makes its television premiere

November 7 Richard Nixon wins reelection, capturing forty-nine states

1973

January 20 Antiwar demonstrations dampen President Nixon's inauguration

January 22 By a 7–2 margin, the Supreme Court legalizes unrestricted abortion during the first trimester of pregnancy in *Roe v. Wade*

January 23 President Nixon announces that Henry Kissinger and North Vietnamese foreign minister Le Duc Tho have agreed in Paris "to end the war and bring peace with honor in Vietnam and Southeast Asia"

March After fourteen years of war in Vietnam, American combat deaths number 46,226 and 10,326 noncombat deaths

May 17 The seven-member Select Committee on Presidential Campaign Activities opens televised hearings on the origin and activities related to the Watergate break-in

October 10 An advocate of law and order, Vice President Spiro Agnew resigns from office after pleading nolo contendere to charges of income tax evasion

December 6 Representative Gerald R. Ford is sworn in as the new vice president

1974

August 24 The Supreme Court rules, 9–0, that President Nixon cannot invoke executive privilege to block the release of sixty-four Watergate-related tapes to U.S. District Court Judge John Sirica

August 8 Nixon is the first president to resign from office

August 9 Gerald R. Ford is sworn in as the the thirty-eighth president

1975

January 18 *The Jeffersons* makes its television debut

April 4	An American airlift delivers 1,400 Amerasian orphans to the United States
April 10	Congress denies President Ford's request for nearly $1 billion in military and humanitarian aid for South Vietnam
April 29	When the North Vietnamese launch a massive rocket attack on the Saigon airport, President Ford orders the remaining 1,000 Americans and 5,500 South Vietnamese evacuated to offshore ships
April 30	South Vietnam surrenders to the North Vietnamese communists
August 10	First Lady Betty Ford reveals during a *60 Minutes* interview that all of her children may have tried marijuana, that she might have tried it when she was young, and that the Supreme Court made a "great decision" legalizing abortion
September 1	*Gunsmoke*, the last western airing on prime-time television, concludes a twenty-year run

BIBLIOGRAPHY

Kleinfelder, Rita Lang. *When We Were Young: A Baby-Boomer Yearbook*. New York: Prentice Hall, 1993.

Kurian, George Thomas. *Datapedia of the United States, 1790–2000: America Year by Year*. Lanham, MD: Bernan Press, 1994.

Webster's *Guide to American History: A Chronological, Geographical, and Biographical Survey and Compendium*. Springfield, MA: G.&C. Merriman Company, 1971.

I

Historical Overview

When history produces an era as momentous and as electrifying as the 1960s, we should anticipate a very durable legacy. We also can assume that such a turbulent era will foment historical repercussions for decades to follow. Progressing at a dizzying, frenetic pace, the sixties were seemingly synonymous with rebellion and conflict. If, in every century, one decade stands out from the rest as a time of challenge and trial, anguish and achievement, in the twentieth century in the United States that decade is the 1960s. No other decade, save the 1860s, when the nation was at war with itself for four years, has been so tumultuous. The 1960s was a revolution by almost any definition. Americans revolted against conventional moral conduct, civil rights violations, authoritarianism in universities, gender discrimination, the establishment, and, of course, the war in Southeast Asia. Within a generation, the national consensus forged during the nation's victorious effort in World War II had come under attack. A counterculture of hippies, or young people distressed with mainstream society, challenged widely accepted cultural practices and espoused an alternative lifestyle. Conflict and disillusionment, as expounded in Tom Hayden's 1962 *Port Huron Statement*, a declaration of counterculture political ideology inaugurating the emergence of the New Left, abruptly shattered social harmony. Traditional conformity gave way to unprecedented individualism and a reexamination of the conventional code of conduct. Change is inevitable and seldom a graceful operation, but the cultural revolution it produced in the 1960s was as profound as it was pervasive, touching virtually every aspect of American life. The sixties was an era when Americans did not so much greet the dawn as confront it.

Decades may adhere to a rigid chronology dictated by the calendar, but historical eras are more amorphorous and fluid. Years start and end precisely, but events that define and shape the human experience are not so easily demarcated. Determining when causes, struggles, and campaigns that are often more idealistic than pragmatic start and end is nearly impossible. Social, political, and intellectual movements frequently produce tangible effects, but their chronological hash marks are more blurred than distinct. Even if they begin abruptly, they usually fade gradually before disappearing entirely. We cannot assume, however, that because a particular event no longer generates public or media interest, it lacks significance or impact, for its influence may endure for generations.

The events set in motion during the 1960s did not simply and abruptly conclude in 1969, and determining the appropriate chronological brackets for such a busy decade is a difficult task. Beginning and ending the sixties is analogous to operating a VCR remote control. For example, to open the decade we press Play on January 20, 1961, when a hatless and coatless John F. Kennedy took the presidential oath in twenty-degree weather. The country, anxious about a missile gap with the Soviets that jeopardized the delicate balance of terror between the two superpowers, was in need of vigorous leadership. His proclamation that day that "the torch has been passed to a new generation of Americans" transcended political oratory. His inauguration was more than just the transfer of power from one party to another. Kennedy was a new generation in the White House. The nation's youngest elected president was a contrast in style and substance to the outgoing Dwight D. Eisenhower, who at seventy years old easily could have been Kennedy's father. This may have been the first clue that the 1950s were rapidly winding down.

Still in the Play mode, the tape continues to the spring of 1970, before we push the Pause button, when dozens of college campuses erupted in response to President Richard M. Nixon's decision to expand the Vietnam War zone to include Cambodia. On May 4, four Kent State University students in Ohio were killed and nine were wounded during the largest series of antiwar demonstrations in the nation's history. Ten days later, two more students were killed following protests at Jackson State College in Mississippi. These tragedies perceptibly diminished the impact of the antiwar movement, but the sixties were not over.

For closure we must move through the first half of the 1970s. At the conclusion of the Kent State and Jackson State tragedies, we then "fast-forward" the tape five years to April 30, 1975. After watching Saigon and

South Vietnam fall to the communists, bringing a dramatic, inglorious conclusion to the American experience in Southeast Asia that began more than
a decade earlier, we can push Stop.

One year in this chronological span—1968—was particularly difficult.
Even before the year began, Americans had endured dozens of destructive
race riots, frequent episodes of violence, countless inhumane acts against
civil rights activists in the South, but always, it seemed in 1968, Vietnam
dominated the front pages. Americans throughout the nation had to be wondering, "When will it end?" The country was coming apart, and in 1968,
there was no Pause button.

Beginning on January 30, 60,000 Vietcong communists launched their
Tet offensive against South Vietnam. The communists overran South Vietnamese cities and even punched their way into the American embassy in
Saigon. Although eventually thrown back with high losses, the communists
had won a psychological victory of sorts. When General William C. Westmoreland labeled the Tet struggle a communist defeat—the "last gasp" of
the enemy—and then called for 206,000 more troops to follow up the
American "victory," White House policy advisers were contentious;
American public opinion was suspicious.[1] Even many hawks—supporters
of American intervention in Vietnam—now conceded that the war was going badly. Two months later, after Minnesota senator Eugene McCarthy
made a surprisingly good showing in the Democratic primary in New
Hampshire as an antiwar candidate, Lyndon B. Johnson, elected four years
earlier by the largest margin of any twentieth-century president to that time,
announced he would not run for reelection in November. On April 4, Martin
Luther King, Jr., was shot to death in Memphis, triggering riots in more than
100 communities across the United States. About two weeks later, Students
for a Democratic Society (SDS) took over five campus buildings to protest
Columbia University's ties to Pentagon-related research and effectively
forced administrators to cancel the semester. On June 6, after winning the
California Democratic primary, Robert F. Kennedy died from an assassin's
bullet. In late August, about 1,000 people required hospitalization when police and National Guardsmen dispersed protesters outside the Democratic
National Convention in Chicago. By the end of the year, American combat
fatalities in Vietnam reached 30,057—about one-third of them, 9,557, during the first six months of 1968—and troop levels exceeded half a million.
To an outside observer, the nation must have appeared on the verge of collapsing from within. *Newsweek* columnist Kenneth Crawford was hardly
being pessimistic when he wrote in January that "if our institutions and basic freedoms come through the next twelve months intact, as they doubtless

will, there will be cause for self-congratulation. We shall have passed a test of adaptabiity, tolerance, and maturity."[2]

SIXTIES POLITICS

Vowing to "get the country moving again," President Kennedy hoped to capitalize on what he believed was a national willingness to abandon the Eisenhower conservatism and embrace his vision of a "New Frontier." The administration's major domestic proposals were essentially an extension of Franklin D. Roosevelt's New Deal and Harry Truman's Fair Deal: health insurance for the elderly, aid to depressed areas, federal aid to public schools, highway construction, reform of immigration laws, and a cabinet-level Department of Housing and Urban Development (HUD). Even with a Democratic congressional majority, however, Kennedy's legislation lacked sufficient support to translate the New Frontier into law. Because he won the 1960 presidential election by the slimmest popular vote margin—49.7 percent to Richard Nixon's 49.5 percent—Kennedy lacked leverage on Capitol Hill, and conservative southern Democrats in the 87th Congress frequently sided with Republicans; of the twenty-three bills he sent to the House of Representatives in 1961, only five were passed into law.

Although civil rights was a critical plank in the Democratic platform in 1960, Kennedy was not aggressive in pushing legislation that would confer equal status for blacks and whites. He did fill more high federal government positions with blacks than any other president, but he preferred to use his executive powers and the courts rather than introduce civil rights legislation, fearing he would alienate southern members in Congress hostile to civil rights and lose what little support he had for his New Frontier agenda.[3] He did, however, issue an executive order in 1961 that created the President's Committee on Equal Employment Opportunity to eliminate discrimination in the civil service. Kennedy and his brother, Robert, the attorney general, did abandon for a moment their cautious approach to civil rights in 1962 when Mississippi governor Ross Barnett defiantly boasted that "no school will be integrated in Mississippi while I am your governor" and ignored a federal court order to admit James Meredith as the first black student to attend classes at the University of Mississippi. After urging citizens to comply with the court order, President Kennedy federalized the state's National Guard and deployed four hundred federal marshals. "Ole Miss" was integrated, but not before two people were killed and 375 persons were injured; five hundred federal troops remained on the campus until Meredith graduated in June 1963. The Kennedy administration found it even more difficult to remain passive on civil rights when, a year later, police commissioner

Eugene "Bull" Connor's officers assaulted civil rights demonstrators, including children, with high-pressure fire hoses and cattle prods in Birmingham, Alabama.

But events forced Kennedy's hand. Black civil rights advocates, using such direct action tactics as sit-ins and demands for admission to public facilities, kept the pressure on for government to guarantee respect for law and equal rights, while segregationists defied the federal government. Newly elected Alabama governor George C. Wallace articulated the southern whites' commitment to racial separation, proclaiming, "Segregation today, segregation tomorrow, segregation forever." When Wallace threatened to "bar the entrance" of two black students wanting to enroll at the University of Alabama's Tuscaloosa campus in 1962, Kennedy again federalized the National Guard to ensure their registration. The president may have supported civil rights reluctantly, but by the time of his assassination in November 1963, his administration had done more than any previous one to advance equal rights.[4]

Bolstered by an overwhelming public affirmation of his own presidency in November 1964, Lyndon Baines Johnson moved quickly to push Kennedy's New Frontier legislation through a Congress controlled by sizable Democratic majorities in both houses. In the most comprehensive reform program since the New Deal, Johnson's Great Society included Kennedy's tax cut, the Civil Rights Act of 1964 and Voting Rights Act of 1965, Medicare (and Medicaid), and federal aid to education. It also included the new Office of Economic Opportunity to wage a war on poverty; Head Start for preschool-aged children; the Neighborhood Youth Corps that provided jobs for teenagers; VISTA, a domestic Peace Corps; and Upward Bound for precollege youths. The administration was successful in creating the Department of Housing and Urban Development and getting legislation passed on highway beautification, air and water pollution control, and immigration reform.

Despite the numerous education and health reforms, proposals to eradicate poverty and prohibit discrimination in public accommodations, and legislation to establish and enforce voting rights, Great Society gains were soon offset by conservatives who opposed high expenditures for poverty programs and many unemployed and economically depressed black Americans who became frustrated with the uneven application of Johnson's civil rights initiatives. Widespread black frustration and dissatisfaction with de facto segregation, discrimination in housing and employment, and poverty eventually erupted in dozens of violent race riots between 1965 and 1968.

IN AND OUT OF VIETNAM

Sputnik anxieties and an alleged missile gap between the two superpowers prompted Kennedy to announce during his inaugural speech that the United States must be "the watchman on the wall of world freedom."[5] To counter communist "wars of national liberation" in the Third World, he adopted a strategy of flexible response that included augmenting the Polaris missile program and using intercontinental Minuteman missiles launched from underground sites to counter any Soviet attacks. Special military forces like the Green Berets, trained for guerrilla counterinsurgency warfare, were used to thwart insurrections or revolutions. The administration also established the Alliance for Progress, a quasi–Marshall Plan for Latin America, to help underdeveloped countries and prevent the spread of communism in that part of the world, though some critics observed that the program was neither much of an alliance nor progress. Significantly more successful was the creation of the Peace Corps in March 1961, an organization of American volunteers who directed economic, educational, and agricultural projects in Third World countries. Within the first two years of its existence, more than five thousand mostly young men and women were sent to forty-six countries, where they helped foster a favorable image of the United States.

Kennedy employed his flexible response in several venues, including the April 1961 Bay of Pigs invasion attempt to overthrow Cuban premier Fidel Castro, increasing America's 300,000 armed forces to defend West Berlin two months later, and the brinkmanship strategy he displayed with the naval blockade around Cuba to prevent Soviet missiles from reaching the island in October 1962. Convinced that the domino theory applied to Southeast Asia, he beefed up American military aid in Vietnam to counter the growing influence of the communists and expanded the number of military advisers to 16,000—including 3,000 Green Berets—by the end of 1963.[6]

At the time of his death, Kennedy expressed misgivings about an all-out military commitment in Vietnam, as did President Johnson, who pledged that "we are not about to send American boys nine or ten thousand miles away from home to do what Asian boys ought to be doing for themselves."[7] But Johnson also vowed, "I am not going to be the President who saw South Vietnam go the way China went," and in the fall of 1964, after Congress overwhelmingly passed the Gulf of Tonkin resolution granting the president virtually unlimited authority "to take all necessary measures . . . to prevent further aggression in Southeast Asia," he began to expand America's role in Vietnam, increasing the military contingent to 23,000 by the end of the year.

After defeating Republican challenger Arizona senator Barry Goldwater in 1964, winning 61 percent of the total popular vote and forty-four states, Johnson had emerged as a national leader in his own right. With a convincing mandate and solid Democratic majorities in both houses of Congress, he could act decisively and aggressively in Vietnam. By the end of 1965, there were 180,000 American troops in Vietnam, a figure that rose to 350,000 by the end of 1966 and to approximately 500,000 by the end of 1967.[8] Despite the increase in military personnel and an annual expenditure of $30 billion, the war was going badly for the United States. When the Tet offensive in early 1968 refuted the president's claim that the United States was winning in Vietnam, Johnson's political vulnerability was exposed by Senator Gene McCarthy, who did unexpectedly well in the New Hampshire Democratic primary. Six weeks later, in a nationally televised address, Johnson withdrew from the presidential race.

With Johnson no longer a candidate and Vietnam the dominant issue in the 1968 presidential campaign, Democrats desperately needed a candidate who could unite the party. In addition to McCarthy, Robert Kennedy and Vice President Hubert H. Humphrey also campaigned for the nomination. When Kennedy was assassinated after narrowly winning the California primary in June, Humphrey became the party's candidate, but his nomination in Chicago—where Abbie Hoffman, Jerry Rubin, and other antiwar radicals clashed with police and disrupted convention proceedings—only highlighted the intense dissension and turmoil in the Democratic party. Exploiting the widespread disenchantment over party policies and a white backlash to civil rights activists, George C. Wallace formed the American Independent party and created a three-way race. He was not able to force a run-off election in the House of Representatives as he had hoped, but with 13.5 percent of the popular vote, he did better than any other third-party candidate since Robert La Follette in 1924. Campaigning on a "law and order" theme and benefiting from a divided Democratic party, Nixon, who promised to "bring America together again," narrowly defeated Humphrey.

During the 1968 election, Nixon generated optimism about resolving the conflict in Vietnam when he claimed to have a secret plan "for the complete withdrawal of all United States ground combat forces and their replacement by South Vietnamese forces."[9] He never did reveal his secret plan, but his two-phase Vietnamization policy took effect in mid-1969. As the United States gradually reduced its fighting forces and relinquished military responsibility to the Army of the Republic of South Vietnam (ARVN), the U.S. Air Force stepped up its role, dropping 130,000 tons of bombs on North Vietnam each month, beginning the previous March. Coinciding with Nixon's Vietnamization plan was the CIA's Operation Phoenix, a systematic covert effort to neutralize the Vietcong infrastructure. By the time the CIA terminated Phoenix in 1973, more than 40,000 Vietnamese people suspected of supporting Vietcong insurgents had been assassinated.[10]

In June, 25,000 American troops were called home. Six months after the first withdrawal, an additional 50,000 GIs were sent home; by September 1972, only 40,000 of the more than a half-million American troops in Vietnam three years earlier remained. Antiwar sentiment was still high, however, and when Nixon announced on April 30, 1970, that he ordered ground troops to destroy North Vietnamese sanctuaries in neighboring Cambodia, protests erupted at Kent State University and hundreds of other college campuses around the country.

A formal settlement was finally negotiated in December 1972, and on January 27, 1973, White House national security adviser Henry Kissinger and North Vietnamese Foreign Minister Le Duc Tho signed an agreement that required the United States to withdraw all its troops from Vietnam within sixty days. For Nixon, American withdrawal according to the prescribed terms was achieving "peace with honor." The conditions both sides agreed to were virtually the same as those presented the previous October. During the four years Nixon was executing his "secret plan," 21,000 casualties, or about 40 percent of the total casualties in Vietnam occurred. On April 30, 1975, the North Vietnamese communists occupied Saigon and renamed it Ho Chi Minh City, and North and South Vietnam were reunited. But the rest of Southeast Asia did not fall to the communists, who fell to fighting among themselves. The domino theory was not valid, and the Pacific Ocean did not become, as President Eisenhower had predicted, "a Communist lake."[11] The Vietnam War was America's longest and most divisive conflict since the Civil War a century earlier. For "resolving" the conflict in Vietnam, Duc Tho and Henry Kissinger were awarded the 1973 Nobel Peace Prize. But the memory of the war at home—its bitter divisions between hawks and doves, its corruption of the political process, its drain on the federal budget and diversion of money from domestic programs, its corrosion of public trust in government, and more—survived in American culture. The music, films, and other American cultural expressions revealed a cynicism that would be one of the legacies of the war and the decade.

THE TEMPER OF THE TIMES

Just as we must encroach on a subsequent decade for closure of the 1960s, it is also true that virtually none of the major events that so traumatized and terrified Americans in the 1960s suddenly appeared between 1960 and 1969. A. Philip Randolph, president of the Brotherhood of Sleeping

Car Porters, was the first person to propose a massive march on Washington to promote racial equality in July 1941, but in the national consciousness, the modern civil rights movement did not begin until December 1, 1955, when after a hard day's work, black seamstress Rosa Parks refused to give her seat to a white rider on a city bus in Montgomery, Alabama. When Parks was arrested, a year-long bus boycott ensued, launching the career of Martin Luther King, Jr., and demonstrating that direct, nonviolent action could challenge Jim Crow in the South.[12]

The American feminist movement was rooted in the antislavery, temperance, women's suffrage, and other reforms in the nineteenth century and reemerged as a major social force in the 1960s. By the mid-twentieth century, women had begun to move into occupations traditionally dominated by men, but they were still generally relegated to subservient positions, whether in the workplace or in the home. Despite a dramatic change in women's roles after World War II, they had not achieved full equality, and there was little indication of a mass movement to alter that reality. In the 1960s, an era of protest, a "solution" to the women's problem would require creating new roles for men and women, and they seriously began to question their "proper place" when Betty Friedan, a suburban housewife and writer, published *The Feminine Mystique* in 1963, exposing the tedium and frustrations of domesticity—"the problem that has no name."[13] Shortly after she founded the National Organization for Women (NOW) in 1966, "women's liberation" found its way into the American vernacular.

The 1960s was a time of coming of age for many Americans, literally, and for the nation as a significant proportion of the baby boomers entered their teens. Many such baby boomers, who turned college campuses into veritable hothouse environments for social reform and counterculture lifestyles in the 1960s, were born in the late 1940s and early 1950s and rebelled against the supposed middle-class conformity and consensus of their parents' era.

In fact, the first rumblings of such protest and calls for alternative lifestyles emanated from the 1950s. Hippies, who embodied the counterculture lifestyle in the 1960s, were the spirited counterparts of the beats, or beatniks, a term derived from the Soviet satellite *Sputnik*. Although small in number, their advocacy of free love and a lifestyle that insolently rejected mainstream values grabbed the media's attention.[14] Even rock 'n' roll, a new genre of popular music that won over a generation of teenagers inclined to rebel against a generation of parents, first appeared in the 1950s.

Americans in the 1960s were divided by race, but there were also cleavages caused by class and economics. Despite President Johnson's promise of a "Great Society" and his declaration of "an unconditional war on poverty" in his 1964 State of the Union address, as many as 40 to 50 million people suffered from inadequate housing, malnutrition, and poor medical care. According to sociologist Michael Harrington, the country had been swept by a "new segregation of poverty" that created a less visible but suffering "other America," an America "populated by failures, by those driven from the land and bewildered by the city, by old people suddenly confronted with the torments of loneliness and poverty, and by minorities facing a wall of prejudice." Despite the existence of a vast "other America," Harrington was concerned that "the middle class no longer understands that poverty exists."[15]

Racial segregation meant physical separation. In the 1960s, while the U.S. government was promoting freedom and claiming to be fighting for democracy all over the world, many of its own citizens could not even exercise their fundamental constitutional right to vote. The Supreme Court's *Brown v. Board of Education of Topeka* ruling in 1954, overturning the "separate but equal" doctrine, had little immediate impact on black peoples' lives in the South where White Citizens Councils, the Ku Klux Klan, and Jim Crow ensured second-class citizenship for African Americans. Ironically, the formal institutionalization of segregation gave blacks the strength to challenge whites-only laws and the status quo. The hardships that poor, and often undereducated, black Americans endured as a repressed minority engendered a sense of community and collective accomplishment that enabled them to campaign for civil rights and launch the greatest social movement in modern history.

With the high expectations of the Great Society, almost every group with a cause anticipated a new order. Perhaps interpreting President Johnson's domestic reforms as a signal for societal change, members of the college-age population challenged authority. Women wanted to eliminate sexism in the workplace and at home as they redefined their traditional inferior roles. Black Americans, impatient with the unfulfilled promise of political and social equality, pressed for an end to their status as second-class citizens, their lack of access to public accommodations, and the denial of the right to vote by staging many protests and direct confrontations against Jim Crow institutions. Amid such turmoil, the United States resembled less a nation indivisible than a swirl of competing interest groups and contesting social classes. Americans became increasingly divisive. Initially the American public supported the government's effort to contain communism in Vietnam; during the latter half of the 1960s, however, Washington's insistence on putting down a communist insurgency in Southeast Asia divided families, generations, and political parties in America. Americans were a nation at war abroad and fighting with each other at home about the war abroad.

Social rebellion and outrageous behavior—virtually synonymous with the sixties—challenged mainstream values and conventional lifestyles. Few institutions escaped some kind of structural change.

TALKIN' 'BOUT MY GENERATION

If the axiom is true that when we are young we want to change the world, the 1960s were ripe for revolution, since at no other time in American history were there so many young Americans. The earliest members of the baby boomers, as the generation became known, greeted the world in May 1946, nine months after the Japanese surrender officially ended World War II.[16] The boomers were products of a generation born in the 1920s that survived a decade-long depression—the worst in the nation's history—and then went off to war—the most expansive in American history—to make the world safe for democracy one more time. Their children, 76 million of them by 1960, born into a child-oriented society Landon Y. Jones calls "babyvilles," were nurtured in the 1950s with no recollection of the hard times and sacrifices endured by their parents.[17] With a strong economy in the 1950s and more disposable income than previous generations, boomer parents who long had delayed gratification could finally afford the American dream: marriage, children, automobiles, televisions, and homes in the suburbs. The depression generation wanted their children to have a better and easier life than they had; they wanted their children to be the first in the family to have a higher education. Because they reached parenthood in an era of prosperity, such aspirations were hardly unrealistic.

As much as the depression generation might have tried to protect their children and be good parents, they were not aware that what they regarded as eternal truths were merely time-bound opinions for the new generation. Baby boomers grew up when the rules adhered to by teachers and parents were changing and often conflicting. In the 1960s, "Obey authority" and "Don't ask questions" were commands supplanted by "Question authority." Instead of learning to control their emotions, they were encouraged to "express yourself and satisfy your inner self." Rather than value 1950s conformity, they were urged to "do your own thing."

When the boomers came of age, more of them than ever before went off to college. Growing to 20 million by the end of the 1960s, they filled college campuses throughout the country. There they were exposed to new ideas about issues, people, and the world. They became aware of different points of view and attitudes that often clashed with their own, or worse, their newly acquired "worldview" sometimes conflicted with that of their parents. For some young people, making the transition from a small hometown to a col-

lege campus was quite literally an eye-opening experience. One woman recalled how, in 1964,

I graduated from high school, and in September I started at the University of
Wisconsin and it was as if I had stepped onto another planet. Everything was so free
and loose there. It was as if I had become another person. I felt as though I was myself for the first time. . . . Suddenly from this little enclave of nothing in high
school, in one month the whole world opened up. I flew on a plane and I went a
million miles from home. I started to hear about Vietnam, and I'd never even heard
of that country.[18]

Not all members of the sixties boomer generation shared the same ideology, the same passion, or the same interest in the issues of the day. In that
sense, the sixties generation was no different from any other. While it may
tempting, if not expedient, to categorize this generation as a monolithic en-
tity, we must resist the perception that the under-thirty-year-old birth cohort
in the 1960s was composed predominantly of long-haired college students
who burned their draft cards, dropped "acid" listening to psychedelic music, wore flowers in their hair, occupied a campus building, and welcomed
any opportunity to defy or ridicule authority.

The stereotypical notion that a small number of the younger generation
represented the majority was more perception than reality. Such an image of
the 1960s frequently came from mass media distortions and the tendency to
focus on the outrageous behavior of a very small minority of a large demographic group. In the first half of 1968, 221 major antiwar demonstrations at
101 colleges and universities involved approximately 39,000 students, or
less than 1 percent of the college population.[19] Between 1965 and 1968,
when the war in Vietnam escalated and White House war planners dramatically increased the monthly draft quotas, no more than 3 percent of college
students considered themselves activists, and only 20 percent of the college
population participated in one demonstration. The chilling photograph of
an incredulous and anguished fourteen-year-old Mary Ann Vecchio kneeling over a mortally wounded student during an antiwar protest at Kent State
appears in many American history textbooks. Because it is one of the most
recognized images from the 1960s, readers might conclude that such violent confrontations between students and government troops were typical.
The tragedy did ignite demonstrations involving perhaps 2 million students
on campuses across the nation, but that represented only about one-fourth
of the 7.9 million students enrolled in college at the time.[20]

A similar demographic pattern also emerges when we examine the impact of the Vietnam War on the boomer generation. Again, just as only a
small number of them actively participated in campus protests, only a frac-

tion of males who were eligible were directly affected by the draft (women were exempted). Between August 1964, when Congress ratified the Gulf of Tonkin Resolution, to the withdrawal of the last U.S. forces from Vietnam in March 1973, 27,000,000 American men were of draft age. Of this number, 8,600,000 served in the military, and 2,150,000 of those were assigned to a tour of duty in Vietnam. Of all the men eligible for military duty during the Vietnam War, only 32 percent served in the military, and only 8 percent of that number spent time in Vietnam. Most boomers were part of a silent majority who neither participated in demonstrations against the war in Vietnam nor fought in it.[21]

Generational disaffection in the 1960s was not unprecedented. But the younger white middle-class generation—the boomers—did not know hard times. They had no experience with scarcity, suffering, or sacrifice. They were ambivalent about modeling their lives to conform to the very clearly defined issues pertaining to gender, race, materialism, and inequality. Many of them were confronted with a fundamental ideological dilemma: Should they embrace the status quo or challenge it?

Not all boomers were like-minded. Members of any generation have different experiences that shape their values and guide their behavior. An eighteen-year-old freshman sitting in a comfortable university classroom, perhaps eagerly anticipating the "big game," would have had little in common with his former high school classmate who did not have the benefit of a 2-S deferment and was anxiously weighing his options: enlist, if possible, in a "safe" branch like the navy or air force, or be drafted and spend a year of his life (and face the real prospect of death) in Vietnam. Even those not affected by the draft likely would have looked at the same issues with a different eye. Recent high school graduates who opted to stay home to hold a steady job and raise a family rather than go off to college shared little with those who felt victimized by in loco parentis and authoritarian university officials who "violated" their "free speech." The same intragenerational dissimilarities also applied to gender. Middle-class white women agitating for feminist causes did not perforce share the concept of "sisterhood" of a black woman, who might be jeopardizing her livelihood and her life for the right to vote.

Similarly, we must not presume that group membership is interchangeable. A member of the counterculture—a hippie—almost certainly would have opposed American intervention in Vietnam, though such a person did not necessarily engage in any active, organized antiwar protest. However, an antiwar activist affiliated with the New Left and the SDS was not necessarily part of the counterculture. Initially, the New Left commended the hippies for their candor, though disillusioned, militant New Leftists criticized them because they lacked "stability and they were intellectually flabby."[22] An activist in the Students for a Democratic Society (SDS) might partici- pate in the Student Non-Violent Coordinating Committee (SNCC), but an SNCC member would not have to be affiliated with the SDS. Even within the SDS, always an unstable coalition, factions emerged, the most militant being an underground group that called itself the Weathermen. Black mili- tants clashed with feminists, both waging a struggle for social, political, and economic equality. Civil rights activists who marched and demonstrated with Martin Luther King, Jr., for voter registration rights were not necessar- ily supportive of SNCC's more aggressive tactics, and rarely were they the same people assaulting police and setting fires in Watts and other inner-city locales.

IMPACT OF THE MEDIA

No other medium in history has had the impact of television, and in the 1960s, it profoundly affected how Americans looked, thought, and be- haved. Initially, programming was dominated by westerns (*Gunsmoke, Bo- nanza*), comedies (*Father Knows Best, The Danny Thomas Show*), and variety shows (*The Ed Sullivan Show* and *Red Skelton Show*); by the end of the decade, when television sets were more prevalent in American homes than refrigerators, bathtubs, or indoor toilets, popular shows had not changed significantly. Americans still watched westerns (*Gunsmoke, Bo- nanza*), comedies (*Here's Lucy, Mayberry, R.F.D.*), and variety shows (*The Carol Burnett Show* and *The Dean Martin Show*).[23] The most popular pro- grams a decade later had changed little in format, but some of the characters portrayed were noticeably different. Commercial television mirrored social changes by featuring more blacks and women.

In the 1960s, network news more than network programming contrib- uted to social and political criticism. For the first time, a majority of Ameri- cans could watch events as they occurred. Many historic moments, such as John Kennedy's inauguration, First Lady Jackie Kennedy's televised tour of the White House, and astronaut Neil Armstrong's walk on the moon had a positive impact that tended to coalesce the nation. But the same audience also witnessed film replays of Kennedy's assassination, the arrests of 668 persons during the bloody confrontation between protesters and the Chi- cago police outside the Democratic convention, Birmingham police dogs attacking civil rights protesters, and nightly footage of the "living room war" in Vietnam.

Television coverage of the war in Southeast Asia, which was more exten- sive than any other subject, had a powerful impact on public opinion, though admittedly it is difficult to document precisely how television coverage alone affected attitudes in the 1960s when most Americans relied on newspapers rather than television as the principal source for news. Television coverage made the distant war vivid, real, and terrible. Viewers of the evening news watched as the weekly number of American troops reported killed soared from an average of 26 in 1965, to 96 in 1966, to 180 in 1967. The camera captured the trepidation on the faces of defenseless Vietnamese civilians as they watched their homes being destroyed and the painful, terrified expressions of American GIs in combat. Viewers were aghast after watching grisly footage of American soldiers lopping the ears off Vietcong troops, and NBC's clip of South Vietnamese police chief General Nguyen Ngoc Loan publicly executing a Vietcong prisoner in a Saigon street symbolized the brutality and inhumanity of war. More devastating to the Johnson administration's handling of the war, though, was CBS news anchor Walter Cronkite's gloomy assessment of the war from Saigon, just after the Tet offensive in February 1968, that "it seems now more certain than ever that the bloody experience in Vietnam is to end in stalemate . . . [and] the rational way out . . . will be to negotiate, not as victors, but as honorable people who lived up to their pledge to defend democracy and did the best they could."[24] A month later, much of the American public and even members in his own party repudiated President Johnson, whom *Time* magazine had recognized just three months earlier as its Man of the Year for 1967.

Hollywood filmmakers were not yet responding to events in Vietnam, but they were arousing the public's sensibilities and forcing Americans to redefine their moral standards. *Bonnie and Clyde* (1967), a loose interpretation of the 1930s gangsters, contained scenes of unprecedented graphic violence. In *The Graduate* (1967) an older woman seduces an alienated baby boomer just out of college. *Guess Who's Coming to Dinner* (1967) tests the liberal views of a white woman's parents when she introduces them to her black fiancé. *Easy Rider* (1969) romanticized independence, drug use, and casual sex in its depiction of the counterculture lifestyle; *Alice's Restaurant* (1969) was an antiwar vehicle; and *Midnight Cowboy,* which won Best Picture of the Year in 1969, featured drugs, male prostitution, and homosexuality. With the liberalization of obscenity laws, the taboo against unconventional sexual conduct was removed, or at least eased, when a beast and a human had intercourse in *Rosemary's Baby* (1968). *I Am Curious Yellow* (1969) showed nudity and coitus, and *Bob and Carol and Ted and Alice* (1969) was a comedy about wife swapping.

The generally more tolerant view of pre- and extramarital affairs was not limited to film. The more sexually permissive atmosphere in the sixties was probably inevitable when, in May 1960, the Food and Drug Administration approved the sale of an oral contraceptive. Pharmaceutical manufacturers were overwhelmed by the demand for Envoid, "the Pill" that offered women the option to engage in sexual relations without the fear of pregnancy.[25]

SEX, DRUGS, ROCK 'N' ROLL?

It would be erroneous to characterize the 1960s as an era of "sex, drugs, and rock 'n' roll." Sexual taboos were frequently challenged, but it is more myth than reality that sexual permissiveness was introduced and flourished in the 1960s. Easy divorce, relatively easy access to contraceptives, and an openness toward promiscuity were common to the 1920s. What did make the sixties unique was the change in attitude. Even so, there was great ambivalence about "sexual perversion," and society seemed to be sending an ambiguous message. Free love might have been the mantra for some, but it was not widely practiced or accepted. Enforcement of anti-fornication laws, albeit applied unevenly, was not unheard of; contraceptives were difficult to obtain, especially for single women; legal abortions were severely limited; and homosexuals were persecuted almost everywhere.[26] Sex was more explicit. In movie houses *Barbarella*, *Blow-up*, and *I Am Curious Yellow* did well at the box office. Theatrical work reflecting the new sexual openness included *Hair*, billed as "an American tribal love-rock musical" and featuring nudity and four-letter words. *Oh! Calcutta* was a popular nude review. Each production enjoyed more than 1,000 performances on and off-Broadway. The older generation wrung its hands in despair over a supposed collapse of morality, but perhaps unnecessarily. The displays of nudity and promiscuity in some films and plays had shock value because they did not speak for all. In July 1967, *Seventeen* magazine published the results of its survey of female teenagers' attitudes about sexual activity. Contrary to popular thinking, 85 percent of the respondents said they were virgins, and fewer than 5 percent of them approved of premarital sex for couples with no intention of marrying.[27]

Before the 1960s, drug use in America was unprecedented. In 1959 doctors prescribed over 579 tons of tranquilizers and were writing nearly $2 million worth of prescriptions for barbiturates, amphetamines, antidepressants, and other mood-altering drugs.[28] A drug subculture did not suddenly and inexplicably emerge in the 1960s. Drugs have been part of American culture throughout American history. Prior to the 1960s, the "big three"—marijuana, heroin, and cocaine—were most commonly associated with marginally social groups. In the sixties, the use of illicit drugs, especially marijuana, had filtered up into the white middle class. When drug use was a means to demonstrate a rejection of mainstream values, marijuana was adopted as the unofficial drug of the counterculture. The establishment had its drugs, too—alcohol and tobacco—but they were legal and did not produce the same mind-enhancing effects as marijuana, almost always experienced in a communal setting.[29]

In the 1960s, the media focused predominantly on the counterculture associated with antisocial behavior as the typical drug users. In Vietnam, however, marijuana, hashish, and opium were widely available, and thousands of American soldiers became addicted to heroin that was 90 percent to 98 percent pure, as compared to 2 percent to 10 percent purity in the United States. American military commanders estimated that in 1970, 65,000 GIs were using narcotics.[30] Drugs were easily accessible in Vietnam, a problem compounded when officials in the South Vietnamese government participated in the drug trade, often in collusion with the CIA. Although President Nixon pledged that "all our servicemen must be accorded the right to rehabilitation," the military discharged more than 1,000 addicted GIs a month who were "of negligible value to the United States Army." In 1973 a White House task force found that 34 percent of American soldiers had "commonly used" heroin.[31]

An accurate accounting of the number of illicit drug users in the United States is nearly impossible, but Henry Brill, head of the American Medical Association's committee on drug dependency, estimated that the number rose from a few hundred thousand at the beginning of the decade to 8 million by 1970. That figure and even higher estimates, however, may be misleading, since a *Playboy* survey in the late 1960s reported that 47 percent of college students said they smoked marijuana, but only 13 percent acknowledged frequent use.[32]

If "ordinary" psychoactive substances could not sufficiently alter one's conscience, a more powerful psychedelic drug, lysergic acid diethylamide (LSD), possessed hallucinogenic effects discovered accidentally in Switzerland in 1943. The substance had no apparent medical or therapeutic value, but in the cold war era, the CIA, in the interest of national security, used LSD in truth drug experiments with unwitting civilians in its controversial MK ULTRA project, a secret program carried out by CIA agents.[33] By the late1960s, LSD was used for experimentation in a different context.

Relatively obscure in 1962, by 1966 LSD, or "acid," was widely recognized. Although there were a number of LSD proponents prior to the 1960s, they attracted little attention until Timothy Leary, a faculty member in Harvard University's Center for Research in Human Personality, began promoting LSD as a means of achieving spiritual growth.[34] In 1965, urging the younger generation to "turn on, tune in, and drop out," he founded the League for Spiritual Discovery, which advocated the mass production and distribution of LSD. A year later, the federal government criminalized the hallucinogenic substance, making the drug even more alluring to devotees of the counterculture interested in social protest.

In the 1960s, the music also made a dramatic transformation from "doo-wop" to lyrics with an edge. Some would say the music grew up in the 1960s. Probably those same people also would say the music died in the six-ties. Whatever the view, rock 'n' roll exploded on the national scene in 1954 when Bill Haley and the Comets sold 16 million copies of their hit song "Rock Around the Clock." As a cultural barometer, the evolution of music provides important clues about how American social and political attitudes were in flux.

Through the first half of the 1960s, the music topping the Billboard charts and played on *American Bandstand* still echoed the fifties in lyrics and sound: fluffy, sentimental, naive, occasionally subtly suggestive. It was also comprehensible; a listener to a 45rpm (still the principal medium for popular music) or radio could discern the words. Not being able to discern the lyrics caused suspicion and led people already leery of rock 'n' roll to as-sume the worst. In 1963 the Kingsmen's "Louie, Louie" (written in 1956) generated widespread controversy because no one knew the words. Three years later, some radio stations would not play Tommy James and the Shon-dells' hit song "Hanky Panky" because it was too suggestive. Although El-vis Presley and other early rock 'n' rollers shook up an entire generation in the 1950s, the new genre had made its way into the mainstream of popular music. After the initial shock, many Americans realized that the music was pretty tame after all, more rhythm than revolution. More often than not, the popular rock 'n' roll reinforced, rather than deprecated, the virtues of tradi-tional, wholesome relationships and extolled the virtues of love and fidelity, not sex or drugs.

In 1963, for example, three of the number-one hits were innocuous and simplistic. In "He's So Fine," the Chiffons longed for the security of "his embrace." In "My Boyfriend's Back," advice to girls wanting to remain faithful to their steady guys, the Angels set straight a would-be suitor about his less than honorable intentions. "Hey, Paula," is an uncomplicated view of love and marriage when Paul and Paula delight in their anticipation of blissful togetherness.

By 1965, though, something was happening to popular music. The Top Forty hits still included sentimental boy-girl favorites like "You've Lost

That Lovin' Feeling," and "Stop! In the Name of Love," and light-hearted sing-alongs such as, "I Got You Babe," "Wooly, Bully," and "Help Me, Rhonda," but a "British invasion," led by the Beatles, the Rolling Stones, the Animals, and several other bands with peculiar names and a new sound revolutionized rock 'n' roll. In the United States, artists such as Joan Baez, Pete Seeger, and Bob Dylan influenced popular music when they introduced folk rock: provocative lyrics with radical implications that promoted an intellectual rebellion and hinted about an impending revolution. Peter, Paul, and Mary's recording of "Blowin' in the Wind" (written by Bob Dylan), which sold 300,000 copies and reached the number-one spot in 1963, became the adopted anthem of the antiwar movement. Two years later, the Byrds' "Mr. Tambourine Man" (also written by Dylan) was a number-one hit song, and Barry McGuire's "Eve of Destruction," a protest song about racism, social injustice, and nuclear annihilation, reached the number-one spot, even though many radio stations banned it—this time because listeners did know the words.[35]

The musical metamorphosis was only beginning, and no rock 'n' roll band had transformed itself more dramatically or more abruptly in the 1960s than the Beatles. In 1967 they moved beyond singing about male-female relationships and light-hearted lyrics to music that was more political and complex. The Beatles, now influenced by Eastern mysticism, drugs, and the "psychedelic" sound, confounded many of their listeners with the nonsensical and enigmatic lyrics about surreal people exhibiting bizarre behavior.

"Doo-wop" had become passé. "Lucy in the Sky with Diamonds" ("LSD") did not make the Top Forty list, but the Beatles' *Sgt. Pepper*'s *Lonely Hearts Club Band* was the album of the year. By the end of the decade, rock 'n' roll had undergone a profound change, stylistically and substantively. No longer was it about broken hearts and Saturday nights. The contrast was unmistakable, and for some, distressing.

Instead of reinforcing teenagers' concerns about decency and reputations listening to "Wake Up, Little Susie," adolescents heard the Rolling Stones suggesting "Let's Spend the Night Together." The music was "evolving" from "Candy Girl" to "Sister Morphine," from "Johnny Angel" to "Sympathy for the Devil," from "Blue Moon" to "Purple Haze," from "I Want to Hold Your Hand" to "Why Don't We Do It in the Road?" In 1969 the music reflected the broader social conflict when two popular songs were "Okie from Muskogee," Merle Haggard's affirmation of patriotism, and John Lennon's "Give Peace a Chance," a plea for policymakers to end the Vietnam War.

Many people seem inclined to recall the sixties music as either antiwar or drug related. Some of it was political; some of it did condone and promote drug use or was written to heighten drug euphoria. Most of the music, though, was politically benign. *Billboard* magazine's Top Five hits for each month from 1965 through 1970 did not include any antiwar or drug-related songs. Even in 1968, a critically eventful and pivotal year when many Americans had to be wondering if the nation was going to survive the decade, none of the top ten songs for that year reflected political or social issues.[36] Because *Billboard* tracks only Top Forty hits—determined by the number of sales—acid rock album cuts that got airplay on FM radio stations were omitted. Antiwar and drug-related music had its following, but the songs did not show up in a mainstream publication, suggesting that a majority of record buyers might have listened to "Lucy in the Sky," but they were also buying "Help Me, Rhonda."

Surveying what the country was listening to in 1968 was not much different from analyzing what the mainstream population was watching. During one of the most turbulent years in American history, the three most popularly watched television programs were *The Andy Griffith Show*, *The Lucy Show*, and *Gomer Pyle, U.S.M.C.* The only prime-time program that made frequent reference to political and social events shaping peoples' lives was *Rowan and Martin's Laugh-In*, which did not debut until September that year.[37]

Such a disparity between popular entertainment and political and social reality may not be especially noteworthy; what people do to amuse themselves seldom does reflect political and social reality. But the incongruity between what was affecting so many people's lives and their source of entertainment in 1968 was so uncommonly extreme that it seems to contradict how we remember the sixties. While a minority of Americans were actively involved in creating social and political upheaval, the "silent majority" likely welcomed the escapism of Mayberry and the antics of Lucy Ricardo.

Writing in the January 1960 issue of *Esquire* magazine, noted historian Arthur Schlesinger, Jr., made the prescient observation that "the Eisenhower epoch—the present period of passivity and acquiescence in our national life—is drawing to a natural end," that the mood was apparent in

freshening attitudes in politics; in a new acerbity in criticism; in stirrings, often tinged with desperation, among the youth; in a spreading contempt everywhere for reigning cliches. There is evident a widening restlesness, dangerous tendencies toward satire and idealism, a mounting dissatisfaction with the official priorities, a deepening concern with our character and objectives as a nation.

Schlesinger may not have been anticipating an emerging counterculture, but he recognized the "rise of the Beat Generation" and attributed it in part to "the failure of our present society to provide ideals capable of inspiring the youth of the nation."[38]

Social rebellion is virtually synonymous with the 1960s, a confusing and challenging era when conflict delineated blacks and whites, young and old, liberals and conservatives, men and women, hawks and doves, demonstrators and hard hats, students and draftees. Public protests, assassinations, violence in the streets, and the war in Vietnam define the sixties as an era of swift and dramatic changes. The 1950s legacy of social complacency and personal conformity was altered forever as Americans in the 1960s questioned the quality of American life and values.

A THEMATIC INTERPRETATION

The chaotic 1960s are packed with personalities, images, and movements, making it difficult to identify just a few events. That reality notwithstanding, however, this study focuses on three topics—the New Left, the antiwar movement, and the counterculture—because they represent the turmoil of the era and effectively contribute to our understanding of the cultural revolution that profoundly changed America.

Baby boomers were far more numerous but much less passive than their parents' generation, as evidenced by the popularity of the Peace Corps and demonstrations against capital punishment. The New Left, and in particular the SDS and the Free Speech Movement at the University of California's Berkeley campus, where students demanded the freedom of political expression, effectively articulated and advanced the concept of participatory democracy throughout the 1960s. Perhaps more significant, the New Left introduced nonviolent protest tactics adopted by Martin Luther King, Jr., and the civil rights movement. Not an organization in the pure sense, the New Left was more a manifestation of student activism than a political constituency. The New Left is also significant because for the first time in history, members of the younger generation were the catalysts for sweeping social and political changes.

One change in particular that students targeted was the Selective Service System, which discriminated against young men of low economic status and racial minorities. Numerous loopholes also existed for draft-aged males with political connections or the financial resources to enable them legally to evade military duty. Several groups opposed the Vietnam War, including pacifists, Quakers, and conscientious objectors. The most vocal and the most visible doves, or critics of the war, however, were college students who were exempted from the draft—and probably Vietnam—because they held a deferment. Not even a significant minority of the "draft generation" took to the streets, but the largest antiwar demonstration in American history occurred in October 1965, when antiwar organizers mobilized about 100,000 people to demonstrate in ninety American cities. In April 1967, about 300,000 in San Francisco and New York City expressed their opposition to the war.[39] Some young men, either more desperate to escape the draft or more committed to the antiwar cause, risked a prison sentence when they burned their draft cards; about 40,000 others forfeited their citizenship and left the country for Canada and Sweden. Others more fortunate and less inclined openly to oppose the draft avoided a tour in Vietnam by enlisting in the National Guard. While Americans were debating whether the war was justified, many among the coming-of-age generation, too young to vote for their political leaders, became cynical, embittered, and alienated.

Some members of the under-twenty-five population who were less political but more disaffected than those active in the New Left or the antiwar movement adopted counterculture values based on drugs, sexual promiscuity, and communal living. "Flower children" provided colorful subject matter for the media and curiosity seekers. Although their alternative lifestyle was never widely accepted, they portended what historian Allen J. Matusow describes as "the erosion of liberal values that had sustained bourgeois society, the character type that had been its foundation, and the ethic that had undergirded efforts to accomplish its reform."[40] Concentrated primarily in the Haight-Ashbury section of San Francisco, the long-haired counterculture "freaks" were probably more disturbing and threatening to the establishment than either the New Left "radicals" or the antiwar protesters. The latter groups questioned governmental policies, but the counterculture challenged Americans' long-held and cherished values pertaining to religion, work, and the family.

Young people were not the only ones to express their discontent or disillusionment in the 1960s. Throughout the twentieth century, black civil rights activists pursued equality through legal means, either in the courts or by nonviolent marches and demonstrations. Sit-ins, Freedom Rides, Freedom Summer, and the march to Selma were successful actions that employed peaceful resistance to end segregation and discriminatory legislation. But by the middle of the decade, a phenomenon social scientists described as "rising expectations," and a perception among some activists that the government was moving too cautiously to eliminate racial inequality caused more militant factions like SNCC, the Black Muslims, and the Black Panthers to rise in influence and command public attention. Their advocacy of "Black Power" and their rejection of Martin Luther King, Jr.'s, emphasis on reconciliation with the white power structure once it recognized equal rights seriously weakened the civil rights movement. Many young blacks, influenced by Malcolm X's admonition to confront white racism rather than yield to it, and SNCC leader H. "Rap" Brown's call to "Burn, Baby, Burn," ultimately became involved in sometimes brutal confrontations with police. In August 1965, the first of numerous urban, race-related riots over the next three summers broke out in the Watts area of Los Angeles, resulting in thirty-four deaths and $35 million in property damage.

Collectively, these four themes played a vital and influential role in shaping the era. They illustrate how the baby boomer generation exposed social injustice and challenged authority. They also reflect the pervasive social and political unrest of the day, and exemplify racial and generational conflict. These events produced a legacy that has marked American political, social, and cultural life to this day.

NOTES

1. William Manchester, *The Glory and the Dream: A Narrative History of America, 1930–1972* (New York: Bantam Books, 1974), 1125; and Irwin Unger and Debi Unger, *Turning Point: 1968* (New York: Charles Scribner's Sons, 1988), 109–21. After Secretary of Defense Clark Clifford's commission evaluated Westmoreland's request, it concluded that further escalation would likely result in a counterescalation with no gain; President Johnson decided the number was unacceptable. By mid-April 1968, the number of American troops in Vietnam had risen to 549,000. In May, the North Vietnamese proposed peace talks in Paris, but it took many weeks for the diplomatic delegations to agree on the shape of the table and other peripheral matters before they could address critical war-related issues. While early negotiations were going on, 2,000 more Americans were killed in Vietnam.

2. Kenneth Crawford, "Tense New Year," *Newsweek*, January 1, 1968, 16.

3. Geoffrey Hodgson, *America in Our Time: From World War II to Nixon—What Happened and Why* (New York: Vintage Books, 1978), 155–56. Kennedy's federal appointments included Thurgood Marshall to the U.S. Court of Appeals in 1961; in 1967, Marshall became the first black associate justice to sit on the U.S. Supreme Court.

4. Dewey W. Grantham, *Recent America: The United States Since 1945* (Arlington Heights, IL: Harlan Davidson, 1987), 246–51; Allen J. Matusow, *The Unraveling of America: A History of Liberalism in the 1960s* (New York: Harper & Row, 1984), 83–85.

5. Kennedy is cited in Grantham, *Recent America*, 219.

6. Joseph R. Conlin, *The American Past* (San Diego: Harcourt Brace Jovanovich, 1990), 861. In early May 1961, Kennedy "was considering the wisdom of using U.S. forces in South Vietnam if such action became necessary to save that

country from Red domination," and noted that further involvement in Vietnam "is a matter still under consideration." "U.S. Weighs Use of GIs in Vietnam," *Philadelphia Inquirer*, May 6, 1961, 1.

7. Johnson is quoted in Conlin, *The American Past*, 863.

8. The Gulf of Tonkin resolution passed in the Senate by a margin of 88–2; after just forty minutes of discussion, the House of Representatives approved the measure 416–0.

9. Manchester, *The Glory and the Dream*, 1165.

10. The CIA developed Operation Phoenix in 1967 and terminated it when the peace accords were signed in January 1973.

11. Michael Schaller, Virginia Scharff, and Robert D. Schulzinger, *Present Tense: The United States Since 1945* (Boston: Houghton Mifflin, 1996), 151.

12. A. Philip Randolph mobilized his supporters to march in response to his claim that the government was "subsidizing discrimination" by refusing to hire blacks in defense plants, and set July 4, 1941, as the date they would march on Washington. President Roosevelt headed off the demonstration, however, when he signed Executive Order 8802, which established a Fair Employment Practices Committee.

13. William H. Chafe, *The American Woman: Her Changing Social, Economic, and Political Roles, 1920–1970* (New York: Oxford University Press, 1972), 224–25.

14. William L. O'Neill, *Coming Apart: An Informal History of America in the 1960s* (Chicago: Quadrangle,1971), 234.

15. Michael Harrington, *The Other America: Poverty in the United States* (New York: Macmillan, 1962), 4, 10.

16. Landon Y. Jones, *Great Expectations: America and the Baby Boom Generation* (New York: Ballantine Books, 1981), 4.

17. Ibid., 38.

18. Joan Morrison and Robert K. Morrison, *From Camelot to Kent State: The Sixties Experience in the Words of Those Who Lived It* (New York: Times Books, 1987), 159–60.

19. Rita Lang Kleinfelder, *When We Were Young: A Baby-Boomer Yearbook* (New York: Prentice Hall, 1993), 472.

20. Terry H. Anderson, *The Movement and the Sixties* (New York: Oxford University Press, 1995), v–vi.

21. Lawrence M. Baskir and William A. Strauss, *Chance and Circumstance: The Draft, the War, and the Vietnam Generation* (New York: Knopf, 1978).

22. Manchester, *The Glory and the Dream*, 1116.

23. Conlin, *The American Past*, 819; and Alex McNeil, *Total Television: A Comprehensive Guide to Programming from 1948 to the Present* (New York: Penguin Books, 1980), 901–6.

24. Charles Kaiser, *1968 in America: Music, Politics, Chaos, Counterculture, and the Shaping of a Generation* (New York: Weidenfeld & Nicolson, 1988), 69.

25. Manchester, *The Glory and the Dream*, 849, 1109.

26. O'Neill, *Coming Apart*, 220–21.

27. Kleinfelder, *When We Were Young*, 444.

28. Manchester, *The Glory and the Dream*, 1111.

29. John C. McWilliams, "Through the Past Darkly: The Politics and Policies of America's Drug War," *Journal of Policy History* 3 (1991): 365–67.

30. Schaller, Scharff, and Schulzinger, *Present Tense*, 339.

31. Alfred W. McCoy, *The Politics of Heroin: CIA Complicity in the Global Drug Trade* (New York: Lawrence Hill Books, 1991), 257–58.

32. Manchester, *The Glory and the Dream*, 1114.

33. Edward M. Brecher, *Licit and Illicit Drugs* (Boston: Little, Brown, 1972), 346, 366.

34. Ibid., 368–69; and David Steigerwald, *The Sixties and the End of Modern America* (New York: St. Martin's Press, 1995), 175.

35. Richard Sorrell and Carl Francese, *From Tupelo to Woodstock: Youth, Race, and Rock and Roll in America, 1954–1969* (Dubuque, IA: Kendall/Hunt Publishing Company, 1993), 59, 69, 164. The Beach Boys, most closely identified with music glorifying fast cars, surfing, songs, and the pursuit of an "endless" summer, could also be sassy—a kind of protest—when they rebelled against parental control chortling how much fun they would have cruising in daddy's T-Bird.

36. Fred Bronson, *Billboard's Hottest Hot 100 Hits: Facts and Figures about Rock's Top Songs and Song Makers* (New York: Billboard Publications, 1995). The top ten songs for 1968 were "Hey Jude" (Beatles), "I Heard It Through the Grapevine" (Marvin Gaye), "Love Is Blue" (Paul Mariat), "Love Child" (Supremes), "Honey" (Bobby Goldsboro), "Sittin' on the Dock of the Bay" (Otis Redding), "People Got to Be Free" (Rascals), "This Guy's in Love with You" (Herb Alpert), "Judy in Disguise" (John Fred and His Playboy Band), and "Woman, Woman" (Gary Puckett and the Union Gap).

37. McNeil, *Total Television*, 905. Other top ten television shows during the 1967–1968 television season included *Gunsmoke* (4), *Family Affair* (5), *Bonanza* (6), *Bewitched* (7), and *The Beverly Hillbillies* (12). The number-one nonfiction best-seller was *Better Homes and Gardens' New Cook Book*. The number-one fiction best-selling book was *Airport*. Americans were watching *The Graduate* and *Planet of the Apes* in the movie theaters.

38. Arthur Schlesinger, Jr., "The New Mood in Politics," *Esquire* 53 (January 1960): 58–60.

39. Jules Archer, *The Incredible Sixties: The Stormy Years That Changed America* (New York: Harcourt Brace Jovanovich, 1986), 54.

40. Matusow, *The Unraveling of America*, 307.

2

The New Left and the End of Consensus

At 4:30 P.M., on February 1, 1960, four unknown "well-dressed Negro students" from North Carolina A&T College entered the Woolworth store in Greensboro. An hour later they had secured their place in history. In an impulsive act of defiance, they challenged the store's discriminatory policy by refusing to leave until they were served a cup of coffee at the "whites-only" lunch counter. The bold action of these student activists set in motion a revolution that won the admiration of young white northerners and forged an informal alliance between them and southern blacks. By the end of February, the Woolworth sit-in was repeated in twenty southern cities.[1] The sit-ins helped set a pattern for other attacks on the status quo in the early 1960s and had a catalytic effect on the emergence of what sociologist C. Wright Mills called the "New Left."[2] A combination of idealism, rising expectations, and a huge baby boomer generation fueled "the Movement," as it was more popularly referred to. It was short-lived, lasting only a decade, but by 1970, it had profoundly altered the nation's institutions, its citizens, and even its conscience.

"WE DIDN'T START THE FIRE": REVOLUTIONARIES IN THE MAKING

The wave of radicalism that swept over the United States in the 1960s was part of the same thread interwoven in American political culture since the colonial era. Samuel Adams and his Sons of Liberty, almost always portrayed in history textbooks as American patriots, were radicals in their views and actions relative to British administrative policies. Frederick Douglass, Elizabeth Cady Stanton, W.E.B. Du Bois, Margaret Sanger, Eugene V. Debs, Malcolm X, and numerous other individuals whose ideology kept them on the fringes of the political mainstream were labeled "radical." Acting as the nation's conscience, they advanced causes as diverse as abolitionism, feminism, environmentalism, and civil rights.

Radicalism has a long history in the United States that includes not only adults championing causes but also student activists. During the Civil War, for example, students were involved in anti-conscription activities, and in 1931, the National Student League agitated for a "revolutionary movement against capitalism."[3] In the 1930s the Old Left was a coalition of socialists and communists whose activities were sharply muted after World War II by blacklists and witch hunts in the era of McCarthyism—an irrational fear and heightened suspicion of communists that ruined the lives and damaged the reputations of many loyal Americans. In the early 1950s, the total number of leftist student activist groups probably numbered fewer than one hundred.[4] "Old Left" children grew up exposed to ambiguous politics, believing that "Communism was 20th century Americanism" while revering Abraham Lincoln and Thomas Jefferson. The "red-diaper babies" also learned that while communists were not as committed to humane and libertarian ideals as they professed, America, the leader of the free world, did not always epitomize democratic ideals.[5]

Several factors figured prominently in the eruption of the loosely defined umbrella-like radical revolution that has become inextricably linked with the 1960s. That there were causes for radicals to strike out against—institutional racism, poverty, and social injustice—prompted a grass-roots, student-led revolutionary movement. But more responsible than these salient issues was the matter of demographics. Not only was the baby boom generation the largest to that time, so was the number of Americans striving for a higher education. Before World War II about 14 percent of college-aged Americans were in university classrooms; by 1960 that figure had nearly tripled to 38 percent, and it surpassed 50 percent by the end of the decade. In raw numbers, the growth in college enrollments was explosive, soaring from 2 million in 1946 to 8 million by 1970. The college population also was more heterogeneous than it had been prior to World War II. More women were attending college, and although college students were still overwhelmingly white, by 1970, more black Americans than ever before—9 percent—were attending college. Equally significant, a number of these college students came from affluent homes and were children of liberal and radical professional people, some persecuted by the red hysteria in the 1950s.[6] Eventually many "mainstream children" who initially might have been apolitical as they headed off

for their freshman year found themselves in highly politicized environments. On many college campuses, where they were segregated from everyday realities and encouraged to think critically about concrete and abstract
issues, students enjoyed four years of academic isolation to experiment
with different philosophies about the role of government and what some of
them regarded as the corruption of American democratic principles.[7] Students had ample opportunity to contemplate Henry David Thoreau's query
as to whether a citizen should "resign his conscience to the legislator."[8] In
this milieu future revolutionaries came of age.

A REVOLUTIONARY MANIFESTO

Student activism in the 1960s was rooted in the 1950s. The Supreme
Court's 1954 *Brown v. Board of Education of Topeka* ruling reversing the
"separate but equal" doctrine opened the door for black equality. That ex-
pectation, unfulfilled in the sixties, thrust the Student Non-Violent Coordinating Committee (SNCC) and the Congress of Racial Equality (CORE) to
the forefront of a militant civil rights movement. White civil rights activists
in turn fostered a growing concern about the role of the university in supporting military research and making herbicides and pesticides, nuclear annihilation in the cold war, and the growth of a Left movement.
"Radicalized" students were determined their participation in the American
democratic process would make a difference.

Named by Al Haber and Andre Schiffrin, Students for a Democratic Society (SDS) came into existence on January 1, 1960, and separated itself
from the Student League for Industrial Democracy (SLID) and the Marxist
Left. In its infancy, according to historian Allen J. Matusow, "the new left
was wholly innocent of ideology."[9] That spring it sponsored its first activity,
a conference on "Human Rights in the North" at the University of Michigan
to bring together southern civil rights workers with northern college students sympathetic with the civil rights movement. In June 1962, one of the
"northerners" in attendance was Tom Hayden, the twenty-two-year-old student editor of the *Michigan Daily*.[10] Politically inspired by the Old Left,
Hayden had just returned from the South where, as a civil rights activist, he
had been beaten by the Ku Klux Klan in McComb, Mississippi, and arrested
for "blocking the sidewalk" and "obstructing traffic" while waiting to board
a train for a Freedom Ride to Albany, Georgia.[11]

With the support of its parent organization, LID (League for Industrial
Democracy), SDS met June 11–15, 1962, at a United Auto Workers educa-
tional camp in Port Huron, Michigan, about fifty miles north of Detroit.[12]
After three days of intense deliberations, they produced a sixty-four-page,

25,000-word document. Hayden, the principal author, called attention in the *The Port Huron Statement* to the lack of popular control of political, economic, and educational institutions that had been contaminated by American liberal capitalism. Believing that racial segregation and discrimination, the emergence of poverty on a national level, and the possibility of nuclear extinction made fundamental changes necessary, he set the tone for the New Left in the prologue, "Agenda for a Generation": "We are the people of this generation, bred in at least modest comfort, housed now in universities, looking uncomfortably to the world we inherit."[13] Hayden also expressed concern about "disturbing paradoxes": in a supposed egalitarian nation, blacks and whites were not treated equally; America's stated desire for peace contradicted sharply with its huge military investment in the cold war; and dispossessed Americans lived in poverty in a nation of abundance and prosperity.

Hayden was apprehensive, disillusioned, and alienated, but he did not advocate radical or revolutionary action. Only when he stated his desire that "we seek the establishment of a democracy of individual participation" did he conjure up images of revolution. Hayden's concept of participatory democracy was controversial not so much because it suggested the introduction of a new kind of democracy, but because it lacked specific definition. Hayden's vision was that

we would replace power rooted in possession, privilege, or circumstance by power and uniqueness rooted in love, reflectiveness, reason, and creativity. As a *social system* we seek the establishment of a democracy of individual participation, governed by two central aims: that the individual share in those social decisions determining the quality and direction of his life; that society be organized to encourage independence in men and provide the media for their common participation.

Because Hayden did not clarify precisely what the concept was or how it was to be applied, some interpreted the *The Port Huron Statement* as being antidemocratic—something that would replace American democracy. Hayden was vague about what "participatory democracy" meant, but he was clear about who would be responsible for transforming the New Left's objectives into reality: "the university is a relevant place for all of these activities."

The New Left leadership believed that educated young people would be most receptive to its message, and it concentrated its efforts on college campuses, anticipating that students would be its agents of change. There was an abundance of baby boomers—5.5 million of them by the middle of the decade—in higher education. Even if only a very small minority of this huge group were radicals, it was clear this generation would have a significant impact on the university system. As journalist Milton Viorst put it, "Students, in fact, seemed to be acquiring a special sense of themselves, and of their political potential."[14]

THE MUSIC IS THE MESSAGE

When discussing the influence of popular music in 1958, cultural historian Jacques Barzun wrote that it leads to "an increasing resistance to words." Few parents would have disagreed with him that in the 1960s, Top Forty songs lacked harmonious lyrics.[15] But if popular music ever functioned as a cultural barometer that evoked social protest, it was during its transformation in the 1960s.

Several years before the music became "hard rock" or psychedelic, folk rock enjoyed a revival among the younger generation. Incorporating into their lyrics more social commentary than the typical Top Forty songs, some artists began to express their disaffection, alienation, and disillusionment with American institutions. Rather than lamenting the end of a romantic relationship as popular music frequently did, folk singers more serious about the repressive nature of a supposedly democratic government in the 1960s found receptive audiences on college campuses, where millions of students related to songs about personal freedom.[16] The singers were more than composers; they were interpreters, and in the 1960s their songs conveyed a message about contemporary social and political issues. Phil Ochs was often critical of southern attitudes toward blacks, and in 1962, he composed "Talking Vietnam" three years before the first antiwar demonstration.[17] Pete Seeger popularized on old labor song, "We Shall Overcome," which became a standard during the civil rights movement, while Peter, Paul, and Mary recycled the Old Left anthem, "If I Had a Hammer," first sung by Seeger's group, the Weavers; it made *Billboard*'s Top Ten hit list in 1962. That year the Kingston Trio had the number-twenty-one hit song, "Where Have All the Flowers Gone?" the first protest song to reach the Top Forty list.[18] In 1963 Peter, Paul, and Mary enjoyed popularity with Bob Dylan's call to arms, "Blowin' in the Wind," when it sold a million copies and was ranked number thirty-six for the year.[19] No rock 'n' roll song in the early 1960s would have made *Billboard*'s Top Ten list with lyrics aimed at Americans who were indifferent to a highly charged political atmosphere when Dylan questioned how many times young men must go to war for the world to have peace.

In the 1960s, Dylan, who adopted his name from the Welsh poet, Dylan Thomas, was the most influential songwriter of his generation, if not the twentieth century. An antiwar troubadour, Dylan's run-on sentences linking literature and popular culture were a radical departure from contemporary popular songs. In "Oxford Town" he told of James Meredith's struggle to enter the University of Mississippi in 1962, and his "Hard Rain A-Gonna Fall" was a somber look at the Cuban missile crisis. In "The Times They Are A-Changin'," released in February 1964, he warned the older generation they might be drowned in a youth-inspired social revolution, pleading with parents to be more tolerant of generational differences and to accept a newer ideology.

Also influential in the early folk rock era was Joan Baez, who often led protesters in singing motivational songs at peace demonstrations. Inspired by Seeger, Baez herself stirred 200,000 people when she led them in "We Shall Overcome" on August 28, 1963, in Washington, D.C., when Martin Luther King, Jr., delivered his historic "I Have a Dream" speech. During Freedom Summer in 1964, Judy Collins, Phil Ochs, and other folk singers formed a Mississippi Caravan of Music and sang in freedom schools to encourage black voter registration.[20]

Glen Campbell sang about the horrors of war and killing in Buffy St. Marie's "Universal Soldier" in 1965. That year the Byrds had the number-nine hit song for the year with "Turn! Turn! Turn!" a song Seeger adapted from the Book of Ecclesiastes, and their electrified version of Dylan's "Mr. Tambourine Man," more psychedelic rock than folk rock, was the number-twenty-nine hit song. Perhaps more surprising, however, was the popularity and commercial success of "Eve of Destruction." Recorded by Barry McGuire, a former member of the folk group the New Christy Minstrels, "Eve," the fastest-rising song in history, made it to number one in September 1965, after only five weeks. The song finished the year at number thirty-two, despite an organized campaign by the Radical Right to ban the record and several radio stations and ABC television's refusal to play it because it was "communist propaganda."[21] Written by nineteen-year-old P. F. Sloan, "Eve" was a much less complex view of world issues than "Blowin' in the Wind" or "The Times They Are A-Changin'," but the lyrics were a micro-documentary history of the era that captured the frustration and anxiety of the younger generation pondering an uncertain future with emotionally charged lyrics warning that violence, hypocrisy, and racism would determine the fate of the human race.

As a rebuttal to the hard-hitting "Eve of Destruction," the Spokesmen released "Dawn of Correction," a dismal flop. Despite the success of protest songs, traditional rock songs still dominated the charts; indeed, the Beatles' early songs worried more about holding hands than ending war. Although protest songs appealed to a narrow segment of the popular music audience, folk rock musicians of the sixties were exulting a mood of limitless hope and achievement as they "educated" their audiences about peace, racial justice, and tolerance while sometimes promoting idealistic expectations of a better tomorrow and a brighter future.[22] The influence of their music with a message, in which they grafted literary and social themes, helped transform that medium, as it also raised the collective conscience of the younger generation, who began to view the world differently. Guitar-playing activists, seemingly omnipresent at political demonstrations and rallies, and their songs provided encouragement and courage for those in the movement agitating for civil rights, women's rights, gay rights, the environment, and ending the war in Vietnam.

THE FREE SPEECH REVOLUTION

The Greensboro sit-ins were a warning to America's majority white populace in 1960 that it could anticipate similar acts of civil disobedience in the future. Few Americans, however, would have expected that the next similar eruption would be led by middle-class white university students largely indifferent to political activism.

The University of California's 27,000-student Berkeley campus, recognized as one of the nation's premier public universities, had a history of activism long before the 1960s. But on October 1, 1964, when university police tried to arrest twenty-four-year-old CORE activist Jack Weinberg, one of several students violating a university ban against distributing political literature on campus property, a rebellion broke out. A veteran of civil rights confrontations, Weinberg passively resisted arrest by going limp. Almost immediately, hundreds of onlookers surrounded the police car and held it and the officers inside hostage. Mario Savio, the chief student leader and twenty-one-year-old philosophy major who had taught in a freedom school in McComb, Mississippi, that summer, climbed on top of the car roof (after he had removed his shoes so he would not damage the car) to announce a rally. The Free Speech Movement (FSM) was born.

Over the next several weeks, as the administration considered its options to reassert in loco parentis and negotiated with FSM leaders, eight students were suspended and nine hundred graduate students went on strike, as students continued to hold rallies. About 6,000 people gathered at Sproul Hall Plaza where the demonstrators sang Dylan's "The Times They Are A-Changin'."[23] For inspiration, Joan Baez sang the "Lord's Prayer" and "Blowin' in the Wind."[24]

Addressing the crowd on December 2, Savio fused Martin Luther King, Jr.'s eloquent "Letter from Birmingham Jail" defining civil disobedience and the discontent expressed in Hayden's *Port Huron Statement* with an alienating and impersonal university by declaring that,

There's a time when the operations of the machine become so odious, makes you sick at heart, that you can't take part; you can't even passively take part. And you've got to put your bodies upon the gears and upon the wheels, upon the levers, upon all the apparatus, and you've got to indicate to the people who own it that unless you're free, the machines will be prevented from working at all.[25]

After Savio's speech, more than one thousand students staged a sit-in at Sproul Hall, marking the first time in the 1960s that students committed an act of civil disobedience against their own campus.[26] Early the next morning, after the demonstrators had been warned to disperse, 635 police officers entered the building and took 814 of them into custody (540 were students), making it the largest mass arrest in California's history.[27] Campus disorders erupted nationwide. In 1965, 114 students were arrested at the University of Kansas during a sit-in protesting racial discrimination in fraternities and sororities. Students at Yale University demonstrated when the university fired a popular philosophy professor. At St. John's University on Long Island, students protested a ban on controversial speakers, and three Stanford University deans resigned during a student government-related dispute.[28] The Free Speech Movement at Berkeley was the beginning, not the end, of student activism and a resurgence of the Left.

BARBARIANS AT THE GATE

During the first half of 1968, nearly 40,000 students participated in 221 major demonstrations at 101 colleges and universities. Although most of them were peaceful and ended without incident, some involved bombings, physical assaults on university officials, and scuffles between students and the police. Some of the radical elements who wanted peace in Vietnam declared war against the university. The year was one of constant turmoil for the nation, which stimulated a boost in the membership of the SDS to about 5,500 in chapters at two hundred colleges.[29]

In the first few months of the year, several issues converged to create a climate on America's college campuses conducive to rebellion. The North Vietnamese surprise Tet offensive in January was a clear indication that the war was going badly for the United States. The Selective Service System's decision to abolish draft exemptions for graduating seniors and first-year graduate students intensified antiwar activities, including demonstrations against ROTC and the Dow Chemical Corporation for manufacturing napalm, an incendiary jellied gasoline that American troops in Vietnam used.

Potential draftees also deplored universities' complicity in the war through contracts with the Institute for Defense Analysis (IDA), a consortium of twelve schools to evaluate weapons and conduct research for the Department of Defense.[30]

Few major campuses escaped some sort of conflict in 1968, but student dissatisfaction with the conduct of the war and college administrations was most dramatically demonstrated at Columbia University in New York City. That spring, in addition to the national-level issues, the Ivy League school was confronted with its own thorny local political concerns that made the campus ripe for a revolt.

As a landlord in Harlem, Columbia had an uneasy relationship with area tenants. When it announced plans to build a gymnasium in Morningside Heights Park, the university alienated the residents of the Harlem neighborhood and the campus Student Afro-American Society (SAS). Since the area had a high crime rate and people would be permitted access to the facility, Columbia trustees saw the gym as an amenity that local residents would welcome. Instead, Harlem residents resented the university's "invasion" of their neighborhood. The SDS had an active chapter at Columbia, but unlike the SAS, it had taken little interest in the gym project.

On April 23, 1968, less than three weeks after the assassination of Martin Luther King, Jr., Columbia erupted when the SDS held a rally to protest the university's IDA affiliation and disciplinary action against the suspension of six demonstrators in March. An integrated group of SDS and SAS members, chanting "Jim Crow Must Go," tore down a section of fencing and occupied ivy-covered Hamilton Hall, the administrative center for the undergraduate college.[31] There they imprisoned a dean and two other officials. The integrated coalition fractured the next day when the sixty SAS students, who were suspicious of white radicals, told the SDS leaders to take their own building. White students were led by SDS president Mark Rudd, a tough-talking junior who wrote an open letter to Columbia president Grayson Kirk that that closed with a line from the poet LeRoi Jones, "Up against the wall, motherfucker, this is a stick-up." The white students occupied Low Library, where they forcibly broke into the president's office, ransacked his files, smoked his cigars, and drank his sherry.[32]

After a week of chaos, President Kirk called in the police to restore order on campus. Black students occupying Hamilton Hall left without resisting. White radicals did not go so peacefully, and police beat them with nightsticks and brass knuckles and dragged them down the stairs head first. Outside the buildings, the police brutalized spectators, sometimes roughing up faculty members. By the time the melee had concluded, more than 100 people were injured and 698 were arrested. Rudd and 72 other students were suspended for a year. Most classes stopped meeting, and final exams were canceled.[33]

Student activists had forced a major university to shut down. The SDS might have regarded the occupation as its finest hour—SDS membership soared to approximately 100,000 members—but victory was fleeting. Over the next several months, factions within SDS more interested in violence and the seizure of power than opening a dialogue with the authorities ultimately led to its rapid decline.

REVOLUTIONARIES REVOLT

As the New Left, and in particular the SDS, became more radicalized, it became increasingly more difficult for the national leadership to maintain philosophical cohesiveness among interest groups advancing particular causes, such as civil rights, the antiwar movement, the women's movement, and the incipient environmental movement. Thousands of young people participating in hundreds of protests produced no positive, tangible response from the government. But when relatively peaceful demonstrations failed to alter the government's policies in Vietnam, the New Left became acrimonious, and internecine feuding resulted in convincing some extremists that nothing short of a revolution would stop the war. After five days of heated debate during the 1969 national SDS convention in Chicago, SDS was effectively split into three factions. If mainstream Americans thought the New Left threatening to democratic institutions prior to then, the embittered new splinter groups must have terrified them. The Maoist May 2nd Movement (M2M), formed in 1964 as an antiwar front, never had more than a few hundred members and was disbanded in 1966, but its radical ideology was the foundation for later revolutionary groups that would emerge by the end of the decade.[34] The Progressive Labor (PL) faction, a Marxist-Leninist cadre of Maoists, was committed to creating a proletarian dictatorship.

Another faction that erupted after the SDS meeting in October 1968 was an anarchist group calling itself "Up Against the Wall: Motherfuckers," an alliance of disaffected radicals and street toughs who despised ideology, as evidenced in one Motherfucker's justification of his organization's existence: "The fucking society won't let you smoke your dope, ball your woman, wear your hair the way you want to."[35] The Revolutionary Youth Movement (RYM, pronounced "rim"), a Marxist faction that would organize white working-class adolescents to fight beside blacks against capitalism, submitted a barely comprehensible policy paper.[36]

An ultra-left cell called the Weathermen was the most extreme and the most dangerous of the factions to surface in the spring of 1969.[37] Taking their name from "You Don't Need a Weatherman to Know Which Way the Wind Blows," a line in Dylan's apocalyptic "Subterranean Homesick Blues," they composed a 16,000-page position paper expressing their belief that it was the duty of white radicals to wage the anti-imperial struggle, which they would do through guerrilla warfare.[38]

Unlike the SDS and most other New Left groups, the renamed Weather Underground was more action oriented—more interested in blowing up buildings and killing people than engaging in a rational dialogue with authorities. They had no patience with SDS civil disobedience tactics and loathed hippies and Yippies who would not be taken seriously. As one Weatherman put it, "We're against everything that's good and decent in honky America." They sounded as if they were serious. No doubt they acquired a macabre view of the world. After Charles Manson and his "family" slaughtered movie actress Sharon Tate and several of her friends in Los Angeles and then disemboweled Tate with a fork, Bernadine Dohrn, a radical SDS activist, gave the grisly crime a perverted spin, relishing how "dig it, first they killed those pigs, then they ate dinner in the same room with them, and they even shoved a fork into the victim's stomach! Wild!"[39]

In the weeks preceding their self-proclaimed "Days of Rage" in October 1969, the Weathermen promised "the streets of Chicago [would] run with blood." They armed themselves with chains, pipes, and clubs and threatened to "tear pig city apart." Eighty Weathermen, wearing helmets and chanting "Ho, Ho, Ho Chi Minh, the NLF [the North Vietnamese army] is gonna win," charged toward a police barricade trashing automobiles and hurling bricks through windows. They then marched to Lincoln Park in Chicago, where they expected to join with others to "kick ass" and "bring the war home." Six Weather "soldiers" were killed and 250 were arrested, but not before the revolutionaries injured 75 police.[40]

Most of the radical Left did not share the Weather Underground's psychotic desire to commit random acts of violence. The SDS chapter at the University of Wisconsin parodied them with, "You don't need a rectal thermometer to know who the assholes are." The Weathermen quite literally blew themselves up on March 6, 1970, in an Eleventh Street townhouse in Greenwich Village in New York City. Three of them were killed by a blast that ignited the gas mains when someone connected the wrong wires while assembling a pipe bomb.[41] Dohrn was on the FBI's "Ten Most Wanted List" until she turned herself in eleven years later in 1980 in Chicago, after she and others decided "it was counterproductive to live underground without being a part of a political organization."[42]

REQUIEM FOR A REVOLUTION

In the end—and for the New Left the denouement was unmistakable and certain—this radical movement was a victim of overreaching its limits and a fundamental misunderstanding of what America wanted. In 1968, when the SDS claimed it had 100,000 members, the movement appeared to be thriving. Internal conflict, however, soon lead to fragmentation and disintegration. Even within itself, the New Left was dangerously at odds, splitting into competing factions. By 1969 the collapse was complete. That the New Left occurred at all was due primarily to an explosive demographic boom of what *Time* magazine called in its January 1967 issue the "inheritors," a generation of young people under twenty-five years of age who reshaped history. By questioning their parents' values pertaining to racism, materialism, and corporatism, the inheritors forced the establishment to reassess the nation's progress on these critical issues. They saw their self-appointed duty to remake America. New Leftists grossly overrated their importance and were too self-delusional in thinking that middle America would find its cause relevant. Hayden's "Agenda for a Generation," largely ignored by his own generation, was even less enthusiastically embraced by the older silent majority.

In reality, the SDS was never a widely representative movement, and its membership was composed predominantly of a very small elite faction. Because the New Left preferred local autonomy and decentralization, it lacked a bureaucratic cohesiveness, and because, by definition, it heartily supported "participatory democracy," the tendency for factions to emerge was greater. By the time the New Left had self-destructed, several identifiable splinter groups had irreparably damaged any unity that still remained.[43]

If numbers were the issue, it made sense when Tom Hayden and other New Left leaders decided to employ students as their agents of change. Although the SDS stressed students' rights, only a small minority of the student population took a leadership role in radical activities. SDS leaders also apparently did not recognize the universal shortcomings of this young and idealistic age group. Unlike Hayden and other SDS leaders, most college-aged students lacked the emotional stability and the intellectual maturity to sustain a long-term ideological commitment to even a noble cause. Students are transients—temporary residents on a college campus, who presumably are there to fulfill career aspirations. Some could be mobilized to march, demonstrate, or even risk arrest by occupying an administration building illegally. But once they left the campus as graduates, they became busy establishing careers and relationships; their affiliation with radicalism diminished, some of them even becoming part of the establishment they had rebelled against. One woman who participated in the 1968 student takeover as an SDS member at Columbia University to protest the Morningside Park gymnasium years later won a fellowship at the university and noted that "one of the ironies of my life is that now, during my fellowship, I'm spending more time in the gym than any other place on campus."[44]

Students were not the only group to waver in its allegiance to the New Left. Many radicals, waging a struggle to eliminate inequality and discrimination, were not "equal opportunity employers," for they relegated "females to a traditional, subservient capacity." Although as one-time SDS president Todd Gitlin confirms, "many of the women proved to be more effective organizers than many of the more celebrated men," the SDS alienated women by limiting them to performing menial tasks in demeaning roles. In what may have been the ultimate hypocrisy, radical women were not accepted by radical men. On the rare occasion a woman addressed a gathering of activists, she was often greeted with jeers and hoots. Marilyn Webb, a veteran of the movement and organizer of a Head Start program in Chicago, who addressed a MOBE gathering and contended that women were oppressed, was denounced with shouts, "Take her off the stage and fuck her!"[45] SNCC leader Stokely Carmichael once observed the "only position for women in the Movement was prone."[46] Sex—and sexism—also was used as antiwar propaganda. To encourage males to resist the draft, some pacifists used a poster featuring Joan Baez that read, "Girls say yes to guys who say no."[47]

COUNTERREVOLUTION

As the New Left was collapsing from within, external forces hastened its demise. Demonstrators who criticized the war effort in Vietnam and the university's role as a tool of the government could hardly have expected these institutions to be sympathetic. But rather than ignore the protesters, university and public officials frequently polarized the two sides and provoked further protests when they antagonized an already aggressive movement with contemptuous and inflammatory language. When asked about how to silence student revolutionaries, California governor Ronald Reagan, seeking a second term in office, commented during a campaign luncheon in San Francisco that "if it takes a bloodbath, let's get it over with. No more appeasement."[48]

After the University of California's Berkeley campus administration razed several homes as the intended site for a soccer field, neighborhood residents, including radicals, students, businesspeople, and some professors, planted flowers and vegetables. On some weekends as many as three thousand people might show up to cultivate gardens, install playground rides, cook, and perhaps smoke some marijuana. But university officials viewed "People's Park" as an affront, and Governor Reagan decided to respond forcefully. At dawn on May 15, 1968, bulldozers tore up the gardens, and a crew erected an eight-foot-high fence around the park. For several hours deputy sheriffs randomly fired shotguns loaded with birdshot into the crowd, killing one person, blinding another, and injuring more than one hundred people. That night three thousand National Guardsmen established martial law in the area and sprayed the entire university with tear gas, including the campus hospital and nearby schools.

San Francisco State University president S. I. Hayakawa, a hardliner appointed by Reagan, decided to confront protesters when he called in the city police and the National Guard to terminate a student demonstration in September 1968. Sporadic violence occurred over the next several months. After order was restored, Hayakawa remarked, "I enjoyed myself immensely during all the rioting. Whenever there was any trouble I stocked up for lunch in the office. From then on the biggest problem was whether to have sardines or paté de fois gras."[49]

According to J. Edgar Hoover biographer Richard Gid Powers, the FBI director "shed no tears for the students shot at Kent State," believing they "invited and got what they deserved." Hoover's rage against what he perceived as the moral decline of America was manifest in his determination to wage a covert war against the New Left and the SDS in particular. Despising New Left politics and its supporters who had "unloosed disrespect for the law, contempt for our institutions of free government, and disdain for spiritual and moral values," he directed the FBI to infiltrate and discredit the SDS and used provocateurs to instigate violence at demonstrations. He also was concerned that the SDS was "a militant youth group which receives support from the Communist party," and in March 1968, the FBI created COINTELPRO–New Left "to expose, disrupt, and otherwise neutralize" the antiwar movement."[50]

REFLECTIONS

When interviewed nearly two decades after the fall of the New Left, some of the participants recalled their activities and accomplishments. Jack Weinberg, who coined the phrase "Don't trust anyone over thirty" and generally has been credited with fomenting the Free Speech Movement at Berkeley in 1964, wryly recalled, "We were just interested in our own issues, not in setting a pattern for the country." Carl Oglesby, president of SDS in 1965, later recalled that "the best part of the struggle was the surrender." Jeff Jones, one of the Weathermen who participated in the Days of Rage, may have described the rationalization of the violent radicalism in the 1960s most aptly when he reflected that

it [the Weathermen] was based on wrong political ideas, and there was a very limited effectiveness, but how old were we? We were nineteen, twenty, and twenty-one. We were living in this incredibly violent period of history, trying to respond to it in a principled way, in a moral way. And this is how we responded to it.[51]

During an interview with *Time* magazine in 1977, when asked what the movement had achieved, Tom Hayden responded with a more positive assessment of the New Left, claiming that "We ended a war, toppled two presidents, desegregated the South, broke other barriers of discrimination."[52] Hayden dramatically overstated the Movement's accomplishments, but the New Left was not totally ineffective. Young people chanting in the early months of 1968, "Hey, hey, L.B.J., how many kids did you kill today?" reminded the public of American involvement in Vietnam and no doubt contributed to Johnson's decision to withdraw his bid for reelection that spring. SNCC activities did focus the nation's attention on racial inequality in the southern states and pressured Washington to enforce voting rights and abolish Jim Crow legislation.

The New Left did not collapse before achieving some success. Because of the Movement, the Selective Service System implemented a lottery system to replace a draft that called a disproportionate number of black and low-income young men. In part due to the Movement's political mobilization of previously disaffected or disfranchised groups and young people, the government was more inclined to the politics of inclusion that brought racial minorities and women closer to the mainstream. The women's movement in the 1970s owes much of its success to the New Left activism in the 1960s. Because of the Movement, universities abolished in loco parentis, introduced more relevant curricular reforms, recruited more minority students and faculty, and offered minorities and women's studies programs. Generally academia was more responsive to students' concerns about an impersonal administration by empowering them with positions on university committees.

EPILOGUE

Americans accustomed to the supposedly passive college student in the 1950s waving pom-poms at football games and spending hedonistic spring breaks at Florida beach resorts were aghast at the student activism of the 1960s. But the level of student activism and certainly of student civil disobedience and violence in the 1960s was exaggerated. Explosive events make for good media coverage, but only 7 percent of all protests during the first half of 1969 resulted in deaths or injuries.

The demise of SDS did not end the New Left movement; radicals continued to attack college campuses, blow up buildings, and disrupt learning. During the 1969–1970 academic year, campus disorders tended to be more spontaneous and simultaneous, prompted by the invasion of Cambodia and the killings at Kent State and Jackson State. Most institutions experienced an average of five protest incidents, though about one-third of them saw none. By May 10, "448 campuses were either still affected by some sort of strike or completely closed down." Campuses most plagued by student protests tended to share certain characteristics. Large campuses, such as the Universities of California, Wisconsin, and Michigan, were most likely to experience unrest. Protestant colleges were more susceptible to demonstrations than Catholic schools; two-year colleges rarely had to deal with campus disorders.[53]

Historian William J. Rorabaugh has observed that "the challenge to authority, while a part of all the sixties movements, was most closely identified with the New Left, and that challenge led Americans in all sorts of situations to be much bolder about questioning authority."[54] In *The Port Huron Statement*, Tom Hayden addressed the ongoing challenge to his generation when he envisioned the university as the agent for the New Left's social change. But Hayden was a visionary with a blind spot, and like many other revolutionaries, he and the SDS planted the seeds of their own demise. Hayden's *Port Huron* manifesto was an ambitious, encompassing conception of a political system that confounded most Americans—even the activists skeptical of anything hinting of establishment politics. They could not translate the abstraction of *Port Huron* into application.

In assessing the movement in 1977, Hayden wondered, "How could we accomplish so much and have so little in the end?" The answer was not much of a mystery. By 1970, when the draft was no longer an issue, the unparalleled idealism and frenetic giddiness driving the radical element earlier in the decade no longer sustained the tattered revolutionaries. The New Left made an impact—no tradition was safe and no custom secure—but it was a protest movement without a coherent program. Any radical notions of participatory democracy had faded. Dylan was right. The times, they were a-changin'.

NOTES

1. Clayborne Carson, *In Struggle: SNCC and the Black Awakening* (Cambridge, MA: Harvard University Press, 1981), 10. Blacks were served in Woolworth's but only if they ate standing up at the end of the lunch counter. Ironically,

the store management hired blacks to cook the food and wash the dishes. Michael Walzer, "A Cup of Coffee and a Seat," *Dissent* (September 1960): 112.

2. Mills may have popularized the term *New Left* but he did not originate it. The movement first gained recognition in France when Claude Bourdet founded the New Left in the aftermath of the Hungarian Revolution in 1956, taking the name *Nouvelle gauche*. It gained greater publicity in 1960 when it sponsored the "Declaration of the Right of Refusing to Serve in the Algerian War." Christopher Bone, *The Disinherited Children: A Study of the New Left and the Generation Gap* (New York: Schenkman Publishing Company, 1977), 2; and Kirkpatrick Sale, *SDS* (New York: Random House, 1993), 23.

3. Philip G. Altbach and Patti M. Peterson, "Before Berkeley: Perspectives on American Student Activism," in Philip G. Altbach and Robert S. Laufer, *The New Pilgrims: Youth Protest in Transition* (New York: David McKay Company, 1972), 13, 20.

4. Andre Schiffrin, "The Student Movement in the 1950s: A Reminiscence," *Radical America* 2 (May–June 1968): 27; and Armand L. Mauss, "The Lost Promise of Reconciliation: New Left vs. Old Left," *Journal of Social Issues* 27 (1971): 4.

5. James Miller, *"Democracy Is in the Streets": From Port Huron to the Siege of Chicago* (New York: Simon & Schuster, 1987), 136–37.

6. David Burner, *Making Peace with the 1960s* (Princeton, NJ: Princeton University Press, 1996), 136. For a detailed analysis of the student activists' backgrounds, see Richard Flacks, "The Liberated Generation: An Exploration of the Roots of Student Protest," *Journal of Social Issues* 23 (Fall 1967): 52–75; and Seymour Martin Lipset, "The Activists: A Profile," *Public Interest* 13 (Fall 1968): 39–51.

7. Allen J. Matusow, *The Unraveling of America: A History of Liberalism in the 1960s* (New York: Harper & Row, 1984), 308; and Burner, *Making Peace with the 1960s*, 136–37.

8. Thoreau is quoted from his *Civil Disobedience* (1849).

9. Matusow, *The Unraveling of America*, 309.

10. SLID was an offshoot of Upton Sinclair's Intercollegiate Socialist Society founded in 1905. Maurice Isserman, *If I Had a Hammer . . . The Death of the Old Left and the Birth of the New Left* (New York: Basic Books, 1987), 180–205.

11. Tom Hayden, *Reunion: A Memoir* (New York: Random House, 1988), 64–69.

12. Isserman, *If I Had a Hammer*, 208; and Stewart Burns, *Social Movements of the 1960s: Searching for Democracy* (Boston: Twayne Publishers, 1990), 56.

13. *The Port Huron Statement*, reprinted in Miller, *"Democracy Is in the Streets,"* 329.

14. Milton Viorst, *Fire in the Streets: America in the 1960s* (New York: Simon & Schuster, 1979), 163, 164.

15. Cited in Serge Denisoff and Mark H. Levine, "The Popular Protest Song: The Case of *Eve of Destruction*," *Public Opinion Quarterly* 35 (Spring 1971): 118–19.

16. In the 1930s and 1940s, Woody Guthrie, Pete Seeger, Phil Ochs, and other folk singers were popular among the working class when they performed union songs and Dustbowl ballads. R. Serge Denisoff, "Folk Music and the American Left: A Generational-Ideological Comparison," *British Journal of Sociology* 20 (1989): 429–33.

17. David P. Szatmary, *Rockin in Time: A Social History of Rock and Roll* (London: Schirmer Books, 1996), 105; and Robert A. Rosenstone, "'The Times They Are A-Changin'': The Music of Protest," *Annals of the American Academy of Political and Social Science* 382 (March 1969): 134.

18. In 1945, "We Shall Overcome," written as "I'll Overcome Some Day" in 1900, was sung as "We Will Overcome" by striking Negro Food and Tobacco Workers in South Carolina in 1945. Pete Seeger changed *will* to a more forceful *shall*. James Haskins and Kathleen Benson, *The 60s Reader* (New York: Viking Kestral, 1988), 85; Rita Lang Kleinfelder, *When We Were Young: A Baby-Boomer Yearbook* (New York: Prentice Hall, 1993), 323. "If I Had a Hammer" was number ten. Seeger appeared before the House Un-American Activities Committee and was cited for contempt of Congress when he refused to answer questions about his performances before communist-line groups. He was convicted in 1961, but the U.S. court of appeals reversed the decision in May 1962. "Folk Singing," *Time*, November 23, 1962, 60.

19. Fred Bronson, *Billboard's Hottest Hot 100 Hits* (New York: Billboard Books, 1995), 259, 264–65.

20. Jane Stern and Michael Stern, *Sixties People* (New York: Knopf, 1990), 113, 115–16.

21. Denisoff and Levine, "The Popular Protest Song," 118; and Carl Belz, *The Story of Rock* (New York: Oxford University Press, 1969), 168.

22. Twice as many students polled at San Francisco State University in 1965 who did not comprehend the "Eve of Destruction" did not understand "Universal Soldier." Denisoff and Levine, "The Popular Protest Song," 121.

23. Viorst, *Fire in the Streets*, 294; and Burner, *Making Peace with the Sixties*, 141.

24. Lewis S. Feuer, "Rebellion at Berkeley," *New Leader*, December 21, 1964, 5, 6.

25. Savio's speech is cited in Burner, *Making Peace with the Sixties*, 141.

26. Matusow, *The Unraveling of America*, 318.

27. William L. O'Neill, *Coming Apart: An Informal History of America in the 1960s* (Chicago: Quadrangle, 1971), 280.

28. Ibid., 285.

29. William Manchester, *The Glory and the Dream: A Narrative History of America, 1932–1972* (New York: Bantam Books, 1974), 1131.

30. O'Neill, *Coming Apart*, 289–90; Allen H. Barton, "The Columbia Crisis: Campus, Vietnam, and the Ghetto," *Public Opinion Quarterly* 32 (Fall 1968): 333; and Irwin Unger and Debi Unger, *Turning Point: 1968* (New York: Charles Scribner's Sons, 1988), 256.

31. Manchester, *The Glory and the Dream*, 1132; and O'Neill, *Coming Apart*, 290.

32. Barton, "The Columbia Crisis," 333–34; and Todd Gitlin, *The Sixties: Years of Hope, Days of Rage* (Toronto: Bantam Books, 1987), 307.

33. Manchester, *The Glory and the Dream*, 1134; Hayden, *Reunion*, 281–82; and Unger and Unger, *Turning Point: 1968*, 271.

34. Viorst, *Fire in the Streets*, 475. The May 2nd Movement took its name from the date of the first demonstration against the Vietnam War in the spring of 1964. Teodori Massimo, ed., *The New Left: A Documentary History* (Indianapolis: Bobbs-Merrill, 1969), 56.

35. O'Neill, *Coming Apart*, 292.

36. Viorst, *Fire in the Streets*, 484; and Matusow, *The Unraveling of America*, 338.

37. O'Neill, *Coming Apart*, 295.

38. Gitlin, *The Sixties*, 384; and O'Neill, *Coming Apart*, 296.

39. Viorst, *Fire in the Streets*, 302.

40. Gitlin, *The Sixties*, 393–94.

41. Ibid., 393.

42. Bill Ayers (Dohrn's husband) interview in Joan Morrison and Robert K. Morrison, *From Camelot to Kent State: The Sixties Experience in the Words of Those Who Lived It* (New York: Times Books, 1987), 320.

43. William J. Rorabaugh, *Berkeley at War: The 1960s* (New York: Oxford University Press, 1989), 139, 29.

44. Interview with Nancy Biberman in Morrison and Morrison, *From Camelot to Kent State*, 276.

45. Gitlin, *The Sixties*, 366, 363. Gitlin was president of the SDS in 1963.

46. Carmichael cited in ibid., 388.

47. William J. Rorabaugh, "Challenging Authority, Seeking Community, and Empowerment in the New Left, Black Power, and Feminism," *Journal of Policy History* 8, no. 1 (1996): 117.

48. "'Bloodbath' Remark by Gov. Reagan," *San Francisco Chronicle*, April 8, 1970, 1.

49. O'Neill, *Coming Apart*, 190; William H. Chafe, *The Unfinished Journey: America since World War II* (New York: Oxford University Press, 1995), 406; and Manchester, *The Glory and the Dream*, 1099.

50. Manchester, *The Glory and the Dream*, 1132.

51. Morrison and Morrison, *From Camelot to Kent State*, 230, 307, 315.

52. Lance Morrow, "An Elegy for the New Left," *Time*, August 15, 1977, 67.

53. Alexander W. Astin, "New Evidence on Campus Unrest, 1969–1970," *Educational Record* 52 (Winter 1971): 41–42; and *Report of the President's Commission on Campus Unrest* (Washington, DC: Government Printing Office, 1970), 17–18; and Alexander Astin, et al., *The Power of Protest* (San Francisco: Jossey-Bass, 1975), 41–43.

54. Rorabaugh, "Challenging Authority," 117.

3

Give Peace a Chance: The Antiwar Movement

To protest a $1.50 poll tax to subsidize the Mexican War, literary figure Henry David Thoreau spent a night in jail in July 1846 and urged others to join him in a "peaceable revolution." When his friend Ralph Waldo Emerson paid him a visit and asked, "Henry, what are you doing in there?" Thoreau replied, "What are you doing out there?" The exchange between the two transcendentalists may have been apocryphal, but Thoreau did go to jail rather than support the war. Thoreau was not the first American to question a government-declared war—a peace movement had begun by 1815—nor was he the only person to do so, but he may well be the best known, and he influenced many later antiwar protesters when he declared "The soldier is applauded who refuses to serve in an unjust war by those who do not refuse to sustain the unjust government which makes the war."[1]

Although the 1960s are commonly associated with peace activists and antiwar demonstrations, virtually every major conflict the United States has been involved in since the American Revolution has provoked protests. Opposition to the Vietnam War, however, differed from earlier protests; never before had so many Americans representing diverse organizations publicly questioned and demonstrated against their government in time of war. Whether the antiwar movement was successful in forcing the White House to negotiate an end to American involvement in Vietnam is still the subject of scholarly debate. More certain is that opposition to the America's longest war consumed a generation and left a legacy of ambivalence, bitterness, and animosity.

DISSENT

Two events in early 1965 stimulated and intensified antiwar sentiment in the United States. The first was President Lyndon B. Johnson's decision to initiate Operation Rolling Thunder, a series of B-52 bomber strikes against North Vietnam to "contain communist expansion" and escalate the number of troops in retaliation for a Vietcong attack on an American base at Pleiku on February 6. Throughout the year the number of American soldiers in Vietnam had increased eightfold, from 25,000 to 200,000. Prior to Pleiku, a critical turning point in the war, organized demonstrating against the war was minimal, with only the May 2nd Movement (M2M) providing any opposition.[2]

The second pivotal event occurred on March 24, 1965, at the University of Michigan, when several hundred faculty members and three thousand students conducted a teach-in, the nation's first major campus protest against the war. Several thousand people attended the all-night vigil in Ann Arbor, and during the next few weeks many other universities across the country held teach-ins. On the University of California–Berkeley campus, where the Free Speech Movement occurred a year earlier, the Vietnam Day Committee (VDC) staged the most spectacular teach-in on May 22, attracting 35,000 people over a period of thirty-six hours.[3] Soon antiwar protests spread rapidly beyond the campuses to massive demonstrations in the streets and other public venues. Protest tactics varied widely from passive prayer vigils to forfeiting one's citizenship or even life.

Although initially reluctant to divert its energy from other political activities, Students for a Democratic Society (SDS) sponsored the first mass protest against the war on April 17, 1965. Most observers expected the March on Washington to End the War in Vietnam to draw perhaps several hundred supporters. March organizers, and almost everyone else, were astonished when 25,000 demonstrators showed up to picket the White House and gather at the Washington Memorial, where they heard speeches and listened to Joan Baez and Judy Collins sing encouraging words.[4]

The protesters, whom one weekly news magazine described as "well-scrubbed, well-dressed, and well-behaved," petitioned Congress to consider possible courses of action in Vietnam, including reconvening the 1954 Geneva Conference that partitioned the country into North and South Vietnam at the seventeenth parallel, negotiating with the communist North Vietnamese National Liberation Front (NLF), or immediately withdrawing American troops.[5] By the end of the decade, antiwar demonstrators were vigorously pressing Washington officials to withdraw.

The April 1965 March on Washington was the first of many massive protests over the next several years. Between 1966 and 1967, as the tonnage of bombs dropped on Vietnam surpassed the total dropped in the Pacific theater during World War II, and the number of Americans in Vietnam escalated from 184,000 at the end of 1965, to 385,000 at the end of 1966, to 486,000 in 1967, so did the number of antiwar demonstrations. In April 1967, the Spring Mobilization Committee to End the War in Vietnam held two huge demonstrations that attracted 125,000 people in New York City and about 70,000 in San Francisco. Approximately 20,000 dissidents participated in Vietnam Summer in 1967. Modeled on Freedom Summer of 1964, Vietnam Summer volunteers encouraged civil disobedience by resisting the draft and hoped to mobilize the middle class to vote as a bloc against the war. The most dramatic antiwar demonstration occurred on October 21, when thousands of demonstrators crossed the Arlington Memorial Bridge during the March on the Pentagon. About the same time, during a "Stop-the-Draft-Week" protest in Oakland, California, thousands of students picketed the army induction center for five days to halt draft activities, and in December four hundred people were arrested during four days of protests around the country.

By April 1968, over a half-million American troops were in Vietnam, deaths had reached 22,951, and the war was costing American taxpayers $1 billion a month. In June, Vietnam had become the longest war in American history, surpassing the American Revolution. Thousands of American draft evaders and deserters were living in Canada and Sweden when the U.S. military commander in South Vietnam, General William C. Westmoreland, asked for 206,000 more troops. The Vietnam War continued to tear the country apart, and antiwar protesters grew increasingly antagonistic as it became more apparent the United States had become embroiled in more than a peacekeeping mission.

In 1969 the antiwar movement organized moratoriums. Prior to one scheduled on May 15, President Richard M. Nixon stated unequivocally that "under no circumstances will I be affected by it." His contempt for the protesters, whom he regarded as traitors, ensured a large turnout. Thousands of Americans wore black armbands and carried placards or candles in their antiwar vigils in New York City, Washington, D.C., Boston, and cities across the nation.[6] On October 15, antiwar activists organized the Vietnam Moratorium Committee when as many as 10 million Americans nationwide took time to participate in public discussions about Vietnam.

New Mobe (New Mobilization to End the War in Vietnam) organized yet another orderly march on Washington on September 15, 1969. While President Nixon watched a football game in the White House, 40,000 people passed by outside, each displaying a card with the name of an American killed in Vietnam. They marched four miles from Arlington to the Capitol, where they dropped the cards into a flag-draped coffin.[7]

VIETNAM—AT HOME

In August 1965, Congress passed legislation directed against the antiwar protesters, especially those who burned their draft cards. It was initiated by Congressman L. Mendel Rivers (D, South Carolina), an advocate of harsh penalties for anyone questioning the way the Selective Service System (SSS) administered the draft. Congressman Rivers, who also chaired the House of Representatives Armed Services Committee, called antiwar protesters "scum" and "vermin," and he intended to deter would-be draft protesters. For destroying a draft card offenders could receive a $10,000 fine or five years in prison.[8] The new law was tested two months after it took effect; on October 15, twenty-two-year-old David Miller deliberately burned his draft card during the first International Day of Protest. Three years later he was the first person convicted and sentenced to two years in a federal prison.[9]

Despite the threat of a heavy fine and the risk of a prison sentence, draft resisters continued to defy the law. In April 1967, the "We Won't Go" group at Cornell University sponsored a public draft card burning during a spring mobilization rally in New York City, and between 150 and 200 young men ceremoniously burned their draft cards in Sheep's Meadow in Central Park. Several thousand resisters turned their draft cards in, and about 250,000 others never registered. Perhaps the most famous resister, world heavyweight boxing champion Muhammad Ali, was convicted for refusing induction, sentenced to five years in prison, and fined $10,000. He never did go to prison, but the boxing association stripped him of his title.

Because antiwar activists expressed dissent more frequently and more openly during the Vietnam era than any other war period in American history, peace gatherings and marches were sometimes disrupted by citizens who felt the protesters were unpatriotic. Nevertheless, draft resistance and antiwar demonstrations not only occurred more often; they also were increasingly critical of the Johnson administration's handling of the war. Some protesters blamed the president personally for Vietnam, taunting him with chants of "Hell, no, we won't go." Even outside the context of a demonstration, the president was attacked for his policy. As a guest on the politically partisan *Smothers Brothers' Show*, Pete Seeger was censored by CBS for singing "Waist Deep in the Big Muddy." In the song's refrain, Seeger made a metaphorical reference to the United States' escalation of the war and Johnson's inability to recognize a lost cause.[10]

Although antiwar demonstrators frequently marched in front of the White House, the federal government did not begin to crack down on draft resisters until General Lewis B. Hershey, head of the SSS since 1941, issued a directive on October 26, 1967, ordering the 4,081 local draft boards to re-evaluate all "misguided registrants." Hershey also recommended that some of the protesters holding deferments be reclassified and that their induction into the armed forces be accelerated. Despite objections by several members of Congress and the American Civil Liberties Union, General Hershey wanted to classify anyone who participated in "illegal demonstrations" as 1-A, meaning they would be eligible for immediate induction. Hershey may have augmented the number of inductees, but another result was that about 10,000 young men crossed the border and relocated in Canada.[11] As a consequence of Hershey's mandate, more than one hundred draft registrants were declared "delinquent" and designated as top priority for induction even though the draft boards had no authority to determine if the inductees had engaged in illegal conduct.[12]

On the surface, SSS procedures appeared to be equitable and nondiscriminatory. In reality, however, the operations of the draft were inconsistent and blatantly racist. Because relatively few black Americans attended college in the 1960s, they were not eligible for a 2-S student deferment, and few of them were in occupations—farming and the ministry, for example—that could be draft exempt. When they did try to enlist, most ended up in the army, marines, navy, or air force, as opposed to safer reserve units. Few black men—1.15 percent—joined the National Guard. As a result, 30.2 percent of eligible blacks were drafted, as compared to 18.8 percent of qualified white inductees. The discriminatory impact of the draft was reflected in Vietnam in 1968 when 90 percent of the frontline troops were draftees. The disproportionate number of blacks drafted was attributed to racism, their socioeconomic status, and their lack of representation in the selection process. As late as mid-1968, only 600 blacks sat on more than 4,000 draft boards.[13]

While minorities and working-class whites were overrepresented in the draft, many middle-class white males received deferments. For those not eligible for a deferment but who did not want to be accused of avoiding the draft, another option that allowed individuals to fulfill their military obligation that was minimally disruptive was a six-year hitch with the National Guard, providing there was an opening.[14] If all available slots had been filled, political connections often facilitated an opening.

Lower socioeconomic class whites were victimized by a capricious draft system almost as egregiously as blacks were. Black or white, less privileged young men from poor neighborhoods who were high school dropouts or had no college education were more likely to be drafted. A draftee selected by the army or marines was almost certain to see action during a year's tour of duty in Vietnam. Others who were able to enlist in the air force or navy before they got drafted might serve in Vietnam, but they were less likely to engage the enemy in combat. More fortunate young men could satisfy their military obligation by enlisting in the coast guard, naval reserves, or a National Guard unit.

Many middle-class, draft-eligible men received 2-S student deferments that allowed them to remain in college and complete their education. In 1969, a year after the SSS terminated deferments for students in graduate school, some of them entered other exempt educational institutions such as seminary school. The "divinity" draft evaders with a 4-D exemption who had no intention of becoming clerics received a legitimate "out" when the Nixon administration introduced the first draft lottery since the 1940s. On December 1, 1969, using the same goldfish bowl used to draw World War I and World War II draft numbers, SSS officials drew capsules with birthdates to determine a draft priority list.[15] A high lottery number—over 250—allowed them to forgo their seminary school deferment or other bogus exemption and pursue graduate studies. This option, while not uncommon for affluent whites, was virtually unavailable for poor whites and blacks. Not surprisingly, the racial and economic discriminatory nature of the draft produced cynicism among prospective draftees.

Some draftees could argue, like Muhammad Ali, that religious beliefs prevented them from engaging in combat. If they could convince the draft board their pacifist beliefs were genuine, they would be granted a CO, or conscientious objector, deferment. Other means of escaping the draft included flunking the physical, which was not that difficult when a doctor agreed to certify the person as unfit for military duty. The most frequently sought exemptions were medical deferments, and there were literally thousands of disqualifying physical and mental conditions. The army's *Standards of Medical Fitness* listed more than four hundred defects and disabilities that could result in a 1-Y classification (ineligible under present conditions) or a 4-F (ineligible under any conditions). Missing toes, a congenital heart condition, or diabetes were creditable and unambiguous causes for exemptions. Other conditions, however, such as obscene tattoos, chronic bed wetting, large hairy moles, or dental braces were more subjective.[16]

If an individual was unable to demonstrate any physical deficiency, still other options were available. For a fee of $400 to $500 (during the Civil War exemptions cost $300), attorneys specializing in draft avoidance exploited loopholes to obtain legal deferments. Hardship exemptions, economic or mental, were relatively easy to procure. If a draftee's wife used illegal drugs or was seeing a therapist, most draft boards felt such dependence was "just cause" for an exemption.[17]

Thousands of draft violations during the Vietnam War overwhelmed the legal system. In 1969 federal courts handled over 2,340, nearly seven times the 341 offenders tried in 1965. The average sentence imposed for draft violators was forty-three months, eight months longer than the average sentence during World War II. Warning draft resisters they would he held accountable for their defiance, Congressman Rivers vowed on national television that such "traitors" would be duly punished.[18]

Most protesters stopped at burning their draft cards. A few, however, burned themselves. On March 16, 1965, Alice Herz, an eighty-two-year-old Quaker, poured gasoline over her body on a Detroit street corner and set herself on fire. She died ten days later. Just prior to a scheduled draft card burning ceremony began on November 6, Norman Morrison, a thirty-two-year-old Quaker, cradled his eighteen-month-old daughter as he walked to the river entrance of the Pentagon. A few feet outside Secretary of Defense Robert S. McNamara's office and fifteen feet from his daughter, he doused himself with kerosene and lit a match. Burned beyond recognition, he died before reaching the hospital. A week later, Roger LaPorte, a twenty-two-year-old Catholic worker from New York, sat down in the United Nations' Dag Hammarskjold Plaza, emptied a two-gallon container of gasoline over his body, and set himself afire. He died the next day.

Three immolations, the ultimate form of protest, and numerous draft card burnings indicated the depth of the conviction and moral outrage of some pacifists and antiwar activists. Self-immolation and even destroying draft cards were actions only a very few protesters were willing to take, but they made it difficult for others to remain complacent, passive observers.[19] Indeed, between 1967 and 1971 more than 5,000 men turned in their draft cards, and another 10,000 avoided the draft by going underground or by leaving the country for Canada or Sweden.

WHAT A FIELD DAY FOR THE HEAT

Three months after the student take-over at Columbia University in April 1968, seemingly every activist and radical group in the country was preparing to join forces in Chicago to protest the nomination of Vice President Hubert H. Humphrey as the Democratic presidential candidate. More than eighty peace groups organized by antiwar activist David Dellinger were there. Hippies were there. MOBE, peace activists, and the SDS were there. So were Yippies. A creation of Jerry Rubin and Abbie Hoffman, the Youth International party was in Chicago to hold a "Festival of Life" as an alternative to the Democrats' "Convention of Death." Disgusted with the growing cautiousness of the SDS, Rubin and Hoffman founded the Yippies in December 1967, "blending pot and politics into a political grass-leaves movement." The Yippies were not international and their absurd demand of "Acid for all!" and threats that "we will burn Chicago to the ground!" made it difficult to take seriously their "plank" for the abolition of pay toilets, or their nomination of "Pigasus"—a 200-pound pig—for president, but Rubin and Hoffman were determined to disrupt the Democratic convention.[20] Given the nature of events that had occurred during the first six months of 1968, confrontation and chaos at Chicago were inevitable.

Mounting furor over the conduct of the draft and the Vietnam War, increasing divisiveness within the SDS, a greater tendency of demonstrators to engage in violence, and the sense of exuberance experienced at Columbia contributed to an extremely volatile situation. In Chicago, Democratic mayor Richard J. Daley's intolerance of dissent and his impulse to unleash the police virtually ensured bloodshed, and it happened literally across the street from where elected leaders were participating in the democratic process of selecting a candidate for president.

Chicago in late August 1968 might have reminded some observers of Prague, Czechoslovakia, earlier that month when the Soviets invaded the city to suppress a democratic "revolution." No tanks cleared the streets in Chicago to put down freedom fighters, but Mayor Daley's policy of "zero tolerance" of disorderly behavior turned Chicago into an armed camp. Manholes around the International Amphitheatre, where the Democratic delegates would convene during the last week of August, were sealed with tar, and a seven-foot-high chain-link fence with barbed wire topping it was erected to prevent trespassing protesters. Daley also had at his disposal 11,500 city police and 5,500 National Guardsmen. Another 7,500 federal troops were standing by. The mayor was serious. The situation was so potentially explosive that the Secret Service advised President Johnson, elected four years earlier in a landslide victory, that it was too risky for him to attend. With security officers policing the aisles in the convention hall, the atmosphere inside was nearly as tense as it was outside. Senator Abraham A. Ribicoff (D, Connecticut) was so repulsed by Daley's fortress mentality that he accused the mayor of using "Gestapo tactics in the streets of Chicago."

On Saturday afternoon, two days before the convention opened, about 2,000 people had gathered in Lincoln Park. Protesters included serious

MOBE peace activists and satirical Yippies whose concept of revolution according to Hoffman "is that it's fun."[21] When the protesters ignored Mayor Daley's ban against camping in the city parks, the police ordered them to leave. Hundreds did, charging through the streets yelling antiwar slogans and clashing with the police. Around midnight, undisciplined police used tear gas and clubs to clear the remaining "trespassers" in Lincoln Park and Grant Park, across the street from the Hilton Hotel where tear gas permeated Vice President Humphrey's room. With television cameras recording the melee, Chicago police beat and gassed demonstrators, news reporters, and bystanders who happened to be within reach. People chanted, "The whole world is watching," as some police removed their badges and charged at the protesters shouting, "Kill, kill, kill."[22] The whole world was not watching, but 89 million American TV viewers witnessed the horror of the eighteen-minute mayhem. Twenty-one reporters were physically assaulted, *Playboy* publisher Hugh Hefner was Maced, and CBS correspondent Mike Wallace was punched in the face. When the riot was over, 668 people were arrested, over 1,000 were injured, and 1 person was dead. With "Happy Days Are Here Again" playing in the background, Humphrey absolved the Chicago police of any wrongdoing and accepted the presidential nomination. He narrowly lost the election in November to Richard Nixon because Johnson and the Democratic party would not or could not extricate the nation from the quagmire in Southeast Asia and the increasing domestic disgust with government bullying and deception. Voters desperately wanted to believe that President-elect Nixon would follow through on his pledge to bring Americans home from Vietnam, resolve the crisis, and maintain "peace with honor."

KENT STATE AND AFTERMATH

On April 30, 1970, President Nixon announced on national television that "tonight American and South Vietnamese units will attack the headquarters of the entire communist military operation in South Vietnam. This is not an invasion of Cambodia."

Nixon's action to widen the war contradicted his assurances that he was withdrawing troops. The president might not have defined his order as an invasion, but most viewers did. The student population was outraged, and their reaction was immediate. Princeton University students and faculty members voted to strike. Students took over an administration building at Oberlin College, seized the university center and closed U.S. Route 101 at the University of California at Santa Barbara, and established a strike center at Brandeis University in Waltham, Massachusetts. Four days later, at the unlikely site of Kent State University in Kent, Ohio, National Guardsmen opened fire on protesters, killing four and wounding nine students, several of whom were not engaged in any protest. College campuses experienced another wave of disorder as more than 500 canceled classes. Four million students participated in demonstrations at half the nation's campuses, resulting in hundreds of arrests and the destruction of thirty ROTC buildings.[23]

Within four days of Nixon's Cambodian announcement, student strikes had occurred on nearly one hundred campuses. On May 9–10, more than 100,000 students gathered in Washington. Ten days after the Kent State killings, similar violence occurred at Jackson State College in Mississippi. Although students there were conducting a peaceful antiwar protest on May 7, the confrontation between students and police on May 14 had no connection with either Cambodia or Kent State. Police, overreacting, fired 150 rounds of ammunition into a women's dormitory, penetrating every floor. Two students were killed and twelve wounded, all black. By the end of May, 415 colleges and universities had been disrupted by spontaneous student strikes. Nixon's Cambodian operation had resuscitated what had been a moribund antiwar movement. America was killing its young in Vietnam and at home.

A year after he sent five hundred National Guardsmen to the Kent State University campus, Ohio governor James Rhodes disdainfully characterized the students as "worse than the Brownshirts, and the Communist element and also the night riders and the vigilantes. They're the worst type of people that we harbor in America."[24] Although the presidential-appointed Scranton Commission that investigated the shootings at Kent State concluded that the "61 shots by Guardsmen certainly cannot be justified," Vice President Spiro T. Agnew blasted the report as "pabulum for permissiveness."[25]

During "May Days" in 1971, demonstrators were arrested for violating a park permit in the capital city while nationwide memorials for the students slain at Kent State and Jackson State attracted thousands of people in major cities. In response to Nixon's order to bomb North Vietnam's Haiphong Harbor in April, spontaneous antiwar rallies erupted on campuses nationwide, with the most disruptive at the University of Maryland, where two thousand student demonstrators blocked U.S. Route 1, a major artery linking Baltimore and Washington, D.C. Over the next three years antiwar protests occurred less frequently, but they were generally well supported by opponents of American foreign policy in Vietnam. On July 4, 1974, about two hundred Vietnam Veterans Against the War held a four-day demonstration outside the White House, and in January 1975, when the Gerald Ford administration wanted to save South Vietnam from imminent collapse, several thousand people participated in a candlelight march to the White House to persuade negotiators to save the peace agreement that had been hammered out in 1972–1973 and led to the withdrawal of most American troops.[26] On April 30, 1975, Saigon fell to communist North Vietnamese troops, who renamed the South Vietnamese capital Ho Chi Minh City. Seven years later, on November 13, 1982, a Vietnam Veterans Memorial black granite wall bearing the inscriptions of the names of the 57,939 Americans who died in Vietnam was formally dedicated in Washington.

For eight years, from 1965 to 1973, the draft was a fact of life for every eighteen-year-old male. For some, military induction was nearly a rite of passage, an unquestioned duty. For others, getting drafted, possibly to serve in Vietnam, was not a "patriotic chore"; rather, it forced individuals to make agonizing decisions that might alienate them from their friends and families, especially if their father was a World War II veteran.

Antiwar demonstrators would have negligible influence on public opinion had not the media created the exaggerated impression that the entire under-twenty-five generation was in revolt against the war. Historian Alan Brinkley more accurately noted that "few of the younger opponents of the Vietnam War had ever been true pacifists; they opposed a particular war, not all wars."[27] Unlike World War II, when military service was a unifying experience, during Vietnam it was divisive. To most Americans—then and now—the image of a draft resister is a long-haired, self-serving, "revolutionary" student who would rather burn his draft card and refuse induction than serve his country. Many students did protest against the draft and American involvement in Vietnam, but the Movement encompassed diverse organizations formed before President Johnson committed American troops to Southeast Asia.

In the latter half of the decade, the number of young men prosecuted for refusing to be drafted increased tenfold, from 369 in 1965 to 3,800 in 1970, but the number who refused was only a fraction of the white, middle-class, college-educated youths who evaded the draft quite legally, with no risk of imprisonment. Hypocrisy was characteristic of the SSS bureaucracy. In 1965 twenty-three-year-old Joe Namath, who signed a $400,000 contract with the New York Jets, received a 4-F draft classification. Namath could play quarterback for a professional football team, but he was declared unfit for military duty because of a torn ligament in his right knee.[28] Critics of the SSS and parents of draftees wondered how the SSS could claim it needed men so desperately while rejecting Namath.

SECOND THOUGHTS

Just as the New Left lacked unity among its supporters and eventually fragmented, so the antiwar movement was an amalgamation of various blocs that shared little commonality beyond their opposition to the Vietnam War. The antiwar movement, never guided by a single individual, was hindered internally by dissension and sometimes conflicting principles. Contrary to the media's depiction of the movement as a group of radical "peaceniks," its membership was a melange of supporters, including students, clergy, union members, teachers, and housewives. An element of radicalism in the movement was evident—SDS, the Old Left, and hippies, for example—but antiwar protesters represented a cross section of American society. The media also erroneously gave the impression that the entire boomer generation enthusiastically embraced the antiwar movement.

Regardless of who the antiwar demonstrators were or what they did, mainstream America was uncomfortable with such expressions of public dissent. Although by 1968 many Americans opposed the war, they rejected protesters whom the white, blue-collar middle class perceived as unpatriotic, spoiled anarchists unwilling to make a sacrifice for their country. When antiwar demonstrators chanted, "Hell, no, we won't go" and "Give peace a chance," the older "silent majority" countered with, "My country, right or wrong," "No glory like Old Glory," and "If your heart ain't in it, get your ass out." Disagreement over America's role in Vietnam was influenced as much by social class as it was by politics. Four days after the killings at Kent State, construction workers in Manhattan beat up a group of antiwar demonstrators as police watched passively. Several days later, President Nixon accepted a symbolic hard hat from "patriotic" union leaders imprinted with "Commander-in-Chief."

Whatever the political legacy of the 1960s, Vietnam is the principal reason for it. The war demonstrated to a generation of Americans, particularly the baby boomers, that the United States was not omnipotent, that it was not militarily invincible, and that it could not assume intervention for the "right" cause would produce victory. Americans also learned they could no longer trust or believe their political leaders. Although most of them wanted to forget the disheartening experience of Vietnam, more than thirty years later, the cultural divide resulting from the ordeal manifested itself when public opinion held elected officials accountable for what they did during the war. During the 1992 presidential election, for example, Democratic candidate Bill Clinton's alleged draft dodging and his opposition to the war cost him considerable support among veterans. But if American voters in the 1990s were certain that evading the draft was unacceptable, they were ambivalent about a candidate's war record—or lack of one. Republican Vice-President Dan Quayle's status as a Vietnam-era veteran was seldom a campaign issue, though he benefited from his family's political influence that had enabled him to escape service in Vietnam by enlisting in an Indiana National Guard unit. Senator Phil Gramm (R, Texas), who attacked opponents for their lack of military experience, took advantage of several deferments to complete his college education, later rationalizing that "I thought what I was doing at Texas A&M was important."[29]

Unlike most of the men who served in Vietnam, Clinton, Quayle, Gramm, and others who questioned the government's war were able to avoid active military duty. Typically, many GIs were less well informed about such options or even the war itself. As one enlistee recalled, "I knew almost nothing about it. The war, I thought was like they taught us in high school, you know, you're fighting communism, you know, it was just the good guys against the bad guys."[30]

The antiwar movement also had considerable influence on American popular culture, as evidenced by a spate of Hollywood films that were mostly critical of the Vietnam War. In 1969 folk singer Arlo Guthrie was called for a pre-induction examination in *Alice's Restaurant*, a critical portrayal of the draft system. Later productions with the Vietnam War as their theme included *Coming Home* (with Jane Fonda playing the wife of a U.S. Army officer), *The Deer Hunter*, and *Born on the Fourth of July*. The 1970s Emmy Award–winning television show *M*A*S*H*, set in the Korean War, was an anti–Vietnam War vehicle.

Popular music reflected antiwar sentiment. The folk rock conscience-raising songs of Dylan and Baez in the early 1960s continued to remind audiences about the lack of egalitarianism in American democracy. The message was essentially the same, but the medium had changed. The new hard rock protest sound, largely ignored on AM radio, found an audience on new FM stations that played album cuts and the full version of songs longer than three minutes.

The antiwar movement's influence was perhaps more ideological than cultural. Many white liberals opposed racial inequality and the Vietnam War on the same moral grounds. Civil rights leader Martin Luther King, Jr., an opponent of the war since 1965, said that Americans could hold "peace rallies just like we have freedom rallies," and contended that civil rights and Vietnam "are inextricably bound together." Dr. King's opposition to the war was not limited to speech-making. On April 4, 1967, at Manhattan's Riverside Church, he announced his profound opposition to the war, calling the United States "the greatest purveyor of violence in the world today." Eleven days later, he marched in the spring MOBE demonstration in New York

City and helped launch Vietnam Summer in Cambridge, Massachusetts, the following week. King's opposition to the war was bold; he risked losing financial support for civil rights initiatives and political support from the Johnson administration.[31] But because the government's financial commitment to Vietnam was siphoning off money that might have been spent on ending housing discrimination, school segregation, and the systematic denial of voting rights, King felt compelled to take a more active role against the war.

By taking its message to the streets, the antiwar movement showed activists of other diverse and unrelated causes that they too would be recognized. Supporters of women's rights, gay rights, legalized abortion, and environmentalism achieved gains by publicizing their grievances before the nation. "Taking it to the streets" was an effective means of popularizing a cause, but it also involved confrontation, and in the raucous 1960s, confrontation frequently resulted in violence. In a milieu of racial polarization, political assassinations, the rapid emergence of a spirited youth counterculture, and the proliferation of underground radical organizations, the antiwar movement was merely another manifestation of the era's culture of violence and disdain for authority. Civil rights activists broke laws—albeit unjust laws—students defied campus administrators and the police, and urban rioters turned residential neighborhoods into combat zones. Violence had become such a national concern by 1968 that Republican presidential candidate Richard Nixon successfully campaigned on the theme of law and order.

The passing of time tends to soften or alter popular sentiment. A decade after 50,000 Americans fled the country rather than be drafted or serve in Vietnam, President Jimmy Carter extended full amnesty in 1977 to 11,000 of the expatriates who still had not returned. Time also blurs the public's memory in other ways. The three-pronged peace symbol so closely associated with a fringe element of society and scorned by middle America in the 1960s was frequently displayed, almost nostalgically, in television commercials and prime-time programming in the 1990s.

Many Americans saw protesters and protest as anathema to the democratic principles the nation represented. Questioning government policy was permissible as long as one did so respectfully. Burning draft cards, calling the police "pigs," and jeering the president of the United States were expressions that conveyed disrespect. But by exercising the rights of peaceful assembly, freedom of speech, and petitioning the government, antiwar protesters validated the necessity and value of the First Amendment. Americans may admire or despise what the antiwar movement represented, but it brought about sweeping changes in the American cultural pysche, if not governmental policy. By directing the nation's attention on the terrible costs of human life and the utter futility of the war—which the government attempted to conceal—it galvanized opposition that eventually ended America's involvement in a tragic, protracted, and failed effort to stop the spread of communism. The movement also made political leaders, then and since, more sensitive to sending American troops abroad when the military objectives are not clearly defined.

America's commitment to make the world safe for democracy by intervening in Vietnam's internal affairs and the antiwar movement's determination to force withdrawal brought the country to the brink of revolution. The ideological clash traumatized the nation. At the very least, the conflict led Lyndon Johnson to decide not to run for reelection and forced policymakers to focus on withdrawal. U.S. involvement in Vietnam lasted longer than World War II and the undeclared war in Korea combined. Over a fourteen-year period from 1962, when President John F. Kennedy committed non-combat personnel, to the fall of Saigon in 1975, the Vietnam War cost nearly 60,000 fatalities, more than 300,000 wounded, and $191 billion. Countless lives of veterans and family members were emotionally shattered. Never before had America sacrificed so much for so little.

Whether they were trying to destroy America or remake it, those in the antiwar movement were intoxicated by the belief in limitless possibility during an age of idealism. Regardless of its failures or successes, however, a generation would be forever haunted by the grim legacy of Vietnam.

NOTES

1. Henry David Thoreau, *Essay on Civil Disobedience* (1849).

2. Teodori Massimo, ed., *The New Left: A Documentary History* (Indianapolis: Bobbs-Merrill, 1969), 57–58.

3. Howard Schuman, "Two Sources of Antiwar Sentiment in America," *American Journal of Sociology* 78 (November 1972): 514; Massimo, ed., *The New Left*, 56; and Irwin Unger and Debi Unger, *Turning Point: 1968* (New York: Charles Scribner's Sons, 1988), 304–8.

4. Massimo, ed., *The New Left*, 56; Michael Ferber and Staughton Lynd, *The Resistance* (Boston: Beacon Press, 1971), 33; and Nancy Zaroulis and Gerald Sullivan, *Who Spoke Up? American Protest Against the War in Vietnam, 1963–1975* (Garden City, NY: Doubleday, 1984), 40–41.

5. "Rebels with Cause," *New Republic*, May 1, 1965, 5–6.

6. William Manchester, *The Glory and the Dream: A Narrative History of America, 1932–1972* (New York: Bantam Books, 1974), 1175.

7. Ibid.

8. Jean Carper, *Bitter Greetings: The Scandal of the Military Draft* (New York: Grossman Publishers, 1967), 17.

9. Joan Morrison and Robert K. Morrison, *From Camelot to Kent State: The Sixties Experience in the Words of Those Who Lived It* (New York: Times Books, 1987), 107–11; and Manchester, *The Glory and the Dream*, 1055.

10. Peter Landry, "Staring at Years of Divisiveness: Could This Be Our Era's Vietnam?" *Philadelphia Inquirer*, December 15, 1998, A35.

11. Unger and Unger, *Turning Point*, 330; and Manchester, *The Glory and the Dream*, 1073.

12. John de J. Pemberton, "The War Protestor," *Current History* 55 (July 1968): 23.

13. Ulysses Lee, "The Draft and the Negro," *Current History* 55 (July 1968): 33–34.

14. Tom Morganthau, "Decade Shock, " *Time*, September 5, 1988, 14–16.

15. "Coming Changes in the Draft—Effects of the Lottery," *U.S. News & World Report*, December 1, 1969, 39.

16. "Beating the Draft, 1970 Style," *Newsweek*, November 9, 1970, 28; and "Rx for Draft Dodging," *Newsweek*, August 3, 1970, 42.

17. "Beating the Draft, 1970 Style," 28.

18. John Poppy, "The Draft: Hazardous to Your Health?" *Look*, August 12, 1969, 33.

19. Zaroulis and Sullivan, *Who Spoke Up?* 1–3; Charles DeBenedetti, *An American Ordeal: The Antiwar Movement of the Vietnam Era* (Syracuse, NY: Syracuse University Press, 1990), 129–31; Thomas Buckley, "Man, 22, Immolates Himself in Antiwar Protest at U.N.," *New York Times*, November 10, 1965, 1; and Thomas Powers, *The War at Home: Vietnam and the American People* (New York: Grossman Publishers, 1973), 87–88.

20. James Miller, *"Democracy Is in the Streets": From Port Huron to the Siege of Chicago* (New York: Simon & Schuster, 1987), 284–85.

21. Michael Schaller, Virginia Scharff, and Robert D. Schulzinger, *Present Tense: The United States Since 1945* (New York: Houghton Mifflin, 1996), 320.

22. Allen J. Matusow, *The Unraveling of America: A History of Liberalism in the 1960s* (New York: Harper & Row, 1984), 420.

23. Edward P. Morgan, *The 60s Experience: Hard Lessons about Modern America* (Philadelphia: Temple University Press, 1991), 164.

24. Manchester, *The Glory and the Dream*, 1214.

25. Ibid., 1175, 1214, 1216.

26. Zaroulis and Sullivan, *Who Spoke Up?* 358, 365, 370–73, 381, 386, 413–16.

27. Alan Brinkley, "Dreams of the Sixties," *New York Review of Books*, October 22, 1987, 12.

28. Carper, *Bitter Greetings*, 146.

29. Arnold R. Isaacs, *Vietnam Shadows: The War, Its Ghosts, and Its Legacy* (Baltimore: Johns Hopkins University Press, 1997), 46.

30. Loren Baritz, *Backfire: A History of How American Culture Led Us into Vietnam and Made Us Fight the Way We Did* (New York: William Morrow and Company, 1985), 283.

31. David J. Garrow, *Bearing the Cross: Martin Luther King, Jr., and the Southern Christian Leadership Conference* (New York: William Morrow and Company, 1986), 429–30, 555–58.

4

Tune In, Turn On, Drop Out: The Counterculture

Cultural revolution in the 1960s was evident in civil rights demonstrations, student radicalism, race riots, feminist demands, antiwar protests, and a general rejection of authority and mainstream values. Many Americans were convinced that the established social order was crumbling or already shattered. The appearance of hippies in the mid-1960s and the emergence of a counterculture reinforced the perception that the cultural revolution was more threatening to the post–World War II consensus than political unrest and violence in the streets.[1]

Hippies and their unorthodox creed confounded and alarmed middle America. Hippies were a direct outgrowth of the disillusioned beats in the 1950s, critics of the stifling conformity of the Eisenhower era, and heirs of a long tradition of rebellion, but unlike their forebears, hippies were apolitical and embraced no ideology. The New Left and other ideological groups of the 1960s agitated for tangible social changes; hippies had no aspirations to repeal laws or replace policies. They believed society had placed too much emphasis on conformity, and they were convinced that America had become too materialistic, competitive, and anxiety ridden. Shunning Christianity, nationalism, and private property, hippies preached love and sought bliss. Rather than try to improve a system they saw as irreparably flawed, they rejected it.

Some hippies were "peaceniks" who supported the antiwar movement. About six hundred of them tried to levitate the Pentagon through group meditation during the October 1967 demonstration, but most hippies were otherwise nondoctrinaire and indifferent to political issues. While the Free

Speech Movement, Students for Democratic Society, the Student Non-Violent Coordinating Committee, and other radical groups were striving to create alternatives to mainstream society, hippies offered no such reforms. Mostly they were disengaged from controversial issues. Hippies were for nothing. They had no desire to take to the streets. Although young blacks and hippies suffered from discrimination, hippies did not support the civil rights movement because, as one of them noted, "the Negroes are fighting to become what we've rejected. We don't see any sense in that."[2] Instead, hippies adopted Native Americans' mysticism and their dress—wearing ponchos, serapes, and beads—because they identified with their "primitive naturalness" and victimization by the dominant white American culture. Preaching love, nonviolence, altruism, and honesty, the hippies' only professed aim was to save a decadent America by "flower power," but not forcefully and not by proselytizing. "Do your own thing" was the basic tenet of their leaderless and unorganized culture, and they were mindful not to force "their thing" on anyone else. They wanted mostly to be left alone. Their unwritten golden rule was, "Be nice to others, even when provoked, and they will be nice to you."[3]

Some hippies, sympathetic to New Left causes or the civil rights movement, engaged in political activism. Some appeared in antiwar demonstrations in Berkeley, and in November 1966, a few thousand of them protested in New York City. Hippies even showed up at the Democratic convention in Chicago in 1968 to renounce the Vietnam War and to participate in a "People's Convention." They also were lured to Chicago by Abbie Hoffman's Youth International party, a contrived title for the farcical "Yippies." Hoffman described an unofficial alliance with the Yippies, hippies, and activists as a "blending of pot and politics."

Yippies were not really organized, but they did have a platform, calling for an end to the war, freedom for blacks, full employment, the elimination of pollution, free birth control and abortions, and the legalization of drugs. Some of their less legitimate proposals included the total disarmament of the police, for people to be able to fornicate "all the time, anytime, whenever they wish," and the abolition of money, pay clothing, pay food, and pay toilets.[4] Because Yippies and hippies sometimes intermingled at demonstrations with New Left and antiwar activists, the media and the public had difficulty distinguishing between committed political activists who wanted to influence government policy and counterculture participants whose main objective was to have fun lampooning the establishment.

Other people were hippies because they were disgusted with middle America, wanted to rebel against parental authority, or simply wished to drop out. Many "weekend hippies" adopted the hippie dress and mannerisms but not the lifestyle. A majority of those who saw themselves as hippies were not necessarily "real" hippies, and few young people who adopted the hippie lifestyle did so through any conscious decision.

The counterculture is nearly impossible to define. Its "members" shared no particular goals or ideas. They supported no programs and, except for the desire to seek "real freedom" through sex, drugs, and music, they had no other common objectives. Although true hippies never numbered more than 300,000 nationwide, their colorful appearance and outrageous behavior made them media favorites. As psychedelic dropouts, hippies were a foreboding and bizarre reverse image of the middle-class ethos—what historian Arnold Toynbee called "a red warning light for the American way of life."[5] They seldom regarded anything seriously, but their existence was a serious concern to adults. Counterculture scholar Theodore Roszak observed that when correctly understood, "the psychedelic experience participates significantly in the young's most radical rejection of the parental society." California governor Ronald Reagan's less flattering characterization of a hippie—a view probably shared by most Americans—was one who "dresses like Tarzan, has hair like Jane, and smells like Cheetah."[6]

LSD, TRIPS, AND THE CULT OF HIPPIEDOM: OH, WOW!

Hippies were especially open to experimentation. More than any other characteristic or behavior, the use of experimental drugs most visibly defined the counterculture. Drug use also was the trait of the hippie lifestyle that mainstream Americans found most disturbing. Marijuana, or "grass," which was ubiquitous, easy to grow, inexpensive, and produced a pleasant intoxication, became a staple of the hippie subculture. But lysergic acid diethylamide (LSD) was the favorite, and Timothy Leary, a Harvard University psychology professor, was its self-appointed promoter, even establishing a religion, the League of Spiritual Discovery. LSD was usually consumed in pill form and produced an eight-hour to twelve-hour "trip" that profoundly altered the user's thought, mood, and perception. An LSD "trip" was an experience that heightened sensations so that the user could "feel" colors, soul-search, hallucinate, and perhaps see God, but not without potentially adverse effects, including prolonged anxiety, impaired memory, and emotional breakdown. For Leary and other hippies, LSD was "one of the best and healthiest tools available for the examination of the consciousness."[7]

Alcohol and tobacco were acceptable "mainstream" drugs because they could be consumed in moderation, without necessarily altering the user's level of consciousness. "Hippie drugs" were objectionable to the middle class because they induced almost immediate euphoria. Counterculture drugs—and drug users—were labeled as deviant. For hippies, though, the establishment's fear and loathing of illicit drugs was blatant hypocrisy, not just because of the popularity of alcohol and tobacco, but also from the heavy prescription drug usage by middle-class Americans. When physicians wrote 147 million prescriptions for tranquilizers, sedatives, and amphetamines in 1965, three thousand people died from legal drug overdoses.[8]

More than any other event, the Trips Festival in January 1966 defined the emergence of a new counterculture. Staged by Ken Kesey, author of the 1962 novel *One Flew over the Cuckoo's Nest*, and his followers, the Merry Pranksters, Trips was advertised as "an LSD party without the LSD." Actually there was plenty of LSD, and the festival was a wide-open three-day party drawing 20,000 people appearing in Victorian dresses, Civil War uniforms, four-inch heels, Indian headbands, and clown regalia. Members of Hell's Angels wore leather and chains, and Prankster Neal Cassady dressed as a gorilla bridegroom. The celebrants were entertained by a local band, Mother McCree's Uptown Jug Champions, later known as the Grateful Dead, who introduced "acid rock," a new, forceful psychedelic sound. Hippies relished group experience, and at Trips they could easily identify one another by their distinct dress and patois, and acknowledged one another by forming a "V" with two fingers to indicate "peace." They seemed to embody the lyrics of the Youngbloods' "Get Together," which entreated people to love each other and to treat one another as brothers.[9]

On October 6, 1966, the hippies held a "Love Pageant Rally" on the Panhandle, a small park near Haight Street in San Francisco, to observe the day that California made the possession of LSD a misdemeanor. Characteristic of counterculture types, hippies flaunted the new law when several thousand of them and a few tourists turned out with free food, music, and drugs, giving local residents an exaggerated sense of the hippie influence. "Straight" society usually overstated the impact of anything associated with hippies and had difficulty understanding the hippie mind-set, as the following exchange between a straight person and a hippie demonstrates:

Straight: Why do you wear your hair so long?

Hippie: Because I think I'm beautiful.

Straight: Why are your clothes so colorful?

Hippie: Because I have self-respect. Say, have you ever stopped to think that writing *STOP* on a sign is a pretty silly way to communicate that concept? It'd be much better if stop signs had God's eyes on them, don't you think? People would stop for God's eyes.

Straight: How do you know what God's eyes look like?

Hippie: 'Cause I looked into them, baby.[10]

Not surprising, the hippie philosophy remained an enigma to most Americans, quite possibly due more to its simplicity than its complexity. Hippies often exhibited an almost child-like fascination of the world around them. Flower children seeking a more peaceful, alternative culture seemed bewildered by everyday realities. A typical hippie response when pondering life's complexities, particularly when under the influence of a hallucinogenic drug, was, "Oh, wow!"

WHERE DO ALL THE HIPPIES MEET?

Few other street corners are as famous as the intersection of Haight and Ashbury in central San Francisco. A person walking between 1400 and 1800 Haight Street after 1966 would have noticed immediately that this neighborhood was different. "Hashbury," the epicenter of the counterculture in the 1960s, resembled an adult Disney World where young people sought peace and love away from the material world. Hippies danced, wore flowers, and talked of love. Hundreds of new dropouts and thrill seekers arrived every week. By June 1966, an estimated 15,000 hippies had moved in. But they came without jobs and little or no money, and so they slept on the sidewalks and panhandled for food or sold marijuana or acid tablets. Drugs, sex, parties, psychedelic music, and a continuous street show of "freaks," "heads," dropouts, and nonconformists of all stripes populated the Haight. Hashbury was a unique community where an LSD Rescue Service helped people cope with bad trips, the Psychedelic Shop offered a meditation room, and the *Dope Sheet* was a popular advice manual for hippies on how to avoid a bad drug experience. The Print Mint sold psychedelic posters, the Weed Patch dispensed drug paraphernalia, and the Blushing Peony had an inventory of "non-establishment" clothes. Patrons could meet friends and catch up with the latest news at the Blue Unicorn coffee shop or hang out in "head shops." Because hippies preferred marijuana and LSD to alcohol, the Haight had few bars, theaters, or other entertainment spots. The San Francisco *Oracle*, the hippie capital's underground psychedelic newspaper, carried the comic strip *Captain High* and informed its 100,000 readers about drug busts, love-ins, police activities, microbiotic diets, and rock concerts.[11]

The Haight also had its own social workers—the Diggers, named for seventeenth-century utopian English farmers who raised food for the poor. Forming a street theater group of actors called the Mime Troupe, the Diggers renounced capitalism, declaring that "money lust is a sickness. It kills perception ... almost all of us were exposed to this disease in childhood, but dope and love are curing us." They held a "Death of Money" parade, even burned money, and when anyone inquired who was in charge, they replied,

"You are!" They staged free concerts, provided free shelter, and operated a Free Store that gave away clothing; each afternoon at four o'clock, Diggers distributed free food. All one needed to do was pass through a thirteen-foot square yellow "Free Frame of Reference," a symbolic threshold separating the way things were and how they might be.[12]

For a time almost as many tourists as hippies converged in Hashbury. In 1967 the Gray Line Bus Company charged six dollars for a two-hour "Hippie Hop" excursion through the "Sodom of Haight," advertised as "the only foreign tour within the continental limits of the United States." Drivers "especially trained in the sociological significance" of the Haight used a "glossary of hippie terms" to educate the "square" curiosity seekers. Resentful of being ogled by invading members of the establishment, hippies held mirrors up to the bus windows so gawking tourists could see themselves.[13]

HAPPY CHAOS: BEING IN, THE SUMMER OF LOVE, AND DEATH OF HIP

The summer of 1967, a pivotal year for the counterculture, was a cultural paradox. Americans were waging a two-front war: one in Vietnam that continued to intensify, the other at home with bloody urban riots that destroyed areas of Detroit and Newark, New Jersey, and erupted in several other cities. Meanwhile, the hippies "tuned out" and "turned on." Their seeming peace amid so much violence in Asia and America attracted many young people to Hashbury to share a summer of love. In San Francisco, the hippie population had been increasing, and all over the country young people responded to a "strange vibration." Many of them were "teeny boppers" in early adolescence who arrived in Hashbury by the thousands. They wore beads around their necks and flowers in their hair, smoked marijuana, and "dropped acid." Author Joan Didion expressed the sentiment of most Americans when she observed about the summer of love, "We were seeing the desperate attempt of a handful of pathetically unequipped children to create a community in a social vacuum."[14]

The counterculture entered popular culture by the summer of love. Television was slower to change than music. Through most of the decade, *F-Troop*, *Bewitched*, *The Flying Nun*, and *The Newlywed Game* remained among the top-rated television programs; *The Andy Williams Show* and *The Monkees* were Emmy Award winners in 1967, and in 1968 more Americans watched the final episode of the *Howdy Doody Show* than the coverage of the Vietnam War on the evening news. In popular music, "Groovin'," "The Letter," and "I Heard It through the Grapevine" were best-selling hits, but the Trips Festival helped move acid rock into the mainstream Top Forty.

"Incense and Peppermint," "Ruby Tuesday," and "Penny Lane" got airplay on AM radio stations, and an abbreviated version of the Doors' seven-minute sexually suggestive "Light My Fire" was a number-one song for three weeks in July. The album of the year, the Beatles' *Sgt. Pepper's Lonely Hearts Club Band*, a complex production featuring a forty-one-piece orchestra, displayed the first cover to express a concept.

In addition to the Beatles, other groups that produced top-five albums in 1967 were the Rolling Stones, the Doors, and Jefferson Airplane. Traditional rock 'n' roll still had a large following, but the audience for "acid" or "hard" rock was growing rapidly. Unlike the Top Forty rock 'n' roll songs, the new psychedelic music was not written to sing along with or dance to. Allusion to drug use in the music of the Beatles, Jefferson Airplane, and Sly and the Family Stone were not lyrics reminiscent of the early era of rock 'n' roll. The new music was loud and electronically distorted, and often laced with mystic messages. By the late 1960s, psychedelic songs had become counterculture vehicles for disseminating the hippie philosophy.

Indicative of the popularity of the new psychedelic sound, many performers, such as the Stones, Beatles, Doors, Jefferson Airplane, and the Grateful Dead, profited from the lucrative counterculture music business. Gaining exposure at the Fillmore West in San Francisco, the Fillmore East in New York's Greenwich Village, and similar sites around the country, these and other groups would eventually become music superstars and members of the Rock and Roll Hall of Fame. Thirty years later, their songs are regularly heard as background music in television commercials, in movie soundtracks, and on jukeboxes and AM and FM radio stations.

Drugs and music were inseparable ingredients of the drug-oriented counterculture. Some acid rock songs, written expressly to complement drug use, seemed to induce a sense of euphoria even without drugs. The Beatles' "A Day in the Life," the Chambers Brothers' "Time," and the Iron Butterfly's "In-a-Gadda-Da-Vida" used special effects and eerie rhythms to enhance the listener's natural high. In "White Rabbit," a psychedelicized interpretation of *Alice in Wonderland*, Jefferson Airplane sang about how the listener could determine his drug experience depending on the substance of choice. Several radio stations would not play the Byrds' song "Eight Miles High" because it glorified drug use. In March 1967, teenage hippies, believing Country Joe and the Fish were on the level when they reported getting stoned on banana peels, went on a great banana binge; hardly a vendor in the Haight could keep the fruit in stock. Donovan's "Mellow Yellow" was interpreted as a disguised message that banana peels were hallucinogenic, triggering impromptu banana smoke-ins. Bananas were bananas, but the craze so concerned the United Fruit Company about how such publicity would affect its sales that the Federal Drug Administration investigated the hoax.[15]

On January 14, 1967, a date set by an astrologer, about 25,000 people celebrated the "gathering of tribes" and the birth of the Age of Aquarius. The world's first "Human Be-In" was promoted as an occasion when

Berkeley activists and the love generation of the Haight-Ashbury will join together with members of the new nation who will be coming from every state in the nation, every tribe of the young to powwow, celebrate, and prophesy the epoch of liberation, love, peace, compassion, and unity of mankind.[16]

Thousands of people congregated for no other reason than to do nothing. Leary encouraged people to "tune in, turn on, and drop out," beat poet Allen Ginsberg read poetry and "purified the ground" with Hindu mantras, and Jefferson Airplane and the Grateful Dead provided the music. Diggers distributed free turkey sandwiches for physical nourishment and acid for mental enhancement. The public was aghast at the "psychedelic picnic," but when the be-in concluded, the flower children collected their litter and left the park clean. Two police officers monitoring the festivity had no complaints about the hippies' conduct.[17] The be-in marked the beginning of the media's fascination with the inhabitants of Haight-Ashbury, who were photographed, analyzed, and pondered as radical dropouts.

In mid-June, more than fifty thousand people paid $3.50 to $6.00 to hear Big Brother and the Holding Company, the Grateful Dead, Country Joe and the Fish, the Mamas and the Papas, the Who, and the Byrds at the Monterey International Pop Festival, about one hundred miles south of San Francisco. The hugely successful Monterey Festival gave national exposure to a number of previously unknown bands, and new performers emerged. Otis Redding popularized soul music, Jimi Hendrix electrified the audience with his explosive guitar playing, and Janis Joplin convinced many in the audience she was the greatest white blues singer ever. Monterey police chief Frank Marinello was so impressed with the behavior of "these so-called hippies," he "made arrangements to be escorted through the Haight-Ashbury district by some of my new-found friends."[18]

The Summer of Love did not survive the fall. On October 6, 1967, disillusioned with all the media attention, the abuse of drugs, the rise in crime, and the invasion of "day-trippers," hippies proclaimed their own demise with a "Death of Hip" ceremony and a frolicsome funeral procession through Golden Gate Park. The "corpse" they carried in a gray box labeled "Summer of Love" clutched a zinnia, a symbol of death for the flower children. At the end of the parade two hundred mourners sang "God Bless

America" and "Hare Krishna" as they set the coffin on fire to signify the end of "flower power." Television cameras were on hand to capture all its outrageousness.[19]

COUNTRY PARADISE

The hippies' illusory search for peace and love in the Haight was derailed by reality. Put off by curious tourists and bus tours and disillusioned with mainstream commercialism and materialism, many hippies gave up on Hashbury and fled to rural areas, where they could be close to nature. The communes they established were as varied as their inhabitants. Among the approximately thirty that developed in Canada, Mexico, and the United States, hippies lived as Hindus, Buddhists, Christians, and feminists. Some lived as vegetarians in wigwams, while others preferred log cabins. In going their various ways out of Hashbury, the hippies revealed how little had held them together.

The variety of lifestyles among post-Hashbury hippies made it more difficult for outsiders to understand the counterculture, which had no "center" and no unifying beliefs. The Hog Farm commune near Taos, New Mexico, for example, was a self-described "expanded family, mobile hallucination, a sociological experiment [and] an army of clowns." Eventually Hog Farmers packed up and assumed a nomadic life following rock festival tours.[20] In Drop City, near Trinidad, Colorado, twenty-one hippies lived in nine geodesic domes built from old automobile tops, where they eked out a hand-to-mouth independent life. Morningstar Ranch, along the Russian River north of San Francisco, was a thirty-one-acre apple orchard where hippie farmers grew vegetables for the Diggers. Twin Oaks in Virginia was a version of behavioral psychologist B. F. Skinner's "Walden Two." The Farm in Tennessee and Gorda Mountain in Big Sur were other communes that rejected technology and materialism to practice the communal spirit of cooperation as in "voluntary primitives."[21] A few of the communes thrived, but like the first American utopias established 150 years earlier, most of them were doomed by internal conflict over authority or ownership, economic hard times, or the hostility of their "straight" neighbors.

THREE DAYS OF PEACE AND MUSIC

Outdoor music festivals were not unprecedented in the United States—the first occurred at Worcester, Massachusetts, and it has been an annual event since 1858—but in the 1960s, large outdoor concerts, where patrons could mingle with like-minded friends in a communal setting in the pursuit of peace and love, had become increasingly popular. Rock festivals in Monterey, Atlanta, Seattle, and Atlantic City were financially successful and well supported. The advertisement for the August 1969 Woodstock Music and Art Fair promised the appearance of more than twenty performers, including Joan Baez, the Who, Arlo Guthrie, Canned Heat, Jefferson Airplane, the Grateful Dead, and Jimi Hendrix. As the personification of hippiedom, Woodstock—actually held at Bethel, New York—was the most successful counterculture event.

Anticipating 100,000 people, promoters leased six hundred acres of land from Max Yasgur, a local farmer, and planned to charge an eighteen dollar admission fee. So many people—perhaps a million and a half—began arriving on August 14, the day before the festival began, however, that state police closed the New York Thruway. "Long hairs" from throughout the country parked their cars and walked miles to the site. As the crowd grew to more than 400,000 people, overwhelmed festival promoters realized the futility of trying to collect a fee and allowed everyone in to experience the greatest program of rock talent ever assembled. Richie Havens opened the concert with "Freedom." Joan Baez, John Sebastian, Arlo Guthrie, and others followed on "folk day." The music began again at 1:00 P.M., on Saturday, and continued until Monday morning as Credence Clearwater Revival; Sly and the Family Stone; Canned Heat; the Grateful Dead; Janis Joplin; Santana; Country Joe and the Fish; Blood Sweat and Tears; Crosby, Stills, Nash, and Young; Joe Cocker; the Moody Blues; and others entertained nearly a half-million crowded, dirty, and rain-soaked fans.[22]

The mainstream media predicted that Woodstock would be a catastrophic weekend, and by all measures, it should have been. With very little security and almost no police protection, severe food shortages, a limited medical staff, inadequate toilet facilities, drugs everywhere, and fierce thunderstorms that turned the field into a swamp, disaster did seem inevitable. Some people suffered from dehydration, and several experienced bad drug trips, but, remarkably, there was no rioting. At Woodstock, the hippies gave peace a chance.

After three days of continuous music, three deaths were reported—two drug related and a third when a tractor accidentally ran over a person in a sleeping bag. One woman gave birth. A sense of community among the crowd fostered cooperation and civility. Wavy Gravy and other members of the Hog Farm commune flew in from New Mexico to provide aid for people on bad trips, the army transported doctors and emergency supplies by helicopter, and many local townspeople contributed food and water. Some farmers complained about hippies trying to milk their cows and others expressed their disapproval of the drugs, drinking, and nudity, but generally

Woodstock was as advertised: "three days of peace and music." The police chief in nearby Monticello called the festival throng "the most courteous, considerate, and well-behaved group of kids that I have ever been in contact with in my twenty-four years of police work."[23] Despite the drugs, unsanitary conditions, a three-hour wait to use a pay telephone, and shortages of almost everything, no violence—not even a fistfight—occurred.[24] Jimi Hendrix closed the festival at 8:30 Monday morning before a sparse, fatigued crowd with his psychedelic interpretation of the "Star-Spangled Banner" and "Purple Haze."

Woodstock was a weekend of sex, drugs, and rock 'n' roll. The gathering of "Woodstock Nation," as Abbie Hoffman mythologized it, also was a transition between eras. Joni Mitchell immortalized the historic cultural event that helped define a generation in her song, "Woodstock," performed by Crosby, Stills, Nash, and Young.

In contrast to Woodstock, the free concert staged by the Rolling Stones on December 6, 1969, at Altamont Speedway outside San Francisco, did not pass without incident. With members of the Hell's Angels motorcycle club providing the security for $500 worth of beer, Altamont was a tragedy. Only four songs into the concert, Angels high on acid indiscriminately assaulted people with sawed-off pool cues.[25] Three songs later they stabbed and kicked to death Meredith Hunter as Mick Jagger was singing "Sympathy for the Devil." By the end of the day, four people were dead. If Woodstock was the brightest shining moment of the counterculture, Altamont was its darkest.

LEGACY

Few parents from the generation that learned how to "live tight" during a ten-year depression in the 1930s and "fought the good fight" in World War II in the 1940s would have imagined their children would conscientiously reject riches for rags in the 1960s. Perhaps the most exasperating aspect about hippies for parents was that the social dropouts were not disfranchised blacks, poverty-stricken whites, or oppressed young people, they were white, affluent, middle-class children indifferent to opportunity and status, so highly valued by the establishment. In snubbing their noses at tradition and the Puritan work ethic, hippies widened the gap between the generations to a nearly unbridgeable chasm, or so many parents claimed. Young people with long hair, goofy clothes, a string of beads, and a sprig of flowers with a live-and-let-live philosophy were disconcerting to a society accustomed to social conformity, order, and respect for the American dream. Mainstream America could not comprehend why their sons and daughters would willingly give up a comfortable lifestyle in a suburban split-level home for a life of poverty on the streets.

Part of the mystique and attraction of the hippie movement was its invitation to freedom. It lured young people out of a rigidly structured work world to a life emphasizing individuality and "doing your own thing." "Hippieness" was more a state of mind than a tangible cult that drew all kinds of people: the young and rebellious, naturally, but also the poets, the disaffected, and worse. Hippiedom also was a magnet for emotionally disturbed misfits, some of whom, like psychotic killer Charles Manson, took advantage of vulnerable, alienated persons so devoid of compassion they could commit ritual murders without motive or remorse.[26]

In August 1969, Manson's "family" capriciously and sadistically murdered actress Sharon Tate, who was eight months pregnant, and four of her friends in a Los Angeles suburb. The victims' mutilated bodies were stabbed 102 times. The next night the "family" slaughtered two more people, stabbing them 57 times. Manson represented the darkest side of the counterculture. Most hippies were not senseless killers, but mainstream Americans saw Manson—a deranged proponent of free love, drugs, and rock music—and the ritualistic slayings as confirmation of their paranoia and worst fears about a hippie drug culture. The media reinforced the perception of a violent counterculture when *Newsweek* called Manson "the hypnotic hippie," and *Time* magazine attributed the grotesque crimes to a "weird story of a mystical, semi-religious drug-and-murder cult."[27]

By the end of the decade, the counterculture had burned itself out. Overcrowding, bad drugs, malnutrition, disease, media exposure, and too many weekend "plastic" or pseudo-hippies looking mostly to score drugs and women had chased older hippies out of Hashbury to the communes. The establishment, loathing the hippies' hedonistic lifestyle and disregard for "American" values, had, it seemed, declared war on the hippies. Mayors throughout the country took action to eliminate hippie enclaves in their cities. To police, hippies' were runaways, vagrants, drug users, and a general social hazard. Minority groups were hostile to hippies. Blacks especially resented the hippies' condemnation of the civil rights movement and were repulsed by their living habits. One black resident of the Haight commented, "If some hippies moved next door to me I would move out, because I couldn't tolerate the filth."[28]

To most Americans, anyone who appeared to be a hippie was a hippie. Because hippies were often misrepresented or misinterpreted in the media, the long hair-beads-peace-and-love stereotype became firmly entrenched in the public mind. But hippies, like other groups in the 1960s, were not so easily categorized. True hippies in the Haight rejected establishment val-

ues, espoused peace and love, and viewed drugs as essential to their psychedelic well-being. Although generally apolitical, some of them held political
interests shared by leftist radicals who opposed the Vietnam War. New Left
activists were not convinced that hippies were sufficiently mature to appre-
ciate political ideology and called them "infantile escapists."[29] Other New
Left activists, however, who grew weary of fighting with the establishment
over the war, racism, and social inequities, gave up, dropped out, and joined
the hippies. The establishment particularly abhorred these "pot heads," and
President Richard Nixon, Vice President Spiro Agnew, Alabama governor
and presidential candidate George C. Wallace, and Chicago mayor Richard
Daley had little difficulty convincing the "silent majority," "hardhats," and
middle-class Americans that the hippies' behavior was dangerous and
threatening to the "American way of life."

Indeed, Haight-Ashbury, once the spiritual center of the "love generation," had become a mecca for almost any runaway youth from middle-class
America. A vibrant neighborhood had deteriorated into a decaying low-rent
area infested with vice and crime. The Psychedelic Ship and the Huckle-
berry House, a home for runaways, closed. Instead of gentle, peace-loving
hippies, the area was taken over by "speed freaks," petty criminals, alcohol-
ics, and sex maniacs who turned the Haight into a veritable gauntlet of pan-
handlers and dispossessed homeless people.

Because they scoffed at mainstream values and threatened authority,
hippies were perceived as deviants who threatened social and political
authority. They were attacked for being hedonistic, immoral, and narcis-
sistic subversives representing an alternative culture that had to be controlled. The persecution of the hippies was nationwide. Like black
Americans, they were often denied service in public businesses. In Boul-
der, Colorado, a sign outside a restaurant read "Hippies not served here."
Billboards in New York advertised "Keep America Clean: Take a Bath,"
and "Keep America Clean: Get a Haircut." Young men who wore their hair
long, even though they were not hippies, were often the target of derisive
chants of "hippie" or "faggot."

The final scene in the cult classic film *Easy Rider*, a fictional depiction of
the counterculture, is a violent confrontation between two hippies motorcy-
cling through the South in the late 1960s and two rednecks in a pickup truck.
The scene may have been a stereotypical portrayal, but if big cities were
hostile to hippies, rural America was less than tolerant. Harassment of the
"long-haired freak hippies" was often more than intimidation. In October
1967, the *New York Times* reported that two "pacifists" were "jailed and
shaved" in Wyoming for hitchhiking. The governor of Tennessee was even

more hostile to hippies, declaring, "It's war. We want every long-hair in jail or out of the state."[30]

The establishment simultaneously feared, reviled, and ridiculed hippies, but it unashamedly co-opted their music, fashion, theater, and art. By 1968 members of the under-twenty-five generation who wore flared, bell-bottom pants, long hair, and a scarf or headband were considered stylish, not eccentric. Conventional fashion for both sexes broke down. Women wore mini-skirts, ankle-length maxi-skirts, and blouse necklines that might cover the throat or plunge to the navel. Their hair length would barely touch the ear or fall over the shoulders.[31] Some sociologists speculated that young people who wore military apparel were mocking the war effort in Vietnam. No doubt some were making a fashion statement against the war, but by the early 1970s, before the withdrawal of troops, the fad was commercially successful.

Any fashion style was in, and any form of censorship was out. In 1968 Hollywood produced the movie *The Love-In*. In New York the play *The Freaking Out of Stephanie Blake* opened, and *Hair,* a counterculture musical that included nude scenes and invited the audience to participate with the cast on stage, was an immediate commercial success when it opened on Broadway in April 1968. In San Francisco, a seedy nightclub featured a "Topless Hippie Sex Orgy." In the Haight a tourist could eat a "loveburger," and a Boston radio station called itself the "Station of Flower Power."[32] Pop culture artist Peter Max was one of several capitalists who helped translate the counterculture into consumer items. Claiming he wanted to "give art to the people," Max integrated abstract patterns and natural images in posters, decals, scarves, and other hippie products that were popular among straights and even corporate America. The Metro Transit Advertising Company used his posters for buses and subway cars in Chicago and New York City.[33]

The Haight-Ashbury area still draws tourists, but they are few and they do not ride "Hippie Hop" buses. Diggers no longer hand out food at their Free Store, but the Anarchist Bookstore on the south side of Haight Street is a reminder of the counterculture era. Despite the countless bad trips experienced in the 1960s, a handful of left-over, burned-out hippies still camp out on the sidewalks, wandering aimlessly and still trying to find their way "home."

As a movement, the counterculture was a chronological blip, but its influences are visible everywhere. Long hair for men and women and unisex clothing have become mainstream fashion styles. Blue jeans, prohibited by public schools in the 1960s, now have top designers' names embroidered on the hip pocket and are nearly a universal form of dress. Marijuana smoking and dropping acid horrified parents in the sixties, but thirty years after "tuning in and turning on," illegal drug use in the United States is still very much a social problem—some would say an epidemic. The latest drug craze for many adolescents—"huffing" inhalants—is even more dangerous than tripping on LSD. The most popular drug in the late 1990s, however, is not marijuana, cocaine, heroin, or LSD. Generating sales of $5 billion in 1998, Prilosec does not expand one's conscienceness; it alleviates heartburn.[34]

The counterculture was often scorned for its frivolous behavior, antiestablishment values, and naive idealism, but as historian Allen J. Matusow has concluded, "The hippie movement was profoundly significant, portending as it did the erosion of the liberal values that had sustained bourgeois society."[35] Neither President Lyndon B. Johnson nor supporters of his Great Society reforms aimed at reducing unemployment and ensuring economic security understood why a vocal minority of young people scorned capitalism and opted for poverty. The counterculture was hard on tradition, and its hedonistic philosophy precipitated extensive social and political attitudinal changes that undermined the virtues of hard work, respect for parental and governmental authority, monogamy, sexual fidelity, and organized religion.

Players died, and legends were born. Woodstock might have been the grandest moment of the counterculture, but it also was short-lived for some of its brightest stars. Hendrix (September 1970), Joplin (October 1970), and Morrison (July 1971) barely survived the decade; all died from drug overdoses at age twenty-seven. Joplin, perhaps a victim of her own rage, was more prophetic than she realized when she claimed, "I'd rather have ten years of superhypermost than live to be seventy by sitting in some goddamn chair watching TV."[36]

In 1994 about 250,000 revellers paid $150 to attend a Woodstock twenty-fifth anniversary concert in Saugerties, New York. Like the original, the sequel was muddy and poorly planned. Unlike the first Woodstock, however, it was neither a cultural nor a commercial success. In July 1999 organizers of the original festival sponsored yet another Woodstock reunion featuring more than forty top musical groups and twenty-two emerging bands, none of which performed in 1969. Hoping to draw more than a quarter of a million people to Griffis Air Force Base—an ironic venue for a counterculture event—in Rome, New York, the promoters hired 2,800 security personnel to police the concert site. For fans who could not attend "Woodstock Nation 99" in person, the acts were offered on pay-per-view television for $59.95.[37] The counterculture lives. Oh, wow!

NOTES

1. The term *hippie* has several possible origins. In the 1940s the word *hip* or *hep* was jive talk indicating a familiarity with jazz musicians and hustlers. In the 1950s beatniks used the term to differentiate themselves from "squares." *Hippie*

could be derived from Cab Calloway's music, which made reference to laborers who wore hip-high boots when they picked cotton. Occasionally a drug user was said to be wise, or "hip." When a *San Francisco Chronicle* reporter used "hippie" in 1965, the label stuck. James J. Farrell, *The Spirit of the Sixties: Making Postwar Radicalism* (New York: Routledge Press, 1997), 203; and John Robert Howard, "The Flowering of the Hippie Movement," *Annals of the American Academy of Political and Social Science* 382 (March 1969): 44.

2. Martin Arnold, "Organized Hippies Emerge on Coast," *New York Times*, May 5, 1967, 41.

3. William L. O'Neill, *Coming Apart: An Informal History of America in the 1960s* (Chicago: Quadrangle Books, 1971), 252.

4. Terry Anderson, *The Movement and the Sixties* (New York: Oxford University Press, 1995), 217–19.

5. "The Hippies," *Newsweek*, July 7, 1967, 18.

6. *Turbulent Years: The 60s* (Alexandria, VA: Time-Life Books, 1998), 137.

7. Jay Stevens, *Storming Heaven: LSD and the American Dream* (New York: Atlantic Monthly Press, 1987), 300.

8. David Farber, *The Age of Great Dreams: America in the 1960s* (New York: Hill and Wang, 1994), 173–74.

9. Martin A. Lee and Bruce Shalin, *Acid Dreams: The CIA, LSD and the Sixties Rebellion* (New York: Grove Press, 1985), 142–43; Allen J. Matusow, *The Unraveling of America: A History of Liberalism in the 1960s* (New York: Harper & Row, 1984), 292; Jane Stern and Michael Stern, *Sixties People* (New York: Alfred A. Knopf, 1990), 149; and Gene Ira Katz, "Woodstock at 25," http://www.publiccom.com/14850/9407/coverstory.html.

10. Stevens, *Storming Heaven*, 336.

11. Stern and Stern, *Sixties People*, 151; Arnold, "Organized Hippies Emerge on Coast"; and Neil A. Hamilton, *The 1960s Counterculture in America* (Santa Barbara, CA: ABC-CLIO, 1997), 133.

12. Farber, *Age of Great Dreams*, 169–70.

13. Stevens, *Storming Heaven*, 340; and Edward P. Morgan, *The 60s Experience: Hard Lessons About Modern America* (Philadelphia: Temple University Press, 1991), 183.

14. Joan Didion, *Slouching Toward Bethlehem* (New York: Farrar, Straus, & Giroux, 1968), 94.

15. Stevens, *Storming Heaven*, 336; Stern and Stern, *Sixties People*, 159.

16. Stern and Stern, 152.

17. *Turbulent Years*, 140.

18. Jerry Hopkins, *Festival!* (New York: Macmillan, 1970), 37.

19. "Where Have All the Hippies Gone?" *Time*, October 13, 1967, 30–31; and William Manchester, *The Glory and the Dream: A Narrative History of America, 1932–1972* (New York: Bantam Books, 1973), 1118.

20. *Turbulent Years*, 143.

21. James J. Farrell, *The Spirit of the Sixties: Making Postwar Radicalism* (New York: Routledge, 1997), 225.

22. Anthony M. Casale and Philip Lerman, *Where Have All the Flowers Gone? The Rise and Fall of the Woodstock Generation* (Kansas City, MO: Universal Press Syndicate, 1989), 14; and Matusow, *The Unraveling of America,* 304.

23. Manchester, *The Glory and the Dream,* 1170.

24. Hamilton, *The 1960s Counterculture in America,* 336–37; and Richard Sorrell and Carl Francese, *From Tupelo to Woodstock: Youth, Race, and Rock and Roll in America, 1954–1969* (Dubuque, IA: Kendall/Hunt Publishing, 1993), 100–102.

25. Matusow, *The Unraveling of America,* 304.

26. "Hippies and Violence," *Time,* December 12, 1969, 25.

27. Anderson, *The Movement,* 273; and O'Neill, *Coming Apart,* 263.

28. William W. MacDonald, "Life and Death of the Hippies," *America,* September 7, 1968, 150–51.

29. Anderson, *The Movement,* 210.

30. Michael E. Brown, "The Condemnation and Persecution of Hippies," *Trans-Action* 6 (September 1967): 37; and Hamilton, *The 1960s Counterculture in America,* 150.

31. O'Neill, *Coming Apart,* 246.

32. MacDonald, "Life and Death of the Hippies," 150.

33. Rita Lang Kleinfelder, *When We Were Young: A Baby-Boomer Yearbook* (New York: Prentice Hall, 1993), 453; and Hamilton, *The 1960s Counterculture in America,* 211.

34. "Ulcer Drug Beats Viagara," *Centre Daily Times* (State College, PA), February 17, 1999, A6.

35. Matusow, *The Unraveling of America,* 307.

36. *Turbulent Years,* 140.

37. Murray Dubin, "They're Banging the Drum for Woodstock," *Philadelphia Inquirer,* April 9, 1999, 2C; and Daniel Rubin, "Woodstock.com., Ready to Click on and Rock," *Philadelphia Inquirer,* 27 June 1999, A1. Event information and updates were posted at www.woodstock.com.

Peter Fonda and Jack Nicholson looking for America in the 1969 counterculture classic, *Easy Rider*. Reprinted by permission of Photo Fest.

A crowd gathers at the stage set up for the Woodstock rock concert on the great meadow of Max Yasgur's farm at Bethel, NY (August 1969).

A girl helps herself to free food ration during the "three days of peace and music" in the camp area at the Woodstock Music Festival in Bethel, New York, on August 15, 1969.

A group of hippies raise their arms in the air and taunt bayonet-armed National Guardsmen (August 28, 1968) near Michigan Avenue during the Democratic National Convention in Chicago.

This is a June 20, 1969, photo of Ken Love burning what he claimed was a draft card and his Students for a Democratic Society card in Chicago.

Chicago police lead a protester from Grant Park during demonstrations that disrupted the Democratic National Convention in August 1968. The convention became the focal point of bitter confrontations between police and antiwar demonstrators.

A young barefoot woman examines a friend's necklace during a festival in San Francisco's Golden Gate Park, August 8, 1967, during what became known as the Summer of Love. To insure it will be identifiable with the 1960s, Summer of Love is now a registered trademark.

Thousands of hippies and hippie-watchers converge on a four block section of Haight Street in San Francisco March 4, 1968. Mayor Joseph Alioto responded to requests from artists and business people in the area, closing the street for the day and turning the neighborhood into a counterculture festival.

5

Legacy of the 1960s Cultural Revolution

George Bernard Shaw once observed that "revolutionary movements attract the best and worst elements in a given society."[1] If any decade in American history simultaneously produced "the best and worst elements," it was the 1960s, and the legacy of that era is no less paradoxical. Much of what happened then was divisive. Many of the events that occurred in the sixties split generations, races, sexes, political parties, and even families. People lived together rather than marry. Many young people sent off to be the first college graduate in the family used their knowledge and energy to attempt to dismantle the American system. Members of the baby boom generation, leaving home to improve their minds and their lives, rebelled and attacked the values and traditions their parents had embraced: authority, the work ethic, religion, conformity, marital fidelity, patriotism, and generally whatever "the establishment" represented. Civil rights, women's liberation, sexual permissiveness, the counterculture, the music, and the Vietnam War all contributed to fragmenting or alienating Americans. Americans fought communists in Southeast Asia, and they fought each other at home, often because they were fighting communists in Southeast Asia.

There were some bright spots. In May 1961, Alan B. Shepard was the first American in space; eight years later, in July 1969, Neil Armstrong fulfilled President Kennedy's promise to land a man on the moon by the end of the decade. In 1964 Congress passed the Civil Rights Act, and the Twenty-fourth Amendment prohibiting poll taxes was ratified. The following year Congress enacted an Immigration Act and the Voting Rights Act. VISTA, a domestic Peace Corps, was a tremendous success. Conversely, black militancy in the mid-1960s led to more violent protests and confrontations between citizens and police, student unrest on many college campuses resulted in dramatic changes in higher education, and the divisive antiwar movement was fatal to the post–World War II consensus.

LEGACIES

The New Left lost momentum and influence after the tragedy at Kent State. When the Selective Service System replaced the old draft with a lottery in 1969 and black voting rights were secured in the South, the movement lost its raison d'être. In fact, as the New Left declined, an emerging New Right gained prominence as the national political pendulum began to swing from liberal to conservative. Many revolutionaries went underground or simply retired, but their influence remains evident in the new century. Because of the Free Speech Movement, a manifestation of student discontent, in loco parentis was abolished in higher education; college students now have a wider choice of course electives, and dormitory rules are almost nonexistent or considerably relaxed. Pressured by free speech activists, academia instituted sweeping curricular reforms, including student representation on virtually every faculty and administrative committee whose policies affect campus life.

The New Left raised fundamental issues and questions about the nature and limits of democracy in modern American society. It emphasized participatory democracy, stressing that anything could and would happen. Unfortunately, by 1966, local SDS campus chapters throughout the country had assumed much of the "old guard" leadership. The desire for local autonomy seriously weakened the national organization, and in 1969, ideological differences produced rival factions at its convention.[2] The New Left's goals of achieving peace, racial equality, broad economic restructuring, and increased government intervention to make society moral and just were more idealistic than realistic. The New Left did reshape society, but as historian William J. Rorabaugh concludes, the movement fell short essentially because "radicals demanded a more drastic change in society than could possibly take place in a time as short as impatient youth could wait."[3]

Of all the wars America has fought, only World War II did not provoke organized protest. During the American Revolution, thousands of Tories fled to Canada rather than sever their ties with the British crown; Federalist New England, bitterly opposed to the War of 1812, threatened to secede from the Union; Abraham Lincoln and Henry David Thoreau denounced the Mexican War (1846–1848) as a scandal; the worst antidraft riots in American history occurred in 1863 in New York City; six U.S. senators and fifty congressmen voted against declaring war against Germany in 1917 as the country was about to enter World War I; and American/United Nations intervention in Korea was widely questioned in the early 1950s.

Opinion is divided on how the antiwar movement affected White House policy in Southeast Asia. Antiwar activists did keep Vietnam on the front page as a constant, nagging, painful reminder of a highly distasteful experience, and in that regard they made certain the war was an issue. It is also true that all subsequent presidents since Lyndon B. Johnson have been hampered in the conduct of American foreign policy by the legacy of Vietnam. President George Bush demonstrated this in 1991 when, rather than try to circumvent Congress, he mobilized a broad international coalition of twenty-seven countries to confront a defiant Iraqi government and solicited congressional approval for military action. Similarly, President Bill Clinton, the first baby boomer, Vietnam-generation president, eschewed any unilateral action against Iraq in 1998 when Saddam Hussein opposed on-site arms-control inspections. The image of the forgotten Vietnam veterans also was invoked in political rhetoric supporting Operation Desert Storm, the military operation to liberate Kuwait. After returning from a visit to the Persian Gulf, Congressman John Murtha (D, Pennsylvania), who served in Vietnam as a marine, told audiences that the American troops in the Middle East frequently asked him whether "the folks back home" supported them. Murtha noted that "the aura of Vietnam hangs over these kids."[4]

Although it is difficult to assess whether the antiwar movement's resistance to the draft or protest of the government's military policy influenced the Johnson and Nixon administrations in their handling of the Vietnam War, the impact of Kent State was profound. In 1971, a year after the violent confrontation, a *Playboy* survey of college students found that only 36 percent of them "would protest now," but, they added, "not violently."[5] Perhaps the most evident legacy of the antiwar/peace movement is the federal government's preference for an all-volunteer military, undoubtedly a major reason that there was no mass protest in 1991 against sending American troops to liberate Kuwait from Iraq.

An unofficial hybrid lobby of peace advocates and counterculture hippies concerned about the fragile condition of the environment renewed interest in the Wilderness Society, the National Audubon Society, and the Sierra Club, which boosted its membership by one-third through the 1980s.[6] By the end of the 1960s, the environment had become a national issue when 20 million people celebrated Earth Day in April 1970, the largest demonstration of the era. Congress adjourned to observe the occasion, an estimated 10 million school children participated in the event, and New York City police closed off Fifth Avenue for two hours.[7] In their role as advocates of an environmental movement, hippies politicized the ecology issue, and over the past quarter-century, activists have been promoting a greater awareness of the precarious interdependence between humans and their natural environment. Rachel Carson's *Silent Spring* (1962), an exposé of pesticide use, influenced forty states to adopt legislation restricting the use of pesticides; and Paul Ehrlich's *The Population Bomb* (1968), warning readers about the dangers of overpopulation, stimulated President Nixon to create the Commission on Population Growth and the American Future in 1970. In September 1970, the Nixon administration created the Environmental Protection Agency, and in May 1971, Congress voted against funding supersonic air transport, due mostly to environmental concerns.

Another legacy of the peace/hippie/ecological activists was the *Whole Earth Catalog*, a kind of "how-to" guide for free spirits dissatisfied with the establishment who wanted to create their own hip culture. The publication's basic objective was to show the reader how to "conduct his own education, find his own inspiration, shape his own environment, and share his adventure with whoever is interested." After Stewart Brand sold the publication rights to Random House, the *Catalog* became a best-seller with over a million copies sold.[8]

Although concerns about the environment largely were ignored during Ronald Reagan's presidency in the 1980s, his successor, President George Bush, who campaigned in 1988 as the "environmental president," revived interest in ecological issues and approved the first overhaul of the Clean Air Act in thirteen years.[9] Other environmental concerns, such as what to do with toxic waste and the threat of global warming, have reenergized environmentalists.

Older organizations committed to conservation no longer speak for environmental interests, and paradoxically the environmental movement grew stronger while it fragmented along ideological lines. In the 1990s the environmental movement has become more radicalized than its pioneers could have imagined. *Eco-terrorism* is a term commonly applied to organizations such as Greenpeace, an international pro-environmental group founded in 1971 and currently located in thirty countries around the world, that draws attention to nations that violate policies aimed to "create a green and peaceful world." In the U.S. Northwest, Earth First! environmental activists "tree-sit" for months at a time in Oregon, Washington, and California to prevent logging companies from cutting down trees.[10]

By the early 1970s, the counterculture was fading into memory. The Diggers, hippies, and Yippies were victims of their own excesses and most likely would have become anachronistic under any circumstances. When economic stagflation throughout most of the 1970s and the oil embargo that began in October 1973 exposed the weaknesses of American capitalism and a free enterprise system that promoted unlimited and disproportionate wealth, their socialistic counterparts were deprived of an "enemy." Perhaps Alex Forman, a former Digger, put it best when he later reflected on his life in Haight-Ashbury: "I quickly saw then that the counterculture wasn't going to make it. It wasn't going to work. It was an illusion."[11] Some observers might argue that everything about the counterculture was illusory: the "summer of love" in 1967, be-ins, utopian communes, the notion of a classless society, and a nation at peace—with itself as well as its adversaries.

Although "real" counterculture types were relatively few in number in the 1960s, they and their influence were disproportionately represented in the media. Their colorful appearance, unconventional lifestyle, and anti-establishment values provided entertaining copy for evening news broadcasts and front pages. Surprisingly, however, as bizarre and repugnant as the counterculture was to middle-class America, several hippie characteristics eventually blended in with the mainstream. Long hair was generally accepted in many workplace settings, and by the end of the 1970s, even more conservative, mainstream "hardhats" were wearing their hair longer. Sexual permissiveness and drug use, while not generally condoned, became less offensive and received less severe sanctions. More than a legacy of fashion statements, though, the counterculture spirit survived long after most hippies had gone straight. About 25,000 social rebels convened during a "Rainbow Family" reunion in Modoc National Forest in northern California in 1984; in the 1990s, the Nike sportswear company used the Beatles song "Revolution" in a television advertisement to sell shoes; and until Jerry Garcia died in August 1995, his counterculture rock group, the Grateful Dead, which performed more than 2,300 shows over thirty years, was one of the top revenue-grossing rock 'n' roll bands in the United States.[12]

"Counterculture drugs" are still widely used (perhaps surprising, heroin addiction in the younger population is a serious problem because the purity level of the drug is so high it can be smoked rather than injected, negating the use of a needle and the possibility of contracting the AIDS virus or hepatitis). Although most members of the baby boom generation have "aged out" of illicit substance abuse, many of them are not reluctant to use over-the-counter drugs. Among the most popular drugs consumed by the baby boomers is Viagra, a pill for male impotence that generated about forty thousand prescriptions daily in mid-1998.[13]

Since the Nixon years, a watershed in federal drug control policy, the White House has been actively involved in waging a war on drugs. In the 1980s, during the Reagan-Bush administrations, antidrug policies included stringent measures that sometimes compromised civil liberties, such as mandatory minimum sentences, asset forfeiture, and withholding welfare benefits of drug offenders. In the 1990s, with the public—and public officials—so concerned about drug abuse, it had become a common practice for many businesses to require job applicants and employees to submit to a urine test as a condition of employment.

The civil rights/Black Power movement fell apart, and the race riots that broke out during the long, hot summers in the 1960s that decimated countless cities throughout the country finally came to an end. By the end of the decade, the militant Black Panthers were defunct. In 1969, 348 Panthers were arrested—not for political transgressions, which might have made them martyrs, but for rape, burglary, and robbery.

In 1968, in perhaps the most terrifying year of a terrifying decade, the President's National Advisory Commission on Civil Disorders rejected the theory that race riots in Newark, Detroit, and other cities that destroyed acres of city blocks and left hundreds of people dead and thousands injured, were part of some nefarious conspiracy. In reality, the root causes were far less sensational. Condemning white racism, the Kerner Commission's 1,485-page report warned that massive black unemployment, unfulfilled promises from civil rights victories, and government resistance to civil rights legislation were tearing the country asunder; the United States was a nation moving toward two societies, "one black, one white—separate and unequal." Specifically, the commission listed 160 recommendations to help alleviate unfavorable economic conditions, including on-the-job-training, new low-rent housing units, and more antipoverty funding.[14] Thirty years after the Kerner study, in February 1998, a report by the Milton S. Eisenhower Foundation, *The Millennium Breach*, concluded that

the economic and racial divide in the United States not only has materialized, it's getting wider. While leaders and pundits talk of full employment, inner-city unemployment is at crisis levels. . . . The rich are getting richer, the poor are getting poorer, and minorities are suffering disproportionately.

Noting what works, the report recommended Head Start programs, job training, inner-city economic development, and crime and drug prevention. Solutions proposed in the nineties were part of the Great Society in the sixties.[15]

The civil rights movement did see progress for black Americans. However, civil rights activists must have wondered just how far they had advanced in the 1980s when President Reagan opposed most civil rights legislation, including school busing. Reagan also tried unsuccessfully to stop Congress from establishing Martin Luther King, Jr.'s birthday as a national holiday and infuriated many black Americans by ordering the Justice Department to petition the Supreme Court to restore a tax-free status to segregated private schools and colleges.[16]

When expressing his support for affirmative action in July 1998, which was under attack as unnecessary and unfair in the wake of civil rights gains over the decades, President Clinton cautioned the audience that "the American people have got to decide" if they want diversity and the pain that comes with it, or a more segregated society that will result without it.[17] Although many of the injustices of the 1960s have been eliminated and blacks are more widely represented in politics, professional capacities, sports, and the entertainment industry, racism is as pervasive at the turn of the century as it was in 1968, a sentiment confirmed in a year-long study conducted by the President's Advisory Board on Race in 1998. Headed by historian John Hope Franklin, the commission noted that "racial attitudes among whites had improved over the last 40 years," but also cautioned President Clinton that he must recognize the "continuing existence of prejudice and privilege that relegates people of color to a status inferior to that of whites."[18]

OTHER SIXTIES FALLOUT

Unlike most other sixties protest movements that dissolved shortly after they began, the women's movement has continued into the twenty-first century. Careers are open today that women would not have dared think about entering thirty years ago. Legislation guarantees equal pay and prohibits sex discrimination. In 1981 conservative Senator Orrin G. Hatch (R, Utah) cosponsored a congressional resolution establishing Women's History Week. Most colleges and universities today offer women's history courses using hundreds of women's history books. Many institutions have women's studies programs. Perhaps most important, attitudes are beginning to change. When, at the beginning of the 1960s, most female high school graduates' career aspirations were limited to teacher, nurse, or secretary, now they can realistically hope to be secretary of state. A "woman's proper place" will never be the same.

Women have realized progress in the workforce. A generation ago, only 3 percent of the nation's lawyers were female; in 1998 about half of all law school graduates were women. Still, the average woman worker earns only seventy-six cents for every dollar a man earns, an increase of seventeen cents since the 1970s, but hardly economic parity. In the upper echelon of the business world, only two Fortune 500 companies employ women CEOs, and only 10 percent of corporate officers are women.[19]

Although many women's rights activists are pleased with the greater opportunities available for women in the 1990s, they also are distressed that many younger women seemed to have forgotten—if they were ever aware of—the struggles that "women's libbers" fought and the barriers they succeeded in overcoming a generation earlier. Only 50 percent of eighteen- to thirty-four-year-old women polled in 1998 said they share "feminist" values.[20] Young women frequently resented what they refer to as feminism, while they casually assume the benefits of gender equity, equal pay, and access to traditionally male-dominated occupations.

Just as activists in the 1960s heightened an awareness of racial and sexual discrimination, they also exposed the flagrant harassment of homosexuals. The public moment of truth for gay rights occurred in June 1969 when about two hundred gay patrons fought back rather than submit passively to arrest by police who wanted to shut down the Stonewall Inn, a private gay club in the heart of a three-block homosexual community in Greenwich Village.[21] The incident stimulated a sense of identity among many gay men and women and the formation of the Gay Liberation Front, and ultimately redefined the boundaries governing sexual orientation. In 1971 the American Psychological Association reclassified homosexuality as a normal sexual preference, and four years later, the U.S. Civil Service Commission ended its ban on employing homosexuals. At the 1984 Democratic National Convention, the party officially welcomed gays and promised to support research for AIDS victims, and in 1993, the military adopted a "don't ask, don't tell" policy regarding the sexual orientation of recruits.

Gay rights remain an important issue on the national political agenda, and homosexuality is viewed by many public figures not so much as a perversion but as a legitimate sexual identity. The mass marriage of gay couples in San Francisco and a superior court judge's 1993 ruling in Hawaii that it was unconstitutinal to ban homosexual marriages indicate more favorable public acceptance.[22] It is difficult to imagine that the 1995 movie *Birdcage* would have been a box office hit ten years before, and when Ellen DeGeneres, starring on television's *Ellen* revealed that she was a lesbian in May 1997, some viewers were offended, but public reaction was generally indifferent; nevertheless, viewership fell off so much as gay themes increased that the show was canceled at the end of the season. No doubt few Americans would have thought that in 1998, the House of Representatives would uphold President Clinton's executive order banning discrimination in federal employment on the basis of sexual orientation, or that the Supreme Court would decide that gays as well as "straights" can be victimized by sexual harassment in the workplace.[23]

The gay issue may not be as incendiary now as it was three decades ago, but it is not resolved. "Political correctness" ensures that generally gays are more tolerated but not necessarily widely accepted, not by the mainstream anyway, and certainly not by those who align themselves with the religious right. In June 1998, reacting to a report on "Gay Days" at Disney World and Orlando, Florida, with displays of gay flags along city streets, evangelist and 1988 presidential candidate Pat Robertson sounded more like Jonathan Edwards castigating his congregation in the 1700s than an enlightened, late-twentieth-century religious leader when he warned, "This is not a message of hate; this is a message of redemption. . . . A condition like this will bring about the destruction of your nation. It'll bring about terrorist bombs; it'll bring earthquakes, tornadoes, and possibly a meteor."[24]

On January 27, 1973, American involvement in Vietnam finally came to an end. According to the terms agreed on in Paris, all U.S. forces would withdraw, Hanoi would release American prisoners of war, and North Vietnamese troops would remain in South Vietnam—the same terms the Nixon administration rejected four years earlier. Whether it was that "dirty little war" or the "right fight" depended entirely on one's perception of America's role in global affairs. In the end, it may not have mattered who was right and who was wrong in Southeast Asia. What did matter is that by the end of the 1960s, Vietnam had become an agonizing, painful reminder that the United States had gotten bogged down in a hopeless struggle to stop communism. What also mattered was the staggering economic price—$167 billion—and the human cost—58,655 fatalities, 155,419 GIs physically wounded, and countless lives emotionally and psychologically shattered.[25]

More than thirty years after the Tet offensive, Americans cannot escape lingering reminders of who took sides over the Vietnam War. In a June 1998 "My Turn" essay in *Newsweek*, a brother of a prisoner of war noted that nearly a quarter-century after the North Vietnamese captured Saigon and renamed it Ho Chi Minh City, "the antiwar movement has yet to recognize the pain and heartache that it caused." This is the "unfinished business" of Vietnam.[26] In 1995, twenty years after the fall of Saigon, Robert S. McNamara, former secretary of defense and architect of America's war policy in Vietnam, acknowledged that "we made an error not of value and intentions, but of judgment and capabilities."[27]

Arguably America's darkest hour during the 1960s, Vietnam entanglement remains relatively unknown to many Americans, certainly those born during and after the 1960s, even though its domestic fallout had far-reaching repercussions. American involvement in Vietnam did more than divide the nation over the government's commitment to fighting communism. After a decade of intervention, Southeast Asia became the source of 70 percent of the world's illicit opium and the major supplier of raw materials for America's booming heroin market.[28] In 1971, four times as many American troops were hospitalized for drug abuse as for combat-related wounds. While GIs were succumbing to highly addictive drugs trafficked by U.S.-supported officials in the South Vietnamese government, the Nixon White House declared a war on drugs at home.

It is practically a universal characteristic that each generation disapproves of its successor and all it represents when yesterday's cantankerous children grow up and become tomorrow's disapproving adults. In 1969, during the three-day rock festival at Woodstock, performers such as Arlo Guthrie pleaded with Customs agents not to confiscate his drugs, Jimi Hendrix rendered what the establishment probably regarded as a blasphemous interpretation of the "Star Spangled Banner" on his electric guitar, and Country Joe McDonald's cynical claim that he didn't give a damn about Vietnam, offended the patriotic silent majority.

Three decades after they ended, the sixties have almost become chic. Business and advertising have become more "hip," and the influence of the sixties is everywhere. When contemporary rock 'n' roll is more raucous than anything heard in the 1960s, the older generation seems more amused than offended by the music.[29] In 1998 several television commercials tried to sell products with 1960s nostalgia. Sprint, a long-distance calling company, used the Rolling Stones'—rock's bad boys in the 1960s—"Time Is on My Side" to promote its calling plan. How surprising it must have been to many boomers in 1998 when AT&T—corporate America, the antithesis of everything the counterculture represented—aired a commercial on television showing how its technology was responsible for an employee's rapid promotion using Woodstocker Sly Stone's "I Want to Take You Higher" as background music. In the late 1960s much of Hendrix's music was regarded as risqué, if not rebellious. By the late 1990s, however, General Motors also apparently felt psychedelic had become quaint and sufficiently mainstream to entice television viewers to buy Pontiac Sunfires with Hendrix singing how he wants to "stand next to your fire," stimulating an exciting response for a sporty automobile. In 1998 the main characters on a popular television sit-com, *Dharma and Greg*, were products of the counterculture and the establishment, respectively, but got along. Their quarrels had more to do with style than matters of substance. Americans are now able to find humor in social issues that once polarized them.

Since they passed, the sixties have been a popular subject among later generations. In the late 1980s, some professors needed to move classes to larger auditoriums to accommodate college students who were curious about a decade of racial, sexual, and social unrest.[30] Generally, however, the Vietnam experience seems to have slipped by a younger generation. According to an ABC News/*Washington Post* poll in March 1985, one-third of adult Americans questioned did not know which side the United States supported in the Vietnam War, and more than half did not know what the war was about. Respondents from the general public were not the only people with hazy memories, since 37 percent of the Vietnam-era veterans polled did not have a "clear idea of what the Vietnam War was about."[31] This revelation may be disappointing, but it is hardly surprising. As a university instructor of American history, I know most members of the younger generation have little awareness of the war in Southeast Asia. Many Americans have forgotten important lessons of history.

Constituting the largest generation in American history, the impact of the baby boomers will be at least twofold. First, their values and attitudes were shaped in an environment that contrasted dramatically with that of any other generation. Landon Y. Jones contends that the boomers will also differ from any previous generation because "they will change what has heretofore been the principal stereotype of old people—namely, that they are poor, uneducated, and unemployed."[32]

The second legacy of the boomers is related to numbers, as confirmed by demographic studies. The impact of the boomers was felt immediately in the late 1940s and early 1950s, in the baby business, and their impact in the geriatric field will continue well into the twenty-first century. The oldest baby boomers began to turn fifty years old in 1997, and a boomer has been reaching the half-century mark every eight minutes since January 1, 1997, a trend that will continue until 2014, when the youngest boomers reach their fiftieth birthday. By 2010, more than 19 million Americans will be between fifty-five and fifty-nine years old, a 65 percent increase from 1998. Because there will be so many more retired boomers than in younger generations—although about 80 percent of them say they plan to continue working in some capacity after they reach age sixty-two—they will consume social security benefits faster than they can be collected. They will also enjoy the benefits longer than previous generations, since about 666,000 of them will live to age ninety-five or older, as compared with 38,000 who reached that age in 1998.[33] Because those over seventy-five years old represent the fastest-growing age group, aging boomers will seriously jeopardize social security benefits, since by 2030 two younger workers will be paying a social security tax for each beneficiary. As recently as 1980, the ratio was six to one.[34] By sheer numbers alone, aging boomers will command ever more influence in the consumer culture. They will have more money and more time to spend it than previous generations. Already their influence in the market is evident in advertising, which hawks products and services targeted to older consumers. Madison Avenue has redefined "beauty" and "youth" to include gray-haired, though still firm-bodied, models and recognizes that buying power no longer belongs to youth alone.

THE LOSS OF INNOCENCE?

Americans in the 1960s witnessed a dramatic social and cultural transformation that might well be characterized as a loss of innocence, caused mostly by the war in Southeast Asia. In 1960 the United States had a handful of noncombat personnel in Vietnam; by the end of the decade more than a half-million troops were unable to bring the Vietcong to the bargaining table. The escalation of troops throughout the decade paralleled increasing animus among Americans about their most fundamental beliefs and, of course, about the nation's involvement in Vietnam. It forced Americans to question their basic assumptions about themselves and their country.

Should Americans be surprised at what happened in the 1960s? What happened then may have been a natural, inevitable outgrowth of America's history and cumulative experiences. The cultural revolution of the 1960s might well have been a phase in an ongoing maturation process for the United States that began as early as 1776, when "protester" Thomas Paine wrote that, rather than "British Americans . . . our great title is Americans." After the War for Independence, Americans, increasingly aware of their reliance on Europe for cultural cues, greatly desired to establish an American way of life. In doing so, they rejected the arranged marriage common then in Europe; experienced more frequent divorces; and as parents, ignored other European traditions, including the superior position of the eldest son, deference to parental orders, and assuming responsibility for the care of relatives.[35]

During what might be considered America's first cultural revolution, which occurred in the antebellum era, William Ladd founded the national American Peace Society, a woman's rights movement emerged from abolitionism, and some individuals, believing the millennium was at hand and looking to create a new order rather than improve the existing one, organized theological-oriented communities in Amana, Harmony, and elsewhere. John Humphrey Noyes, an evangelical Protestant, incorporated some unorthodox ideas for his Oneida community. Believing all people belong to each other, Noyes's program included birth control, planned reproduction, and a "communism in love." He also introduced the "complex marriage," more recognizable to a 1960s counterculture member as "free love."[36]

Cultural historian Russell B. Nye has observed of Americans in the early nineteenth century that they "did not reject the past, but they were far more concerned with building a new society than in perpetuating the qualities and values of the older ones."[37] Assuming Nye is correct, America's cultural revolution in the 1960s might be more extreme, but it was not without precedent.

If America did experience a loss of innocence in the 1960s, it can be viewed relatively. One reason some contemporary observers such as former Speaker of the House of Representatives Newt Gingrich (R, Georgia) recall the 1960s as a time when "the whole system began decaying" is that the sixties "Days of Rage" was in sharp contrast to "Happy Days" in the fifties, an era that typically conjures up idealistic images of economic prosperity, social harmony, political unity, and wholesome family values, images created and reinforced by the media, especially television.[38] The family situation comedies, *The Donna Reed Show*, *The Adventures of Ozzie and Harriet*, and *Father Knows Best*, though usually recalled in the 1990s as widely viewed in the late 1950s, were never highly rated; in fact, only *Father Knows Best* (rated sixth during the 1959–1960 season) and *The Donna Reed Show* (sixteenth in 1963–1964), ever appeared among the top twenty highest-rated programs. Interestingly, shows that did began to appear with increasing regularity in the top twenty featured violence: *Wyatt Earp*, *The Restless Gun*, *Wanted: Dead or Alive*, *The Rifleman*, *The Lawman*, and *Have Gun Will Travel* were regular top-twenty programs.[39]

Conversely, what viewers do not see is sometimes as important as what they watch. For his on-the-spot-execution of an enemy Vietcong soldier, General Loan came to symbolize the savagery and cold-bloodedness of the Vietnam War. Eddie Adams's Pulitzer Prize photograph created a powerful, lasting image of what was perceived as an inhumane act that many Americans thought too ruthless, even in war. The photograph captures a spontaneous, violent act, but it does not reveal that the shooting followed a battle between Loan's South Vietnamese marines and the Vietcong, that Loan was admired by his troops, and that he devoted much of his time to having hospitals built in Vietnam for war casualties.[40]

The Vietnam War frequently has been, albeit unfairly, compared with World War II. Consequently, many members of the older generation expected and demanded unconditional patriotism from the younger draftees in the 1960s and severely criticized those who balked at sacrificing their lives for their country. But Vietnam was different from the war the older generation remembered. Vietnam was a civil war, it did not directly affect

American national security interests, it possessed no valuable natural resources, it did not offer potentially lucrative commercial markets, and it did not threaten democratic institutions in the United States. Even if Vietnam did fall to communist domination, it was not likely to threaten America's geopolitical sphere of influence. Tangible differences differentiated the two wars; more significant, Vietnam lacked the nobility and idealism of World War II—the "last good war"—that America fought and won.

THE REAL SIXTIES?

In one of his *Doonesbury* strips, political cartoonist Garry Trudeau uses a character trying to comprehend what "protestors during the sixties were really like," naively assuming they were "larger than life, bonded and driven by commitment, putting their lives on the line for a great cause." Despite the trauma of war, there was a revolutionary spirit in the sixties and a mood of optimism, but only idealists would recall the era so positively. These people also might argue that the sixties was a state of mind. If so, it was also an era of historical distinction, for it represented a collective letdown for a nation that had suffered a depression, fought a world war, and forged a political consensus about the national purpose. Basic assumptions about life in America were turned upside down. The American social landscape changed with startling speed. The America that entered the 1960s eagerly anticipating to benefit from the nation's international prestige and domestic prosperity by 1970 wanted the decade to be over. Assumptions that guided American foreign policy were no longer relevant or valid. The complacency, comfort, and conformity of the fifties became chaos, confusion, and challenge in the sixties. Revolution is synonymous with the 1960s, and it is difficult to know which facet of the cultural revolution had the most impact, since students, women, blacks, gays, radicals, and baby boomers generally all changed the face of America.

For some people, the phrase *1960s* is inherently a derisive characterization, a time when traditional values were challenged, redefined, and rejected, a time when America lost its way. During the Republican National Convention in August 1992, Marilyn Quayle, wife of Vice President Dan Quayle, clearly had the Democratic presidential candidate and fellow baby boomer Bill Clinton in mind when she correctly noted that "not everyone demonstrated, dropped out, took drugs, joined in the sexual revolution, or dodged the draft." This sixties stereotype frequently has been linked with questionable moral behavior among the baby boomers. In September 1998, when President Clinton was mired in the Monica Lewinsky sex scandal, Pat Robertson told three thousand members of the Christian Coalition in Washington, D.C., that the Oval Office has become "the playpen for the sexual freedom of the poster child of the 1960s."[41] Another baby boomer and political leader, House majority leader Dick Armey (R, Texas), is convinced that when considering such social problems as AIDS and drug use, "all the problems began in the 60s."[42] Anything that suggested "traditional" or "establishment" was scoffed at or ridiculed. Conservative Republicans are not the only people reeling from the sixties. In 1996 *Time* essayist Lance Morrow lamented that "most decades have the good grace to go away. Why won't the 60s?" For Morrow, who laments the absurdities of the decade, "The 60s go on and on."[43] Nationally syndicated columnist George Will disparaged the sixties spirit as "infantile" and the era as "noisy with the voices of fundamentally frivolous people feigning seriousness," an "age of intellectual rubbish."[44]

No doubt many Americans would concur with Will's contemptuous assessment. For others, though, the sixties connotes something more positive, perhaps even idealistic—a time of limitless possibilities. Some regard the sixties experiences as exhilarating, while others saw them as terrifying. Perhaps young people confused exuberance with experience when they challenged authority and demonstrated to eradicate social and racial inequities, overturned the longstanding doctrine of in loco parentis, and pressured the government to withdraw from an unwinnable and, in their minds, unjustified and immoral war.

Should we remember the sixties as a spirited time when exuberant and idealistic activists believed anything was possible, or were the sixties an era when naive and overzealous agitators espousing an anti-establishment attitude, the widening of social boundaries, and the challenge of authority caused America to lose some of its greatness? Was the decade one of "peace and love" or "fire in the streets"? Regardless of the perception, postmortems on any historical era are difficult at best, and the 1960s were extraordinarily eventful and uncommonly complex. However we describe or remember them, the sixties ended, and when they did, America—and Americans— had changed. A decade of so many political and social upheavals does not simply fade away, and if the sixties were something less than *Doonesbury*'s image of people "larger than life, bonded and driven by commitment, putting their lives on the line for a great cause," as they are sometimes depicted, they were also much more than a shallow, one-dimensional "sex, drugs, rock 'n' roll nostalgia trip. The sixties are over, but the effects still reverberate and they have produced social, political, and cultural changes that have had a continuing impact on American life and institutions.

NOTES

1. Laurence J. Peter, *Peter's Quotations: Ideas for Our Time* (New York: Bantam Books, 1987), 453.

2. Dick Flack, "What Happened to the New Left?" *Berkeley Journal of Sociology* 33 (1988): 95, 99.

3. William J. Rorabaugh, "Challenging Authority, Seeking Community and Empowerment in the New Left, Black Power, and Feminism," *Journal of Policy History* 8 (1996): 117.

4. Jerry Lee Lembcke, "The Myth of the Spat-Upon Vietnam Veteran and the Rhetorical Construction of Soldiers as Means and Ends in the Persian Gulf War," *Vietnam Generation* 6 (1995): 30. Convinced that unrestricted reporting from Vietnam had negatively influenced public opinion, Bush's Pentagon officials minimized press access to American troops in the Persian Gulf and censored their reports. Chester J. Pach, Jr., "The Vietnam War on the Nightly News," in David Farber, ed., *The Sixties: From Memory to History* (Chapel Hill, NC: University of North Carolina Press, 1994), 113.

5. William Manchester, *The Glory and the Dream: A Narrative History of America, 1932–1972* (New York: Bantam Books, 1973), 1225–26.

6. Terry Anderson, "The New American Revolution: The Movement and Business," in Farber, *The Sixties*, 198.

7. Godfrey Hodgson, *America in Our Time: From World War II to Nixon—What Happened and Why* (New York: Vintage Books, 1976), 403.

8. Ibid., 348; and Anderson, "The New American Revolution," 195. In the 1970s, similar publications included *Our Bodies, Ourselves*, devoted to female nutrition and hygiene, and *Living on the Earth*, which discussed home carpentry, water supply systems, organic gardening, and solar power.

9. Michael Schaller, Virginia Scharff, and Robert D. Schulzinger, *Present Tense: The United States since 1945* (Boston: Houghton Mifflin, 1996), 551–53.

10. "Greenpeace Annual Report, 1992–1993," http://www.greenpeace.org/gpi.html; and Debra Gwartney, "The Moral High Ground," *Time*, August 10, 1998, 61.

11. Alex Forman interview, in Joan Morrison and Robert K. Morrison, *From Camelot to Kent State: The Sixties Experience in the Words of Those Who Lived It* (New York: Times Books, 1987), 221.

12. Schaller, Scharff, and Schulzinger, *Present Tense*, 330; and Jules Archer, *The Incredible Sixties: The Years That Changed America* (San Diego: Harcourt Brace Jovanovich, 1986), 195.

13. "The Most Popular Prescription Drugs," *Parade*, July 12, 1998, 9. Drug prescriptions tend to reflect an aging baby boomer generation. Before Viagra's popularity, Premarin, which replaced estrogen in menopausal women, was the most prescribed drug. Prozac, an antidepressant, selling about 23 million prescriptions, also was a "top-ten" drug among baby boomers.

14. Irwin Unger and Debi Unger, *Turning Point: 1968* (New York: Charles Scribner's Sons, 1988), 184–85.

15. Deb Riechmann, "Report: Nation's Race Gap Widens," March 1, 1998, A1; and "New War on Poverty," *Philadelphia Inquirer*, March 8, 1998.

16. Schaller, Scharff, and Schulzinger, *Present Tense*, 466.

17. Jodi Fonda, "Clinton Says Diversity Is Right Course," *Philadelphia Inquirer*, July 9, 1998, A2.

18. Sonya Ross, "Report Urges Clinton to Confront Prejudice, Privilege in U.S.," *Philadelphia Inquirer*, September 18, 1998, A6.

19. Joanne Jacobs, "Feminism Movement Still Alive," *Centre Daily Times* (State College, PA), July 12, 1998, 13A; and Ginia Bellafante, "Feminism: It's All about Me," *Time*, June 29, 1998, 58.

20. Bellafante, "Feminism," 58.

21. Paul Sann, *The Angry Decade: The Sixties* (New York: Crown Publishers, 1979), 275–76; and Jerry Lisker, "Homo Nest Raided, Queen Bees Are Stinging Mad," *New York Daily News*, July 6, 1969, 1.

22. The potential impact of the judge's decision in Hawaii was nationwide, since the Constitution requires reciprocity among the states relative to statutes and legal bonds. Despite the ruling, the controversy over same-sex unions remains fierce, and in November 1998, voters in Alaska and Hawaii supported amendments banning gay marriages.

23. "Gay Rights," *USA Today*, August 6, 1998, 6A.

24. "Robertson Could Be Held Liable Should a Terrorist Bomb Manifest in Orlando, HRC Asserts," June 1998, website http://gaylesissues.tqn.como/library/content/blpr061298hrc.htm

25. Archer, *The Incredible Sixties*, 195; and Louis Galambos, "Paying Up: The Price of the Vietnam War," *Journal of Policy History* 8 (1996): 167.

26. Robert J. Brudno, "Unfinished Business," *Newsweek*, June 1, 1998, 12.

27. Robert S. McNamara, "'We Were Wrong, Terribly Wrong,'" *Time*, April 17, 1995, 45.

28. Alfred W. McCoy, *The Politics of Heroin: CIA Complicity in the Global Drug Trade* (Brooklyn, NY: Lawrence Hill Books, 1991), 196.

29. "Rock Around the Clock," *New York Times*, September 23, 1985.

30. Michelle N-K. Collison, "Today's Students Flock to Courses about 1960s," *Chronicle of Higher Education*, May 25, 1988, A33.

31. "Americans Confused on Vietnam," *Centre Daily Times* (State College, PA), March 1, 1985.

32. Landon Y. Jones, *Great Expectations: America and the Baby Boom Generation* (New York: Coward, McCann, 1980), 312–13.

33. Michael Vitez, "AARP Reaches Out to New Generation," *Philadelphia Inquirer*, June 7, 1998, A10.

34. Michael Tanner, "Re-Thinking Social Security," *Washington Post National Weekly Edition*, August 17, 1998, 8; and Jones, *Great Expectations*, 319.

35. Russell B. Nye, *The Cultural Life of the New Nation, 1776–1830* (New York: Harper & Row, 1960), 39, 139–41.

36. Ronald G. Walters, *American Reformers, 1815–1860* (New York: Hill & Wang, 1978), 40–41, 56–57, 87, 112.

37. Nye, *The Cultural Life of the New Nation*, 147.

38. Fred Barnes, "Revenge of the Squares," *New Republic*, March 13, 1995, 23.

39. Alex McNeil, *Total Television: A Comprehensive Guide to Programming from 1948 to the Present* (New York: Penguin Books, 1984), 900–3.

40. Eddie Adams, "Eulogy," *Time*, July 27, 1998, 19.

41. Tracy Connor, "Resign? We've Gotta Kick Him Out: Robertson," *New York Post*, September 19, 1998, 16.

42. David S. Broder and Ruth Marcus, "Bush Nominated for 'Fight of Our Life,'" *Washington Post*, August 20, 1992, A1; and Barnes, "Revenge of the Squares," 23.

43. Lance Morrow, "Turn On, Tune In, Trash It," *Time*, May 9, 1996, 92.

44. George Will, "About that 'Sixties Idealism,'" *Newsweek*, August 21, 1995, 72. Will is quoted in Mickey Kaus, "Confessions of an Ex-Radical," *Time*, May 9, 1985, 24.

Biographies: The Personalities Behind the Cultural Revolution

Baez, Joan (January 9, 1941–)

A folk musician with an extraordinary voice who spent most of her life protesting and demonstrating for social causes, Joan Baez was born on January 9, 1941, and grew up on Staten Island, New York. When her parents moved to Palo Alto, California, in the early 1950s, her sensitivity to racism intensified when her classmates shunned her because of the dark skin she inherited from her Mexican father. Her pacifism also originated with her father, a Quaker whose belief in nonviolence motivated him to quit a lucrative job in the defense industry.

After Baez graduated from high school in 1958, the Baez family moved back to the East where Joan's father, a physicist, taught at Harvard University and the Massachusetts Institute of Technology. Baez attended Boston University's School of Fine and Applied Arts, but she was not well suited for the discipline required in academia, dropped out, and began singing in local coffeehouses in nearby Cambridge. By 1959, at age eighteen, she could claim a national following, which was boosted with her appearance before thirteen thousand people at the Newport Folk Festival in Rhode Island that year. Two years later, she signed a record contract and released her first album, *Joan Baez*. She toured with Bob Dylan, usually drawing ten thousand to twenty thousand fans to their concerts, which increased to more then twenty a year, and she began to appear more frequently on television. Mainstream America was introduced to Baez when she was the subject of *Time* magazine's cover story in November 1962. But Baez did not forget her friends or principles as her star rose. She refused to sing on ABC's new show *Hootenanny* in 1963 because the network would not allow activist Pete Seeger to appear.

In the 1960s, Baez was actively involved in protests, especially the antiwar and civil rights movements. She appeared at the Free Speech Movement in Berkeley, California; performed at the 1963 March on Washington, where Martin Luther King, Jr., delivered his "I Have a Dream" speech; and marched with King from Selma to Montgomery. To protest the Vietnam War, she informed the Internal Revenue Service she would withhold 60 percent of the federal income taxes she owed. Because she fervently believed in peaceful protest, she founded the Institute for the Study of Non-Violence in 1965. Her position on nonviolence alienated her from the more radical protest groups such as the Black Panthers, whom she once criticized because they carried guns and called cops "pigs." She also drew the ire of organizations on the opposite end of the political continuum. Army bases around the world banned her albums, and the Daughters of the American Revolution prohibited her from performing at Constitution Hall in Washington, D.C., because of what they regarded as her "unpatriotic activities."

In 1966 she marched in Mississippi to protest a racial crime against black elementary school children and performed at a benefit to aid striking Chicano farmworkers in Santa Monica, California. The following year she was arrested in October and again in December for participating in a sit-in outside the draft induction center in Oakland. While demonstrating against the draft, she also helped finance the Resistance, an organization founded by David Harris, whom she married in 1968 and divorced three years later.

In the late 1960s, Baez released two successful albums, *Baptism* (1968) and *Any Day Now* (1969), about the same time she sang at the Woodstock music festival. She was still committed to social causes in the 1970s, but recorded two commercial hits, "The Night They Drove Old Dixie Down" and "Diamonds and Rust." In 1985 promoters of the Live-Aid rock performance to benefit famine victims in Africa asked her to be the opening act. Sometimes known as the "queen of the folksingers," Baez has performed concerts in Europe, Japan, and Latin America, and has earned eight gold albums and one gold single record. Thirty years later, many fans equate her music with political activism.

The Beatles (1960–1971)

George Harrison (February 25, 1943–)   Paul McCartney (June 18, 1942–)

John Lennon (October 9, 1940–December   Ringo Starr (July 7, 1940–)
  8, 1980)

Mostly superlatives come to mind when describing the Beatles' contributions to popular music in the 1960s. No other group approached the innovative style, evolution (even revolution) of music, or influence on culture. Never before in the history of popular music has a group been so dominant as the Beatles. No other rock 'n' roll band incorporated such diversity in their songs and continually redefined their work. In their rhythms, instrumentation, and lyrics, the Beatles captured the mysticism and drug experimentation of the counterculture, but they also had numerous hit songs that made the mainstream Top Forty. Most critics would agree that the Beatles changed the direction of music.

John Lennon and Paul McCartney had been performing together with different groups since they were teenagers when they added a third member, George Harrison. By the late 1950s, the three musicians from working-class families, calling themselves the Quarrymen, began to draw a local following in their hometown, Liverpool, England. When they made their first trip to Hamburg, Germany, in 1960, with two other members, they were still seeking an identity, having gone through several name changes, from Moondogs to Moonshiners to Beatles to The Beatals, to Silver Beetles, before Lennon suggested spelling the word *Beatles*, as a play on the phrase "beat music."

In February 1961, the Beatles began playing at the popular Cavern Club in Liverpool. Following a second trip to Hamburg, they changed their appearance, wearing sport coats without collars and their hair longer and combed down over their foreheads. They also underwent personnel changes when Stu Sutcliffe left the band and drummer Pete Best was fired and replaced by Ringo Starr (born Richard Starkey). With Brian Epstein—sometimes called the fifth Beatle—as their manager, the Beatles began their rapid ascent to the top of the rock world.

Two Lennon-McCartney original songs, "Love Me Do" and "P.S. I Love You," sold well in England when they were released in September 1962, but the Beatles did not have a number-one hit until they recorded "Please Please Me" in March 1963. By the end of the year, "She Loves You" was the top song in England, selling over 1 million copies, and "I Want to Hold Your Hand" topped the British chart for five weeks, eventually selling more than 15 million copies worldwide. The Beatles had not yet appeared in the United States, but when they arrived in New York City in February 1964, thousands of screaming teenage fans, overcome by Beatlemania, mobbed them at Kennedy Airport. On February 9, the Beatles made their live American debut on CBS television's *Ed Sullivan Show*. A theater that seated only a few hundred people was swamped with 50,000 requests for tickets, and an estimated 73 million viewers watched the televised performance. A week later, after they had played at the Washington, D.C., Coliseum and Carnegie

Hall in New York, they made a second appearance on the *Ed Sullivan Show* broadcast from Miami. In April 1964, "Can't Buy Me Love," "Twist and Shout," "She Loves You," "I Want to Hold Your Hand," and "Please Please Me" were *Billboard*'s top five hit songs.

The Beatles continued to develop as their song writing matured over the next few years. In 1964 they filmed their first movie, *A Hard Day's Night*, a commercial success, and during their first extensive U.S. tour that year, they met Bob Dylan, who introduced them to marijuana. Their music soon reflected the influence of hallucinogenic drugs as evidenced in songs from their second movie, *Help!*, released in 1965. Later that year their albums *Rubber Soul* and *Revolver* showed a more introspective side of the Beatles, who focused more on social issues rather than the more common boy-meets-girl themes of their earlier work.

In 1967 they used forty musicians to create an orchestral sound to produce *Sgt. Pepper's Lonely Hearts Club Band,* an album praised by popular and classical music critics as one of the best albums in rock history. The album, a million-seller before it reached the dealers' shelves, accurately captured the essence of the counterculture and demonstrated how the group pushed the intellectual boundaries of rock music. Creating an alter-ego band—Sgt. Pepper's—the album was unprecedented in its diversity and complexity as it explored problems of alienation.

A year after *Sgt. Pepper*, the group released *The Beatles*, more popularly known as the "White Album," a double-record set containing thirty songs. The album was a critical and commercial success, but with members of the Beatles working separately on some of the songs, their relationship became more acrimonious. In January 1969, they appeared together publicly for the last time when they played "Get Back" on their studio rooftop in London. Their last album, *Abbey Road*, was released in July. By 1971, when the group officially announced the dissolution of the Beatles, Lennon had recorded "Imagine" and, with his wife, Yoko Ono, "Instant Karma"; McCartney had released his album *McCartney;* Harrison had a top single, "My Sweet Lord"; and Starr recorded a solo album, *Sentimental Journey*.

In December 1980, returning from a recording session near his home in Manhattan, Lennon was assassinated. In 1994, the surviving three members sang together again to record "Free as a Bird," with Lennon's voice on one of the tracks.

Carmichael, Stokely (June 29, 1941–November 15, 1998)

This proponent of aggressive, if not revolutionary, tactics in the civil rights movement was born on June 29, 1941, in Trinidad in the British West

Indies. Carmichael attended the Tranquility Boys School through the elementary grades before his parents emigrated to Harlem in New York City. He graduated from the prestigious Bronx High School of Science in 1960. He had become radicalized by watching black sit-ins on television before he joined the Congress of Racial Equality (CORE) while a student at Howard University in the early 1960s. Profoundly influenced by the Greensboro, North Carolina, sit-in, he was convinced that the demonstration was a watershed in the struggle for black freedom. He participated in CORE-sponsored Freedom Rides to integrate interstate travel in the South, and he was arrested—more than twenty-five times by his own count—and beaten several times during civil rights demonstrations. After one arrest, he spent forty-nine days in Mississippi's infamous Parchman Penitentiary.

In 1964 he joined the Student Non-Violent Coordinating Committee (SNCC). As part of the Freedom Summer campaign to register black voters in Mississippi, he was largely responsible for increasing black registration in the state's Second Congressional District from seventy to twenty-six thousand, giving blacks a voter majority in that county. The following year, in Lowndes County, Alabama, where Martin Luther King, Jr., led a march from Selma to Montgomery in March 1965, for a federal voting rights act, Carmichael added two thousand blacks to what had been an all-white voter registration. Violent white resistance to civil rights convinced him to change SNCC's focus from integration to black liberation, form a separate group, and adopt the black panther as its logo. As chairman of SNCC in 1966, he rejected King's nonviolent, integrationist civil rights philosophy and emphasized black freedom instead.

During James Meredith's 225-mile "March Against Fear" that year from Memphis to Jackson, Mississippi, Carmichael shouted "Black Power" to black farmers he encountered along the road, hoping to increase the 30 percent of eligible black Mississippians registered to vote. Asserting that a more militant approach was necessary to secure racial equality, he provoked controversy with blacks and whites with the phrase "Black Power," which many whites interpreted—correctly—as a form of black militancy. Carmichael openly advocated black liberation by "any means necessary," and during a voter registration drive in Mississippi he suggested that blacks should carry guns for self-defense. In a book he coauthored with Charles V. Hamilton, *Black Power: The Politics of Liberation in America* (1971), Carmichael explained Black Power as "a call for black people in this country to begin to define their own goals, to lead their own organizations . . . to resist the racist institutions and values of this society."

Although Carmichael was trying to improve living conditions for black Americans, many people active in civil rights attributed his call for Black

Power to splintering the movement. In 1967 he left SNCC and joined the newly formed Black Panther party, the most revolutionary black organization in the nation. Only a few months later, however, disillusioned with the Panthers' acquiescence toward white radical organizations, he left the Panthers. He was an outspoken critic of the Vietnam War and attacked the Selective Service System because it was "white people sending black people to make war on yellow people in order to defend the land they stole from red people." By the late 1960s, he had embraced pan-Africanism and advocated a homeland in Africa for oppressed black people throughout the world. In 1969 Carmichael and his wife, South African singer Miriam Makeba, left the United States on a self-imposed exile for Guinea-Bissau, a small country in West Africa. Two years later, after he adopted the name Kwame Toure, taken from Kwame Nkrumah and Ahmed Sekou Toure, two pan-Africanists, Toure advocated a homeland in Africa for oppressed blacks. He made occasional visits to the United States to lecture on African culture and promote his African People's Revolutionary party. He died from prostate cancer in Guinea-Bissau on November 15, 1998.

Dylan, Bob (May 24, 1941–)

Exploding onto the music scene in 1963, Bob Dylan quickly became the most influential of the folk protest music artists who challenged the social, cultural, musical, and political status quo. Born Robert Zimmerman on May 24, 1941, in Duluth, Minnesota, into a modest middle-class family, he changed his name while a student at the University of Minnesota. While in school, he performed at a local coffeehouse. Idolizing Woody Guthrie, Dylan left the university in January 1961, to visit the great folksinger in a New Jersey hospital before moving to Greenwich Village, where he spent time with Pete Seeger, Allen Ginsberg, Phil Ochs, and Joan Baez. His unique voice and style soon won him a loyal audience and a favorable review in the *New York Times*, which described him as "one of the most distinctive stylists to play in a Manhattan cabaret in months." His first album, *Bob Dylan*, recorded in March 1962, contained little that was innovative, but his next, *The Freewheelin' Bob Dylan*, released in May 1963, included the civil rights anthem "Blowin' in the Wind," "A Hard Rain's A-Gonna Fall," and "Oxford Town," compositions that confirmed his talent as a folk-protest songwriter and musical genius. Dylan also had written "Talkin' John Birch Society Blues" for the album, but Columbia Records would not include the cut, fearing an adverse reaction from the right-wing group. When the CBS television network would not permit him to sing "John Birch" on the *Ed Sullivan Show*, Dylan canceled his appearance.

Six of the ten tracks on Dylan's third album, *The Times They Are A-Changin'*, released in January 1964, are protest songs that earned him recognition as the musical poet of the student-organized New Left movement. The album sold well, but in his last acoustic release, *Another Side of Bob Dylan*, in May 1964, he shifted his emphasis from social and political issues to deal with personal relationships and the influence of drugs. "Chimes of Freedom" and "My Back Pages," later recorded by the Byrds, were more rock than folk, as was "It Ain't Me, Babe," one of the Turtles's biggest hits. *Bringing It All Back Home* (March 1965), which includes "Subterranean Homesick Blues" and "Mr. Tambourine Man," was the first time he used a backup band. Dylan proved to be an iconoclast even within the genre of folk protest music as he constantly changed styles throughout his career. At the Newport Folk Festival in July 1965, Dylan shocked and disappointed folk purists in the audience, who booed him off the stage for using an electric guitar. In September 1966, he released *Highway 61 Revisited*, which opens with "Like a Rolling Stone," a six-minute song that was popular among mainstream audiences. With his release of the mystical double album *Blonde on Blonde* in mid-1966, which included "Rainy Day Women #12 & 35" and "Just Like a Woman," Dylan became popular with the emerging counterculture and the youth movement, but alienated his Old Left following. In July, just two months after the release of *Blonde on Blonde*, Dylan suffered a broken neck in a motorcycle accident. While convalescing in Woodstock, New York, with the band he again experienced a transformation in his music, recording *John Wesley Harding* in October 1967, signaling his return as a folk singer; two years later, though, his fans heard a country Dylan in *Nashville Skyline*.

Widely regarded as the preeminent poet-lyricist and songwriter of his time, Dylan embraced different social themes and causes in his songs after the 1960s. In 1971 he performed at a concert organized by former Beatle George Harrison in Madison Square Garden to benefit the new nation of Bangladesh. In 1975 he sang at a concert to publicize the incarceration of ex-boxer Rubin "Hurricane" Carter, then serving a life sentence for a murder Dylan believed that Carter did not commit. Because he bridged the worlds of folk and rock, in 1985 Dylan was part of the celebrity group recording *We Are the World*, a fund raiser for starving children in Africa, and that September he sang at the Farm Aid concert to help economically struggling farmers.

Dylan confounded his fans yet again when he embraced Bible-thumping Christianity in *The Last Waltz* (1979), followed by a trilogy of albums: *Slow Train Coming*, *Saved*, and *Shot of Love*. In the 1980s he returned to a more secular but no less moralistic tone in three albums recorded in 1983, 1985, and 1989. He released an album in 1991, and in 1998 he won three Grammy Awards: album of the year (*Time Out of Mind*), best male rock vocal performance, and best contemporary folk album.

As a tribute to his enduring contribution to American music, the American Society of Composers, Authors and Publishers (ASCAP) presented Dylan with the Founders Award in 1986 for influencing the direction of popular music. Two years later he was inducted into the Rock and Roll Hall of Fame.

Dylan's popularity has not been limited to the United States. His music and influence have been perhaps even more popular in Europe and Japan. His work has generated numerous books, articles, and graduate theses by journalists and academics, who have analyzed and interpreted his style, lyrics, and personal life, which generally has been shrouded in secrecy. In the summer of 1999, he began touring with Paul Simon, formerly of Simon and Garfunkel.

Fonda, Jane (December 21, 1937–   )

A political activist and accomplished actor, Jane Fonda, daughter of actor Henry Fonda, was born December 21, 1937, in an affluent section of Los Angeles, where she attended the Brentwood Town and Country School. After her mother committed suicide in 1949, Jane moved to Greenwich, Connecticut, to live with her maternal grandmother. There she continued her secondary education at the Greenwich Academy and in 1955 completed her high school education at the Emma Willard School in Troy, New York. That fall, she enrolled at Vassar College in Poughkeepsie, New York, and worked the following summer as an apprentice actor at the Cape Playhouse in Dennis, Massachusetts. After a year at Vassar, where she spent more time socializing than concentrating on her studies, she dropped out and went to Paris, ostensibly to study art at the Sorbonne. Again, she demonstrated little commitment to her education and soon returned to the United States. In 1958 she began taking acting lessons at the Actor's Studio, where director Lee Strasberg was impressed with her talent. Over the next few years, she appeared in Broadway productions and three movies that brought her little acclaim, though she did receive the New York Drama Critics Award as "the most promising new actress of the year."

In 1968 Fonda attracted a large following within the counterculture when she starred in the comedy–science fiction movie *Barbarella*, directed by Roger Vadim, whom she had married in 1965. By the end of the decade, influenced by her father's New Deal liberalism, student riots she witnessed in

Paris, television broadcasts of the war in Vietnam, and the abject poverty she observed while traveling in India, Fonda became more involved in social-political causes. She supported the American Indians who had occupied Alcatraz Island in 1970 and the revolutionary Black Panthers, visited communist–Black Panther member Angela Davis held in Marin County jail on murder charges, and walked a picket line with migrant workers during Cesar Chávez's national boycott of non-union grapes. In February 1971, the year she won the Academy Award for Best Actress for playing a prostitute in *Klute*, she met Tom Hayden at a peace rally and became active in the anti-war movement.

Wanting to learn firsthand about the conduct of the war in Vietnam, Fonda made a visit to Hanoi, the communist capital of North Vietnam, in July 1972. While there, she toured villages and hospitals that had been destroyed by American bombs, talked with American prisoners of war, and accused American pilots on Radio Hanoi of "betraying everything that American people have at heart, betraying the long tradition of freedom and democracy." Her criticism of the American government and particularly of American troops made her persona non grata when she returned to the United States two weeks later. Several members of Congress contended that she should be charged with treason. An editorial in New Hampshire's conservative *Manchester News Leader* advocated that she should be shot. Because of her actions, her name was added to President Richard M. Nixon's "enemies list" of people the White House considered to be a threat to the administration. The FBI's J. Edgar Hoover, who regarded her as an anarchist, had her telephone tapped, illegally investigated her bank account, and alleged that she possessed drugs when she returned from a trip to Canada. The drugs in her possession were vitamin pills.

Fonda's controversial political activities adversely affected her career for several years until she made *Fun with Dick and Jane* in 1977. Playing the wife of a marine captain fighting in Vietnam in *Coming Home* (1978) and a reporter investigating a meltdown at a nuclear power plant in *The China Syndrome* (1979), she meshed her interest in social issues with her acting career. In 1979 she established the Jane Fonda Workout Studio in Beverly Hills, California, and two years later published the successful *Jane Fonda Workout Book*. Transformed into an American heroine in the 1980s, she starred in her own series of workout books and fitness videotapes. She divorced Hayden in 1989 and is currently separated from cable television mogul Ted Turner.

The Grateful Dead

Jerry Garcia (August 1, 1942–   Ron "Pig Pen" McKernan (September 8,
   August 9, 1995)   1946–March 8, 1973)

Bob Weir (October 16, 1947–   )   *Added in the early 1970s:*

Phil Lesh (March 15, 1940–   )   Donna Godchaux (August 22, 1947–   )

Bill Kreutzmann, Jr. (May 7, 1946–   ) Keith Godchaux (July 19, 1948–   )

Mickey Hart (September 11, 1943–   )

Often recognized as the greatest San Francisco band ever, the Grateful
Dead has not amassed huge record sales over its three decades of performing because of the group's anticapitalistic and antiauthoritarian commitment to their counterculture values. Rather than sign lucrative contracts
with a record company, the group encouraged their loyal fan following—
"Deadheads"—to bring their own tape recorders to concerts so they could
make their own tapes.

Before they were the Grateful Dead, they were known as the Warlocks,
formed from an earlier Jerry Garcia group called Mother McCree's Uptown
Jug Band. Garcia, who spent a short time in the army before he was declared
unfit for service, grew up listening to bluegrass music, rock 'n' roll, and the
beat poets who hung out in the North Beach area of San Francisco. In the
late 1950s, he was one of the more talented folk guitarists performing in the
Bay Area, playing country and folk music with various groups. By the mid-
1960s, Garcia had joined with Bob Weir (who had dropped out of a board-
ing school), Ron McKernan (son of a white rhythm and blues disc jockey
who also quit school), Garcia's longtime friend Phil Lesh (a child violinist),
and Bill Kreutzmann, Jr. (from a middle-class family) to form the Warlocks,
borrowing the name from an Egyptian prayer Garcia discovered in a dictionary. The group changed its name to Grateful Dead after Garcia spotted
the phrase in a dictionary while smoking marijuana at Lesh's house in July
1965.

About the time the group became the Grateful Dead, they entertained
Ken Kesey's Merry Pranksters at a commune in La Honda, California, and
regularly participated in Kesey's "Acid Tests," a series of public experimen-
tations with the hallucinogenic drug LSD, then still legal. The experience
profoundly changed the group's music, which infused blues, folk, and rock
into a new, improvisational psychedelic sound that was well received at
Dead appearances at the first "human be-in" at the Golden Gate Park, the
Monterey Pop Festival, the Newport Pop Festival in Costa Mesa, California, and the ill-fated Rolling Stones concert in Altamont.

Because the group played numerous free shows and did not want to sell
out to corporate America, it never enjoyed a hit record during the sixties. In

1967 the band released an album, *The Grateful Dead*, recorded in three days, but it had little impact and did not sell well initially, though it did eventually earn a gold record. Not until 1970, when the group released its biggest-selling album, *Workingman's Dead*, which reached number twenty-seven in the country and later earned a gold record, did the Grateful Dead begin to attract attention nationwide. Later that year, their album *American Beauty* reached number thirty and brought the group another gold record. Included on this album was "Truckin'," which became the Dead's unofficial anthem. The band's next album, *Historic Dead* also went gold, putting it financially in the black for the first time. They did not produce a top-ten hit single until "A Touch of Grey" reached number nine in September 1987.

Through the 1970s, the Dead experienced several personnel changes, one of them resulting from the death on March 8, 1973, of "Pig Pen" McKernan, who had been suffering from a chronic liver ailment and died from a stomach hemorrhage in a friend's back yard in Marin County, California. Despite, or perhaps because of, the use and influence of LSD and other drugs, band members and many Deadheads who followed the group from city to city had become a cult event by the late 1980s. The Grateful Dead was also one of the most popular bands in the history of rock 'n' roll. *Forbes* magazine's annual list of the forty highest paid entertainment groups in 1989 ranked the Dead twenty-ninth, with an estimated annual income of $12.5 million.

One indication of the popularity of the Dead in the 1990s was Ben & Jerry's Ice Cream's most requested flavor, Cherry Garcia, named for the band's leader. Nearly thirty years after the Dead began playing together, their performances still drew aging hippies and neophytes wanting the social experience of a live Dead concert. Like the band members, Deadheads also appreciated the euphoric experience of hallucinogenic drugs. At three-day series of Dead concerts in April 1991, police in Atlanta, Georgia, arrested fifty-seven people and confiscated 4,856 "tabs" of LSD, 39 bags of "mushrooms," 24 "lids" of marijuana, 1 vial of crack cocaine, and 18 cylinders of nitrous oxide.

On August 9, 1995, Jerry Garcia suffered a fatal heart attack while a patient at a drug and alcohol treatment center.

Hayden, Tom (December 12, 1940–   )

Tom Hayden was virtually synonymous with the New Left and student rebellion in the 1960s. Born on December 12, 1940, to Catholic parents, Hayden attended the Shrine of the Little Flower school in Royal Oak, Michigan, under the administration of Father Charles E. Coughlin, the right-wing "radio priest." Soon after Tom Hayden was born, his father abandoned him and his mother, a school librarian.

Hayden became an activist in 1957, shortly after he enrolled at the University of Michigan, not far from his hometown. He later recalled the campus as "a system of absolutely arbitrary authority." Disillusioned with rules he regarded as irrelevant and antiquated, he took on a new view of the world and briefly flirted with the beat way of life. During his junior year his worldview was more clearly defined by two events that would profoundly shape his future: demonstrations against the House Un-American Activities Committee (HUAC) at the University of California–Berkeley campus and the lunch counter sit-ins in Greensboro, North Carolina. At the conclusion of his junior year, Hayden hitchhiked to California, where he met with students who demonstrated against HUAC and leaders of the southern sit-in movement. From these experiences evolved a new radical perspective on political and social issues that influenced opinions he wrote supporting radical causes as editor of the *Michigan Daily*, the campus newspaper. After completing his studies at Michigan, he worked full-time with the Student Non-Violent Coordinating Committee (SNCC) in Georgia and McComb, Mississippi, where he was physically assaulted by a white racist during a voter registration drive.

In June 1962, during a meeting of the Students for a Democratic Society (SDS), Hayden wrote the first draft of *The Port Huron Statement*, the manifesto of the New Left attacking the arms race, racial discrimination, bureaucracy, and apathy. The New Left's most prolific figure also introduced the concept of participatory democracy, which he defined as individuals sharing in social decisions determining the quality and direction of their lives. Through participatory democracy, Hayden hoped to transform the social, racial, economic, and political structure. In 1964 he moved to Newark, New Jersey, where he administered the Economic Research and Action Project (ERAP), which sponsored rent strikes, organized welfare rights demonstrations, and pressured the city government to create playgrounds and repair streets. Hayden also hoped to mobilize black residents but found the task overwhelming because they were so demoralized and transient. The emergence of Black Power and a race riot during the summer of 1967 in Newark rendered ERAP's influence and activities useless.

By 1965 Hayden had become involved in antiwar activity. Although he was concerned his acts might have been considered traitorous, he made the first of several trips to Southeast Asia for the purpose of establishing contact with the North Vietnamese government. Two years later, the North Vietnamese invited him to attend a conference in Bratislava, Czechoslovakia, where American antiwar members met with leaders from North Vietnam.

On a second trip to Hanoi, Hayden discussed the release of captured Americans as a gesture of good faith with the American peace movement. During a stop-over in Paris on the way home, he received a message that he was to return to Hanoi to escort three prisoners back to the United States. His negotiations with the enemy, however, created deep-seated public animosity that would cloud his future.

In June 1968, Hayden served as a pallbearer for assassinated Democratic presidential candidate Senator Robert F. Kennedy, with whom he had became acquainted while engaging in civil rights and antiwar activities. That August, Hayden was one of the planners of demonstrations at the Democratic National Convention in Chicago sponsored by the National Mobilization Committee to End the War in Vietnam. As one of the Chicago Seven, he was indicted on rioting charges from the confrontations with police during the convention. In February 1970, he was found guilty and sentenced to a five-year prison term. The charges were later voided by an appeals court.

Two months after the final American withdrawal from Vietnam in April 1975, Hayden declared that "the radicalism of the 1960s is fast becoming the common sense of the 1970s," and announced his candidacy for the Democratic nomination for the U.S. Senate from California. Despite an investment of $500,000 from his second wife, actress Jane Fonda, he was defeated in the primary by the incumbent, John V. Tunney, but he did win 40 percent of the vote. Not deterred from politics, in 1982 he won election as a member of California's State Assembly and served five terms, establishing himself as a supporter of environmental education issues. Hayden could win a local race, but his history as a radical sympathetic with the enemy was apparently too much baggage to overcome when he lost a bid for governor of California in 1994. Three years later, he also lost a mayoral race in Los Angeles. In April 1999, apropos of his activist interests, he chaired the California state Senate Committees on Higher Education and Natural Resources and Wildlife.

Hendrix, Jimi (November 27, 1942–September 18, 1970)

Born James Marshall on November 27, 1942, in Seattle, Washington, acid-rock guitarist Jimi Hendrix's father was a gardener, and his mother was a full-blooded Cherokee. Hendrix quit Garfield High School during his senior year and did some handyman work for a while before enlisting in 1959 in the Army's 101st Airborne Division as a paratrooper to avoid being drafted. Two years later, he received a medical discharge after sustaining back injuries during his twenty-sixth parachute jump. From 1961 to 1966, using the pseudonym "Jimmy James," he toured with several rhythm and blues shows, including James Brown's Famous Flames and the Isley Brothers. Late in the summer of 1966, while living in New York City, he played in several clubs and became acquainted with other younger musicians, such as Bob Dylan and Bruce Springsteen. During engagements in Greenwich Village clubs and coffeehouses, the left-handed Hendrix acquired proficiency playing his Stratocaster guitar while holding it upside down and behind his head, and even occasionally playing it with his teeth.

In 1966 the emerging "acid rock" star moved to England, where he formed the Jimi Hendrix Experience band with bass guitarist Noel Chandler and drummer Mitch Mitchell. The group's "Purple Haze," released in March 1967, was immediately popular among the counterculture generation because of its allusions to mind-expanding drugs. Hendrix's live performances, described as erotic and provocative, usually culminated with his dousing his guitar with lighter fluid and setting it on fire. His innovative guitar playing and raucous performances made him an instant hit in Europe, where he broke attendance records at the Tivoli in Stockholm, Sweden; the Sports Arena in Copenhagen, Denmark; and the Saville Theatre in London. With a record contract in hand, he recorded a series of singles—"Hey, Joe," "Purple Haze," and "The Wind Cries Mary," that were top-ten hits in Britain.

Shortly after recording its first album, *Are You Experienced?* the Hendrix Experience made its American debut in June 1967 at the Monterey Pop Festival in California, where Jimi's electrifying guitar playing mesmerized the audience. His tours were standing-room-only events over the next two years, earning him recognition as *Billboard*'s and *Rolling Stone*'s artist of the year in 1968, an honor *Playboy* also conferred on him in 1969. In February 1969, the group split up, and Hendrix was arrested at the Toronto, Canada, airport on charges of possession of heroin; he was acquitted in December. Although he denied using hard drugs at the time of his arrest, he was plagued with a drug addiction problem. In August he gave a memorable performance that included an eerie rendition of the "Star-Spangled Banner" as the closing act at the Woodstock music festival.

On September 18, 1970, at the age of twenty-seven, after leaving a message on his manager's answering machine, pleading, "I need help bad, man," he died in his London apartment from "an inhalation of vomit due to barbiturate intoxication," according to the coroner's report.

Hoffman, Abbie (November 30, 1936–April 12, 1989)

A one-time pharmaceutical salesman who came to prominence as a radical activist in the 1960s, Hoffman was born November 30, 1936, in Worcester, Massachusetts. He was expelled from high school after fighting with his English teacher and eventually graduated from the Worcester Academy, a private school. In 1955 he enrolled at Brandeis University in Waltham, Massachusetts, and graduated in 1959 with a bachelor's degree in psychology. A year later he received a master's degree in psychology from the University of California–Berkeley. His Jewish heritage and the failure of Jews to resist Nazi repression forcefully in the 1930s influenced his advocacy of activist causes, for Hoffman rejected passivity and insisted on active engagement as the test of radical belief. According to Hoffman, two events were especially influential in shaping his thinking about social issues. The first was participating in a protest against the death penalty in California; the second occurred just a few days later during a demonstration against the House Un-American Activities Committee (HUAC) hearings in San Francisco, when police attacked him and other demonstrators with clubs and hoses.

In 1964 and 1965, he participated in the Student Non-Violent Coordinating Committee's Freedom Summers in Mississippi, where he was arrested. Two years later, he moved to New York City and opened Liberty House, a store that sold goods made by poor black people in Mississippi. In 1967, after he had settled in with some hippies, he began to oppose the Vietnam War. More serious about staging outrageous and mischievous "happenings" than organizing legitimate protest activities, Hoffman and a group of cohorts in October 1967 threw dollar bills from the visitors' galley to the floor below of the New York Stock Exchange, sending traders into a frenzy as they scrambled after the money. That October, during a large antiwar demonstration in Washington, D.C., he and Jerry Rubin led a group of hippies in an attempt to levitate the Pentagon and exorcise its evil spirits. He helped organize be-ins in New York's Central Park, sent three thousand marijuana cigarettes with instructions on how to smoke them to people he randomly selected from the telephone book, and was part of numerous demonstrations against the establishment. When appearing on the *Merv Griffin Show*, wearing an American flag shirt, network censors blacked out Hoffman's half of the television screen so viewers would not be offended.

On New Year's Day 1968, Hoffman and Rubin coined the term *Yippies* to describe themselves and founded the Youth International party, boasting that the organization had "no leaders, no members, and no organization." Yippies supported the hippie lifestyle while denouncing the Vietnam War. The Yippies' most memorable event was their guerrilla theater activities at the 1968 Democratic presidential convention in Chicago that resulted in a series of violent confrontations between demonstrators and the police. In March 1969, a federal grand jury indicted Hoffman, Rubin, and six others on charges of conspiracy and rioting. He was convicted in the Chicago Seven trial (defendant Bobby Seale's case was handled separately) of 175 charges of contempt and sentenced to jail for eight months, but the charges were suspended.

During the early 1970s, Hoffman visited Canada, Britain, and Northern Ireland and traveled throughout the United States, speaking in opposition to the Vietnam War at dozens of colleges. In May 1971, discouraged and exhausted after police broke his nose during a demonstration in Washington, D.C., his activism began to wane. Following an extended period of inactivity, in 1972 he campaigned for Democratic presidential candidate George S. McGovern and co-authored a book with Rubin, titled *Vote!*, on the presidential conventions in Miami.

In August 1973, he was arrested for selling three pounds of cocaine, valued at $36,000, to two undercover police officers. To avoid facing charges, in February 1974, just before his trial was to open, he dropped out of sight. For the next six years he went underground, living in Canada and Mexico, and had plastic surgery to alter his appearance, He was never apprehended during his period as a fugitive, but he did suffer two nervous breakdowns. In early September 1980, he appeared on ABC national television with Barbara Walters to announce his surrender the next day. In January 1981, he pleaded guilty to reduced charges and served less than a year in jail before being paroled.

Hoffman wrote several books relating his experiences and activities as a revolutionary. In 1968 he published *Revolution for the Hell of It*, a collection of anecdotes, photographs, and political observations aimed at the youth generation. *Steal This Book* (1971) facetiously advocated actions such as overthrowing the government, experimenting with LSD, and ripping off the telephone company. No radio station and only one mainstream newspaper accepted advertising for it, and most bookstores refused to sell it.

Ever an activist, Hoffman maintained his commitment to civil rights, antiwar, and ecological causes through the 1980s. Suffering from manic depression, he died from an overdose of phenobarbital—an apparent suicide—in a motel room in New Hope, Pennsylvania, on April 12, 1989.

Kesey, Ken (September 17, 1935–   )

A nonconformist who epitomized the rebellious countercultural lifestyle, Kesey was born September 17, 1935, in La Junta, Colorado. His parents, who were in the dairy business, moved frequently throughout the West before settling near Eugene, Oregon, where they operated the highly successful Eugene Farmers Cooperative. While attending Springfield High

School in Springfield, Oregon, where he was a star wrestler in the 174-pound class, he was voted "most likely to succeed." In May 1956, he married his high school sweetheart, and a year later he graduated from the University of Oregon, majoring in speech and communication. His high grades won him a Woodrow Wilson Fellowship, which he used to enroll as a graduate student in Stanford University's Creative Writing Program. The author of the novel *One Flew over the Cuckoo's Nest* came in contact at Stanford with faculty members who were also writers and critics, such as Wallace Stegner and Malcolm Cowley, and fellow students Wendell Berry and Larry McMurtry. Equally important for Kesey during his graduate studies at Stanford was his exposure to cultural experimentation and radicalism while living at Perry Lane, a group of cottages near the campus. He later recalled how, during his stay at Perry Lane, "We pioneered what have since become the hall-marks of hippy culture: LSD and other psychedelics too numerous to mention, body painting, light shows, and mixed media presentations . . . be-ins, exotic costumes, strobe lights, sexual mayhem . . . eastern mysticism, and the rebirth of hair."

Perhaps the most significant discovery for Kesey occurred in 1959. When no publisher had expressed an interest in a manuscript he called his "North Beach novel," and his wife was expecting their first child, he took a job as a night attendant in the psychiatric ward at the Veterans Administration Hospital in Menlo Park. At the suggestion of a fellow graduate student, he also volunteered to participate as a subject in an experimental program to supplement his income. For twenty dollars a session, he took a number of hallucinogenic drugs, including LSD, psilocybin, mescaline, peyote, IT-290, Ditran, and morning glory seeds. This experience influenced him to write *Cuckoo's Nest*, which was published in 1962. Set in a mental ward with the message that people need to get back in touch with their world, *Cuckoo's Nest* was a critical success. In the 1970s, it sold more than 1 million copies and was the most frequently used contemporary novel in college courses. It is also one of few modern American works to be presented as a novel, play, and movie, the last starring Jack Nicholson and winning six Academy Awards in 1975.

The drug experience at the Menlo Hospital also convinced Kesey that certain substances could heighten consciousness and enhance the user's creative personality. In 1964 and 1965, he and his Merry Pranksters planned public events or parties called "acid tests," where participants used Day-Glo paint and other visual and audio aids to enhance their LSD experience. In 1964 Kesey bought a 1939 International Harvester school bus, converted it into a camper, and painted it an array of psychedelic colors. A sign in the front of the bus read "Further"; another sign on the back warned, "Caution:

Weird Load." Kesey and some Pranksters used the bus ostensibly for a trip to visit the World's Fair in New York City, and to be there when his novel *Sometimes a Great Notion* was scheduled for publication. The cross-country bus trek and other Prankster adventures were the subject of Tom Wolfe's *The Electric Kool-Aid Acid Test,* published in 1968.

On two occasions, Kesey's drug activities involved him in legal problems. After a second arrest for the possession of marijuana in early 1966 and concerned he would receive a lengthy sentence if convicted, he and some friends loaded up the bus and fled to Mexico. When he returned six months later, he was arrested in San Francisco and served five months in the San Mateo County Jail and later in the San Mateo County Sheriff's Honor Camp. After his release in November 1967, he moved to the Eugene area, where he apparently lost interest in LSD and declined to participate in any Prankster activities. In the 1990s, Kesey wrote children's stories.

Leary, Timothy (October 22, 1920–May 31, 1996)

Often referred to as the "high priest of LSD," the guru of the "psychedelic utopians," and the "corrupter of youth," the rebellious Leary, folk hero of the counterculture, was born October 22, 1920, in Springfield, Massachusetts. As a student at Classical High School in Springfield, he acquired a reputation as a socializer, served as editor of the school newspaper, and earned mediocre grades. His father, a U.S. Army captain and dentist, and his mother, a schoolteacher, were both Catholics and so were pleased when Leary was accepted at Holy Cross College in Worcester, Massachusetts, in 1938. Disenchanted with the strict Jesuit curriculum, however, he left Holy Cross and was admitted to the U.S. Military Academy at West Point in New York. About half of the eighteen months he spent there was in punitive isolation for rules infractions. During his period of isolation, he read Eastern philosophy and developed an interest in Buddhism. After resigning from West Point in August 1941, he enrolled at the University of Alabama and received a bachelor's degree in psychology in 1942. During the last years of World War II, he served as a psychologist at a U.S. Army hospital in Pennsylvania before earning a master's degree in psychology at Washington State University in Pullman in 1946, and a doctorate in psychology from the University of California–Berkeley in 1950. From 1950 to 1955 he was an assistant professor of psychology at Berkeley, before becoming the director of psychological research at the Kaiser Foundation Hospital in Oakland, California, where he created a personality assessment test that was widely used by private and governmental agencies, including the Central Intelligence Agency.

In 1958 the first of Leary's five wives committed suicide and left him with two children. The following year, after a trip to Spain, Harvard University recruited him for its psychology program and appointed him as a lecturer. At Harvard he explored existential transactional psychology and became a harsh critic of conformist, middle-class society. During a trip to Mexico in 1960, he used the psychedelic drug psilocybin, found in "magic mushrooms," for the first time. Excited over the potential he believed psilocybin had to alter personalities, he began experimenting with it, mescaline, and LSD. Soon, joined by fellow professor Richard Alpert, Leary's research involved weekend gatherings with students who took psilocybin. In 1962 he made a second trip to Mexico, where he continued taking LSD and founded the International Foundation for Internal Freedom (IFIF) to train guides in psychedelic exploration. Returning to Harvard, he was more convinced of the benefits of hallucinogenic drugs, especially LSD. Although the drug proved to be useful in other experiments for treating some cases of alcoholism and schizophrenia, the notoriety he attracted embarrassed the administration and he was dismissed in 1963.

That August, he moved into a sixty-four-room mansion in Millbrook, New Jersey, leased to him gratis by William Mellon Hitchcock, a young millionaire fan of Leary. While living at Millbrook with about sixty other adults and children, he met with numerous visitors interested in his drug experimentation, including Alpert, Jack Kerouac, Allen Ginsberg, Aldous Huxley, and William Burroughs. By 1967 Leary had dropped completely out of society and was living in a tepee with little money and only occasionally earning income from lectures. Appearing barefoot, and dressed in white pants and Indian silk shirts, he urged his audience to turn on to the mystical experience (of LSD), tune in to the message, and drop out of the mainstream. He also claimed that "America will be an LSD country within fifteen years."

In 1965, when he formally converted to Hinduism after a trip to India, and again in 1969, Leary was arrested on two marijuana possession violations—one in Texas, the other in California. Convicted of the charges, he entered a minimal-security correctional facility near San Luis Obispo, California, in March 1970, where he served six months before escaping in September, perhaps aided by members of the Weathermen leftist revolutionary group. In October he turned up in Algiers, where the Algerian government gave him political asylum. After bouncing around Europe for three years, he was apprehended in Kabul, Afghanistan, and extradited to California, where he was incarcerated until 1976.

In the 1980s, Leary was active on lecture tours, including one with convicted Watergate conspirator G. Gordon Liddy, and dabbled in stand-up comedy, books, cyberspace, and the Hollywood party scene. In 1990 his daughter, Susan, accused of shooting her boyfriend, hanged herself while confined in a women's institution.

The foremost prophet and proselytizer of LSD, who had polarized the flower children of the 1960s and their "straight" parents, died from prostate cancer on May 31, 1996. As he had requested, his body was cremated and his ashes were scattered into outer space from a rocket launched in the Canary Islands. In July 1999 the FBI confirmed that in 1974, Leary was an informant on the radical Weather Underground, hoping to win his release from jail.

Morrison, Jim (December 8, 1943–July 3, 1971)

Perhaps the most articulate psychedelic music performer, Jim Morrison, born in Melbourne, Florida, on December 8, 1943, was the son of a career navy officer who frequently had to move his family. After graduating from George Washington High School in Alexandria, Virginia, in 1961, Morrison attended a junior college in St. Petersburg, Florida, transferred to Florida State University for a year, and then dropped out. In 1964 he moved to Los Angeles and enrolled at the University of California at Los Angeles, where he wrote poetry and studied cinema. Two months after he graduated, he met keyboard player Ray Manzarek, who agreed to help recruit two additional members to form a group Morrison called the Doors, an allusion to the doors of perception opening into the surreal worlds as described in Aldous Huxley's quest for hallucinogenic substances, and William Blake's passage, "There are things that are known and things that are unknown, in between the doors." The group's music, which frequently mixed sex with death in their songs, was regarded as immoral and morbid by many people and did not hold great appeal for mainstream rock 'n' roll audiences. Despite his sometimes dark lyrics and outrageous behavior on stage, Morrison quickly gained national attention and a devoted following of his white blues, psychedelic music.

After working several years as a house band at the Whiskey-a-Go-Go, a sleazy psychedelic bar on Sunset Strip in Los Angeles, The Doors released their first single record, "Break on Through (to the Other Side)" from their first album, *The Doors*; it did not make the charts. Another song, "Light My Fire," written by Morrison, also on their first album, spent three weeks as the number-one song and it was *Billboard*'s number-two song of the year in 1967. The song was notable also for its length of nearly seven minutes—more than twice the length of Top Forty songs—and for being sexually suggestive. In 1968 "Hello, I Love You" was the year's number-thirteen song, and José Feliciano's version of "Light My Fire" was number forty-seven for the year. Other Doors' hit songs included "People Are Strange" and "Love Me Two Times."

The Doors' second and third albums, *Strange Days* and *Waiting for the Sun*, compared favorably with *The Doors*, but Morrison had demonstrated a tendency for self-destructiveness, and his volatile behavior caused tension within the group. In May 1968, during a concert in Chicago, he incited the audience to riot and escaped through backstage doors as police tried to prevent fans from stomping onto the stage and destroying equipment. Three months later, a similar incident occurred in New York.

Twice arrested for indecent exposure, Morrison, who was more articulate than most other rock stars, described his live concerts as "a public meeting called by us for a special kind of dramatic discussion and entertainment." During a concert on March 1, 1969, in Miami, Morrison supposedly exposed his genitals and simulated masturbation and oral sex. Obscenity charges were dropped, but the band lost much of its popularity and the confidence of their promoters who were reluctant to commit the Doors to future engagements. By this time Morrison could no longer function in the band, dropped out, and moved to Paris, where he died on July 3, 1971. The official cause of death was listed as heart attack induced by respiratory problems, but because his death notice was delayed and few people saw his body, rumors have circulated that he is still alive. In a 1973 interview, Manzarek was suspicious of Morrison's fate, commenting, "I don't know to this day how the man died and in fact I don't even know if he's dead." Morrison was buried in the Poets' Corner of Pere Lachaise Cemetery in Paris. His grave has become a popular tourist site and even a shrine to devoted fans of the Doors and the counterculture they supposedly embodied.

Rudd, Mark (June 2, 1947–   )

A campus revolutionary, Mark Rudd was born on June 2, 1947, and raised in an upper-middle class Jewish family in suburban New Jersey. His father was a Department of Defense employee and military reserve officer, but Mark Rudd did not follow his father's career path or politics. He enrolled in Columbia University in New York City in 1966 and soon emerged as one of the most visible student protesters in the 1960s. At Columbia, Rudd became active in a campus antiwar group, the Independent Committee on Vietnam. Within a year he joined the newly formed Columbia chapter of the Students for a Democratic Society (SDS), and in November 1967, he was one of forty-six people arrested at a demonstration protesting the appearance of Secretary of State Dean Rusk at the New York Hilton Hotel. Aligning with a group labeled the "action faction" at Columbia, Rudd advocated a militant strategy in building a broad student support base. After a three-week trip to Cuba in February 1968, he was elected the chair of Columbia's SDS chapter.

On March 20, defying an SDS directive, members of the "action faction" threw a pie in the face of an official from the Selective Service System who was speaking at Columbia. Rudd later recalled the event as a turning point in convincing the SDS to adopt more aggressive tactics. A week later, after he led a demonstration inside Low Library demanding the university sever its ties with the Institute for Defense Analysis (IDA), he was placed on disciplinary probation. Outraged with this action, he wrote an open letter to Columbia president Grayson Kirk, declaring that "society is sick and you and your capitalism are the sickness." During a memorial service for Martin Luther King, Jr., who had been assassinated only a few days earlier, Rudd seized the speaker's podium and denounced Columbia for its involvement with the IDA and its proposed new gymnasium, which would disrupt an adjacent black neighborhood.

Over a two-day period in late April 1968, about one thousand Rudd-led students occupied campus buildings, resulting in a bloody encounter with police and 178 arrests, including Rudd, who also was suspended from the university. At a December 1968 SDS meeting he supported a leftist-splinter group, the Revolutionary Youth Movement, and organized working-class youths and students. In 1969 he joined the Third World Marxists, another SDS faction that ultimately became the Weathermen, a radical group committed to violence and revolution. As its national secretary, Rudd was at the front of the Weathermen's "Days of Rage" in Chicago in October 1969 when the radicals assaulted the police.

Rudd was indicted for his role in the demonstrations, but the FBI failed to apprehend him because he and most other Weathermen had gone underground to commit acts of sabotage and violence to stop the war. In 1977 he surrendered and was sentenced to two years' probation. In April 1988, Rudd and several other activists reunited in New York City on the twentieth anniversary of the Columbia University strike. Although some of the revolutionaries were convinced their efforts brought an end to the Vietnam War, Rudd was not so certain, commenting, "I bought into a fantasy." In 2000 he was teaching math and reading at the Albuquerque Technical Vocational Institute in New Mexico.

Savio, Mario (December 8, 1942–November 7, 1996)

One of the most dynamic leaders of the student rebellion, Mario Savio was born on December 8, 1942, and raised in a working-class Italian family in New York City. He graduated at the head of his high school class of twelve hundred, and briefly considered the priesthood before he attended Manhattan College on a scholarship and then Queens College. When his parents moved to Los Angeles in 1963, he transferred to the University of California–Berkeley, where he joined other political activists in the civil rights movement. After spending the summer of 1964 working with black children at a freedom school in McComb, Mississippi, an experience that deeply affected him, he returned to Berkeley angry about racism and oppression in a democratic country whose population placed such a high value on freedom and justice.

While pursuing a degree in philosophy, he became increasingly troubled with the university's bureaucracy, impersonalization, and restrictions on freedom of speech. Influenced by his recent experience in Mississippi and the writings of Karl Marx, who asserted that bureaucratic institutions fostered alienation, Savio joined the Young People's Socialist League and won election as the chairman of the University Friends of the Student Non-Violent Coordinating Committee (SNCC). Savio was skeptical about the future of his generation. In an essay he called "The End of History," he contended that society was too unjust to deserve preservation. But Savio was more interested in making history than reading about it. He and other activists decided to challenge the university's new policy prohibiting students from soliciting funds or recruiting volunteers for unrelated university social causes at tables on a narrow strip of sidewalk at a campus entrance. Arguing that the university was violating First Amendment rights to free speech, Savio's United Front challenged the administration by setting up tables in defiance of university regulations. On October 1, 1964, the university suspended Savio and seven other students.

A brilliant, and often fiery, orator, Savio called the administrators a "bunch of bastards" and compared a police officer to a Nazi who "like Adolph Eichmann, has a job to do." Savio played only a minor role in the negotiations between the student activists and university officials, but he was recognized as the leader of the Free Speech Movement (FSM) demonstrations protesting campus rules regulating free speech. The FSM is generally credited as the first campus sit-in and a model for a larger movement protesting the Vietnam War. The sit-in at Berkeley came to an end after three months of disorders and confrontation with the police. Savio was expelled from the University of California and received to a 120-day jail sentence for his role in the sit-ins. He was elected to the steering committee of the FSM, but soon withdrew from political activities in the spring of 1965, married, and worked as a bartender and labor union organizer.

Savio earned a bachelor's degree and graduated summa cum laude in 1984 and received a master's degree in physics in 1989 from San Francisco

State University. In 1995, while teaching mathematics and philosophy at Sonoma State College, he organized the Campus Coalitions for Human Rights and Justice to oppose the abolition of affirmative action programs. On November 6, 1996, he died in Sebastopol, California, after going into a coma caused by fibrillation of the heart.

Seeger, Pete (May 3, 1919–   )

Once described as a "reincarnated troubadour," Seeger was perhaps more responsible than anyone else for popularizing folk music in the United States. Tracing his ancestry back to the *Mayflower*, he grew up in a small town in New York in a highly politicized family environment. His father was forced to quit teaching at the University of California–Berkeley in 1918 because his pacifism won him so many enemies. Seeger spent two years at Harvard University as a sociology major and joined the Young Communist League before dropping out in 1938 to travel throughout the New England countryside, painting landscape scenes. Seeger made his way to New York, where he met and was influenced by folk-song performer Huddie Ledbetter (Leadbelly) and labor militant Aunt Molly Jackson.

In 1940 Seeger, already an accomplished musician, sang with the legendary Woody Guthrie at a "Grapes of Wrath" migrant worker benefit concert. That same year, Seeger, Guthrie, and two other folk singers formed the Almanac Singers, a group that toured the country singing "sod-buster ballads," union songs, and antifascist songs in migrant camps and union halls in the South and Southwest. In 1940–1941, the Almanac Singers recorded a recruiting song for the Congress of Industrial Organizations. In weekly "hootenannies," or song festivals, they also campaigned against America's entry into World War II until Germany invaded Russia, when the group then sang on behalf of the Allies. Inducted into the army in 1942, Seeger spent three and a half years with the Special Services, entertaining troops in the United States and the South Pacific. After his discharge with the rank of corporal, in December 1945, he was the moving force behind People's Songs, a national clearinghouse for folk and sociopolitical songs. The organization enjoyed a membership of about three thousand at its peak, published a monthly bulletin, and conducted weekly hootenannies.

Seeger helped stimulate a folk music revival in 1948 when he founded a quartet called the Weavers, who were immediately successful with such recordings as "Goodnight Irene," "On Top of Old Smoky" and "So Long, It's Been Good to Know You." By 1952, after radio and television appearances, their record sales exceeded 4 million copies. The Weavers' popularity was short-lived, however, when they and other entertainers were victimized in

1952 by blacklisting, red-baiting, and last-minute cancellations of their performances because of their left-wing politics. Throughout the 1950s Seeger's opportunities to perform were restricted, especially after he was called to testify before the House Un-American Activities Committee in 1955, which was investigating alleged subversive influences in the entertainment industry. Refusing to answer questions about his political beliefs, Seeger invoked the First Amendment guaranteeing freedom of speech rather than the Fifth Amendment protection against self-incrimination. In 1961, when his song "Where Have All the Flowers Gone?" was a hit, the House of Representatives found him guilty of ten contempt charges, and he was sentenced to ten years in prison. Although the U.S. court of appeals unanimously reversed his conviction on a technicality in 1961, television still banned him. When ABC's *Hootenanny* show made its television debut in 1963, the network refused to allow Seeger to appear unless he would sign an affidavit indicating his political affiliations. He refused to do so.

Throughout the 1960s, Seeger performed benefit concerts against racism, poverty, and numerous other social evils. He sang against the Vietnam War and for civil rights, using "We Shall Overcome," "If I Had a Hammer," and other songs to convey his message. In the 1960s, he became involved in environmental causes, focusing particularly on restoring the Hud- son River in New York. To dramatize the condition of the river, he established the "Clearwater Festival" in 1969, named after his sloop *Clearwater.*

By the 1980s, with Seeger holding to his conviction that "socialism is still the only hope for the human race," he had recorded sixty albums and various performers had recorded more than one hundred versions of "If I Had a Hammer." In 1999 he received the Felix Varela Medal, Cuba's most prestigious cultural award, for turning the Cuban poem, "Guantanamera," into an international hit song. To celebrate his eightieth birthday in May 1999, he played the banjo and led a sing-along, campaigning for a clean Hudson River.

Primary Documents of the Cultural Revolution

NEW LEFT

Document 1
THE PORT HURON STATEMENT

In 1962 Tom Hayden wrote the manifesto of the Students for a Democratic Society (SDS). In *The Port Huron Statement*, Hayden introduced the concept of participatory democracy and identified its two central objectives: that the individual share in those social decisions determining the quality and direction of his or her life and that society be organized to encourage independence in men and women and provide the media for their common participation. Following is Hayden's preamble to *The Port Huron Statement*, or the New Left's "state of the nation" declaration.

INTRODUCTION: AGENDA FOR A GENERATION

We are people of this generation, bred in at least modest comfort, housed now in universities, looking uncomfortably to the world we inherit.

When we were kids the United States was the wealthiest and strongest country in the world; the only one with the atom bomb, the least scarred by modern war, an initiator of the United Nations that we thought would distribute Western influence throughout the world. Freedom and equality for each individual, government of, by, and for the people—these American values we found good, principles by which we could live as men. Many of us began maturing in complacency.

As we grew, however, our comfort was penetrated by events too troubling to dismiss. First, the permeating and victimizing fact of human degradation, symbolized by the Southern struggle against racial bigotry, compelled most of us from silence to activism. Second, the enclosing fact of the Cold War, symbolized by the presence of the Bomb, brought awareness that we ourselves, and our friends, and millions of abstract "others" we knew more directly because of our common peril, might die at any time. We might deliberately ignore, or avoid, or fail to feel all other human problems, but not these two, for these were too immediate and crushing in their impact, too challenging in the demand that we as individuals take the responsibility for encounter and resolution.

While these and other problems either directly oppressed us or rankled our consciences and became our own subjective concerns, we began to see complicated and disturbing paradoxes in our surrounding America. The declaration "all men are created equal . . ." rang hollow before the facts of Negro life in the South and the big cities of the North. The proclaimed peaceful intentions of the United States contradicted its economic and military investments in the Cold War status quo.

We witnessed, and continue to witness, other paradoxes. With nuclear energy whole cities can easily be powered, yet the dominant nation-states seem more likely to unleash destruction greater than that incurred in all wars of human history. Although our own technology is destroying old and creating new forms of social organization, men still tolerate meaningless work and idleness. While two-thirds of mankind suffers undernourishment, our own upper classes revel amidst superfluous abundance. Although world population is expected to double in forty years, the nations still tolerate anarchy as a major principle of international conduct and uncontrolled exploitation governs the sapping of the earth's physical resources. Although mankind desperately needs revolutionary leadership, America rests in national stalemate, its goals ambiguous and tradition-bound instead of informed and clear, its democratic system apathetic and manipulated rather than "of, by, and for the people."

Not only did tarnish appear on our image of American virtue, not only did disillusion occur when the hypocrisy of American ideals was discovered, but we began to sense that what we had originally seen as the American Golden Age was actually the decline of an era. The worldwide outbreak of revolution against colonialism and imperialism, the entrenchment of totalitarian states, the menace of war, overpopulation, international disorder, supertechnology—these trends were testing the tenacity of our own commitment to democracy and freedom and our abilities to visualize their application to a world in upheaval.

Our work is guided by the sense that we may be the last generation in the experiment with living. But we are a minority—the vast majority of our people regard the temporary equilibriums of our society and world as eternally-functional parts. In this is perhaps the outstanding paradox: we ourselves are imbued with urgency, yet the message of our society is that there is no viable alternative to the present. Beneath the reassuring tones of the politicians, beneath the common opinion that America will "muddle through," beneath the stagnation of those who have closed their minds to the future, is the pervading feeling that there simply are no alternatives, that our times have witnessed the exhaustion not only of Utopias, but of any new departures as well. Feeling the press of complexity upon the emptiness of life, people are fearful of the thought that at any moment things might be thrust out of control. They fear change itself, since change might smash whatever invisible framework seems to hold back chaos for them now. For most Americans, all crusades are suspect, threatening. The fact that each individual sees apathy in his fellows perpetuates the common reluctance to organize for change. The dominant institutions are complex enough to blunt the minds of their potential critics, and entrenched enough to swiftly dissipate or entirely repel the energies of protest and reform, thus limiting human expectancies. Then, too, we are a materially improved society, and by our own improvements we seem to have weakened the case for further change.

Some would have us believe that Americans feel contentment amidst prosperity—but might it not be better called a glaze above deeply-felt anxieties about their role in the new world? And if these anxieties produce a developed indifference to human affairs, do they not as well produce a yearning to believe there is an alternative to the present, that something *can* be done to change circumstances in the school, the workplaces, the bureaucracies, the government? It is to this latter yearning, at once the spark and engine of change, that we direct our present appeal. The search for truly democratic alternatives to the present, and a commitment to social experimentation with them, is a worthy and fulfilling human enterprise, one which moves us and, we hope, others today. On such a basis do we offer this document of our convictions and analysis: as an effort in understanding and changing the conditions of humanity in the late twentieth century, an effort rooted in the ancient, still unfulfilled conception of man attaining determining influence over his circumstances of life.

Source: SDS Papers, State Historical Society of Wisconsin, Madison, Wisconsin.

Document 2
AN END TO HISTORY
Mario Savio

Mario Savio is generally recognized as the leader of the Free Speech
Movement at the University of California–Berkeley that resulted in a
student strike and an administrative resolution supporting students'
free speech. In the fall of 1964, just a few months after he returned from
participating in SNCC's Freedom Summer voter registration campaign in Mississippi, Savio delivered this speech before a large gathering of Berkeley students, criticizing what he and others in the New Left
perceived as an impersonal campus learning environment and a university bureaucracy that repressed and alienated students. Savio, and
those others who demonstrated at Berkeley for free speech, touched off
a student rebellion that erupted on college campuses nationwide during the latter half of the 1960s.

Last summer I went to Mississippi to join the struggle there for civil
rights. This fall I am engaged in another phase of the same struggle, this
time in Berkeley. The two battlefields may seem quite different to some observers, but this is not the case. The same rights are at stake in both
places—the right to participate as citizens in democratic society and the
right to due process of law. Further, it is a struggle against the same enemy.
In Mississippi an autocratic and powerful minority rules, through organized
violence, to suppress the vast, virtually powerless, majority. In California,
the privileged minority manipulates the University bureaucracy to suppress
the students' political expression. That "respectable" bureaucracy masks
the financial plutocrats; that impersonal bureaucracy is the efficient enemy
in a "Brave New World."

In our free speech fight at the University of California, we have come up
against what may emerge as the greatest problem of our nation—deperson-
alized, unresponsive bureaucracy. We have encountered the organized
status quo in Mississippi, but it is the same in Berkeley. Here we find it impossible usually to meet with anyone but secretaries. Beyond that, we find
functionaries who cannot make policy but can only hide behind the rules.
We have discovered total lack of response on the part of the policy makers.
To grasp a situation which is truly Kafkesque, it is necessary to understand
the bureaucratic mentality. And we have learned quite a bit about it this fall,
more outside the classroom than in.

As bureaucrat, an administrator believes that nothing new happens. He
occupies an ahistorical point of view. In September, to get the attention of
this bureaucracy which has issued arbitrary edicts suppressing student po-

litical expression and refused to discuss its action, we held a sit-in on the campus. We sat around a police car and kept it immobilized for over thirty-two hours. At last, the administrative bureaucracy agreed to negotiate. But instead, on the following Monday, we discovered that a committee had been appointed, in accordance with usual regulations, to resolve the dispute. Our attempt to convince any of the administrators that an event had occurred, that something new had happened, failed. They saw this simply as something to be handled by normal University procedures.

The same is true of all bureaucracies. They begin as tools, means to certain legitimate goals, and they end up feeding their own existence. The conception that bureaucrats have is that history has in fact come to an end. No events can occur now that the Second World War is over which can change American society substantially. We proceed by standard procedures as we are.

The most crucial problems facing the United States today are the problem of automation and the problem of racial injustice. Most people who will be put out of jobs by machines will not accept an end to events, this historical plateau, as the point beyond which no change occurs. Negroes will not accept an end to history here. All of us must refuse to accept history's final judgment that in America there is no place in society for people whose skins are dark. On campus students are not about to accept it as fact that the university has ceased evolving and is in its final state of perfection, that students and faculty are respectively raw material and employees, or that the university is to be autocratically run by unresponsive bureaucrats.

Here is the real contradiction: the bureaucrats hold history as ended. As a result significant parts of the population both on campus and off are dispossessed, and these dispossessed are not about to accept this ahistorical point of view. It is out of this that the conflict has occurred with the university bureaucracy and will continue to occur until that bureaucracy becomes responsive or until it is clear the university can not function.

The things we are asking for in our civil rights protests have a deceptively quaint ring. We are asking for the due process of law. We are asking for our actions to be judged by committees of our peers. We are asking that regulations ought to be considered as arrived at legitimately only from the consensus of the governed. These phrases are all pretty old, but they are not being taken seriously in America today, nor are they being taken seriously on the Berkeley campus.

I have just come from a meeting with the dean of students. She notified us that she was aware of certain violations of University regulations by certain organizations. University friends of SNCC, which I represent, was one of these. We tried to draw from her some statement on these great principles, consent of the governed, jury of one's peers, due process. The best she could do was to evade or to present the administration party line. It is very hard to make any contact with the human being who is behind these organizations.

The university is the place where people begin seriously to question the conditions of their existence and raise the issue of whether they can be committed to the society they have been born into. After a long period of apathy during the fifties, students have begun not only to question but, having arrived at answers, to act on those answers. This is part of a growing understanding among people in America that history has not ended, that a better society is possible, and that it is worth dying for.

This free speech fight points up a fascinating aspect of contemporary campus life. Students are permitted to talk all they want so long as their speech has no consequences.

One conception of the university, suggested by a classical Christian formulation, is that it be in the world but not of the world. The concept of Clark Kerr [Berkeley president], by contrast, is that the university is part and parcel of this particular stage in the history of American society; it stands to serve the need of American industry; it is a factory that turns out a certain product needed by industry or government. Because speech does often have consequences which might alter this perversion of higher education, the university must put itself in a position of censorship. It can permit two kinds of speech, speech which encourages continuation of the status quo, and speech which advocates changes in it so radical as to be irrelevant in the foreseeable future. Someone may advocate radical change in all aspects of American society, and this I am sure he can do with impunity. But if someone advocates sit-ins to bring about changes in discriminatory hiring practices, this cannot be permitted because it goes against the status quo of which the university is a part. And that is how the fight began here.

The administration of the Berkeley campus had admitted that external, extra-legal groups have pressured the University not to permit students on campus to organize picket lines, not to permit on campus any speech with consequences. And the bureaucracy went along. Speech with consequences, speech in the area of civil rights, speech which some might regard as illegal, must stop.

Many students here at the University, many people in society, are wandering aimlessly about. Strangers in their own lives, there is no place for them. They are people who have not learned to compromise, who for example have come to the University to learn to question, to grow, to learn—all the standard things that sound like clichés because no one takes them seriously. And they find at one point or other that for them to become part of society, to become lawyers, ministers, businessmen, people in government, that very often they must compromise those principles which were most dear to them. They must suppress the most creative impulses that they have; this is a prior condition for being part of the system. The University is well structured, well tooled, to turn out people with all the sharp edges worn off, the well-rounded person. The University is well equipped to produce that sort of person, and this means that the best among the people who enter must for four years wander aimlessly much of the time questioning why they are on campus at all, doubting whether there is any point in what they are doing, and looking toward a very bleak existence afterward in a game in which all of the rules have been made up, which one cannot really amend.

It is a bleak scene, but it is all a lot of us have to look forward to. Society provides no challenge. American society in the standard conception it has of itself is simply no longer exciting. The most exciting things going on in America today are movements to change America. America is becoming ever more the Utopia of sterilized, automated contentment. The "futures" and "careers" for which American students now prepare are for the most part intellectual and moral wastelands. This chrome-plated consumers paradise would have us grow up to be well-behaved children. But an important minority of men and women coming to the front today have shown that they will die rather than be standardized, replaceable and irrelevant.

Source: Alexander Bloom and Wini Breines, eds., *"Takin' It to the Streets": A Sixties Reader* (New York: Oxford University Press, 1995), 111–15.

Document 3
BRING THE WAR HOME

Although Students for a Democratic Society (SDS) initially did not intend to function as an antiwar organization, by the end of the 1960s SDS members were actively participating in and coordinating protests against American involvement in Vietnam. Mass protest and confrontation with establishment authorities became SDS objectives. In the following excerpt from the August 1, 1969, issue of *New Left Notes*, SDS leaders make a nationwide call for members to attend an antiwar demonstration in Chicago and express SDS thinking on the corruption of American culture caused by and revealed in America's Vietnam policy. The document also speaks to the SDS's and other New Left antiwar groups' linkage of the war to racism and the need for black liberation.

This is the National Action brochure that the national office has produced. So far they have been going as fast as we can print them. They can be ordered from the n.o. [national office] at a price of $5 per thousand.

It will also be printed as a part of the mass newspaper that SDS will have ready within a week. Send in orders for the paper, too, and pass them both out wherever you go.

It has been almost a year since the Democratic Convention, when thousands of young people came together in Chicago and tore up pig city for five days. The action was a response to the crisis this system is facing as a result of the war, the demand by black people for liberation, and the ever-growing reality that this system just can't make it.

This fall, people are coming back to Chicago: more powerful, better organized, and more together than we were last August.

SDS is calling for a National Action in Chicago on October 11. We are coming back to Chicago, and we are going to bring those we left behind last year.

LOOK AT IT: AMERICA, 1969

The war goes on, despite the jive double-talk about troop withdrawals and peace talks. Black people continue to be murdered by agents of the fat cats who run this country, if not in one way, then in another: by the pigs or the courts, by the boss or the welfare department. Working people face higher taxes, inflation, speed-ups, and sure knowledge—if it hasn't happened already—that their sons may be shipped off to Vietnam and shipped home in a box. And young people all over the country go to prisons that are called schools, are trained for jobs that don't exist or serve no one's real interest but the boss's, and to top it all off, get told that Vietnam is the place to defend their "freedom."

None of this is very new. The cities have been falling apart, the schools have been bullshit, the jobs have been rotten and unfulfilling for a long time.

What's new is that today not quite so many people are confused and a lot more people are angry: angry about the fact that the promises we have heard since first grade are all jive; angry that, when you get down to it, this system is nothing but the total economic and military put-down of the oppressed peoples of the world.

And more: it's a system that steals the goods, the resources, and the labor of poor and working people all over the world in order to fill the pockets and bank accounts of a tiny capitalist class. (Call it imperialism.) It's a system that divides white workers from blacks by offering whites crumbs off the table, and telling them that if they don't stay cool the blacks will move in on their jobs, their homes, and their schools. (Call it white supremacy.) It's a system that divides men from women, forcing women to be subservient to men from childhood, to be slave labor in the home and cheap labor in the factory. (Call it male supremacy.) And it's a system that has colonized whole nations within this country—the nation of black people, the nation of brown people—to enslave, oppress, and ultimately murder the people on whose backs this country was built. (Call it fascism.)

But the lies are catching up to America—and the slick rich people and their agents in the government bureaucracies, the courts, the schools, and the pig stations just can't cut it anymore.

Black and brown people know it.

Young people know it.

More and more white working people know it.

And you know it.

LAST YEAR, THERE WERE ONLY ABOUT 10,000 OF US IN CHICAGO

The press made it look like a massacre. All you could see on TV were shots of the horrors and blood of pig brutality. That was the line that the bald-headed businessmen were trying to run down—"If you mess with us, we'll let you have it." But those who were there tell a different story. We were together and our power was felt. It's true that some of us got hurt, but last summer was a victory for the people in a thousand ways.

Our actions showed the Vietnamese that there were masses of young people in this country facing the same enemy that they faced.

We showed that white people would no longer sit by passively while black communities were being invaded by occupation troops every day.

We showed that the "democratic process" of choosing candidates for a presidential election was nothing more than a hoax, pulled off by the businessmen who really run this country.

As we showed the whole world that in the face of the oppressive and exploitative rulers—and the military might to back them up—thousands of people are willing to fight back.

SDS IS CALLING THE ACTION THIS YEAR

But it will be a different action. An action not only against a single war or a "foreign policy," but against the whole imperialist system that made that war a necessity. An action not only for immediate withdrawal of all U.S. occupation troops, but in support of the heroic fight of the Vietnamese people and the National Liberation Front for freedom and independence. An action not only to bring "peace to Vietnam," but beginning to establish another front against imperialism right here in America—to "bring the war home."

We are demanding that all occupational troops get out of Vietnam and every other place they don't belong. This includes the black and brown communities, the worker's picket lines, the high schools, and the streets of

Berkeley [University of California]. No longer will we tolerate "law and order" backed up by soldiers in Vietnam and pigs in the communities and schools; a "law and order" that serves only the interests of those in power and tries to smash the people down whenever they rise up.

We are demanding the release of all political prisoners who have been victimized by the ever-growing attacks on the black liberation struggle and the people in general. Especially the leaders of the black liberation struggle like Huey P. Newton, Ahmed Evans, Fred Hampton, and Martin Sostre.

We are expressing total support for the National Liberation Front [NLF] and the newly-formed Provisional Revolutionary Government [PRG] of South Vietnam. Throughout the history of the war, the NLF has provided the political and military leadership to the people of South Vietnam. The Provisional Revolutionary Government, recently formed the NLF and other groups, has pledged to "mobilize the South Vietnamese armed forces and people" in order to continue the struggle for independence. The PRG also has expressed solidarity with "the just struggle of the Afro-American people for their fundamental national rights," and has pledged to "actively support the national independence movements of Asia, Africa, and Latin America."

We are also expressing total support for the black liberation struggle, part of the same struggle that the Vietnamese are fighting against the same enemy.

We are demanding independence for Puerto Rico, and an end to the colonial oppression that the Puerto Rican nation faces at the hand of U.S. imperialism.

We are demanding an end to the surtax [federal income tax], a tax taken from the working people of this country and used to kill working people in Vietnam and other places for fun and profit.

We are expressing solidarity with the Conspiracy 8 [defendants charged with rioting during the Democratic convention] who led the struggle last summer in Chicago. Our action is planned to roughly coincide with the beginning of their trial.

And we are expressing support for GIs in Vietnam and throughout the world who are being made to fight the battle of the rich, like poor and working people have always been made to do. We support those GIs at Fort Hood, Fort Jackson, and many other army bases who have refused to be cannon fodder in a war against the people of Vietnam.

IT'S ALMOST HARD TO REMEMBER WHEN THE WAR BEGAN

But, after years of peace marches, petitions, and the gradual realization that this war was no "mistake" at all, one critical fact remains: the war is not just happening in Vietnam.

It is happening in the jungles of Guatemala, Bolivia, Thailand, and all op-pressed nations throughout the world.

And it is happening here. In black communities throughout the country. On college campuses. And in the high schools, in the shops, and on the streets.

It is a war in which there are only two sides; a war not for liberation but for an end to domination, not for destruction, but for liberation and the un-chaining of human freedom.

And it is a war in which we cannot "resist"; it is a war in which we must fight.

On October 11, tens of thousands of people will come to Chicago to bring the war home. Join us.

Source: *New Left Notes*, August 1, 1969, 2–3.

ANTIWAR

Document 4
SDS CALL FOR A MARCH ON WASHINGTON

By the mid-1960s the Students for a Democratic Society (SDS), the New Left organization that questioned injustices in the American eco-nomic and political system, had begun to participate in protests against the war in Vietnam. In April 1965, it sponsored a March on Washington that attracted 25,000 people. Following is an SDS call for another March on Washington in November that reiterates its commitment to "participatory democracy."

In the name of freedom, America is mutilating Vietnam. In the name of peace, America turns that fertile country into a wasteland. And in the name of democracy, America is burying its own dreams and suffocating its own potential.

Americans who can understand why the Negroes of Watts can rebel should understand too why Vietnamese can rebel. And those who know the American South and the grinding poverty of our Northern cities should un-derstand that our real problems lie not in Vietnam but at home—that the fight we seek is not with Communism but with the social desperation that makes good men violent, both here and abroad.

THE WAR MUST BE STOPPED

Our aim in Vietnam is the same as our aim in the United States: that oli-garchic rule and privileged power be replaced by popular democracy where the people make the decisions which affect their lives and share in the abun-dance and opportunity that modern technology makes possible. This is the only solution for Vietnam in which Americans can find honor and take pride. Perhaps the war has already so embittered and devastated the Vietnamese that that ideal will require years of rebuilding. But the war cannot achieve it, nor can American military presence, nor our support of repressive unrepresentative governments.

The war must be stopped. There must be an immediate cease fire and demobilization in South Vietnam. There must be a withdrawal of American troops. Political amnesty must be guaranteed. All agreements must be ratified by the partisans of the "other side"—the National Liberation Front and North Vietnam.

We must not deceive ourselves: a negotiated agreement cannot guarantee democracy. Only the Vietnamese have the right of nationhood to make their government democratic or not, free or not, neutral or not. It is not America's role to deny them the chance to be what they will make of themselves. That chance grows more remote with every American bomb that explodes in a Vietnamese village.

But our hopes extend not only to Vietnam. Our chance is the first in a generation to organize the powerless and the voiceless at home to confront America with its racial injustice, its apathy, and its poverty, and with that same vision we dream for Vietnam: a vision of a society in which all can control their own destinies.

We are convinced that the only way to stop this and future wars is to organize a domestic social movement which challenges the very legitimacy of our foreign policy; this movement must also fight to end racism, to end the paternalism of our welfare system, to guarantee decent income for all, and to supplant the authoritarian control of our universities with a community of scholars.

This movement showed its potential when 25,000 people—students, the poverty-stricken, ministers, faculty, unionists, and others—marched on Washington last April. This movement must now show its force. SDS urges everyone who believes that our warmaking must be ended and our democracy-building must begin, to join in a March on Washington on November 27, at 11 A.M. in front of the White House.

Source: Alexander Bloom and Wini Breines, eds., "Takin' It to the Streets": A Sixties Reader (New York: Oxford University Press, 1995), 226–29.

Document 5
WE REFUSE TO SERVE

In 1967 a major network of draft resisters was established at the University of California–Berkeley and Stanford University. Unlike other groups protesting the Vietnam War, this organization advocated active opposition to the draft. Calling itself "The Resistance," this more radical group promised to fill the jails with civil disobedient demonstrators who vowed to "put their bodies on the line." With new chapters springing up across the country, The Resistance sponsored a mass turn-in of draft cards on October 16, 1967, and a Stop the Draft Week to begin the same day. Following are excerpts from their position paper outlining their antiwar activities.

I. WE REFUSE TO SERVE

In the past few months, in many parts of the country, a resistance has been forming . . . a resistance of young men—joined together in their commitment against the war. . . .

We will renounce all deferments and refuse to cooperate with the draft in any manner, at any level. We have taken this stand for varied reasons:

opposition to conscription

opposition only to the Vietnam war

opposition to all wars and to all American military adventures.

We all agree on one point: the war in Vietnam is criminal and we must act together, at great individual risk, to stop it. Those involved must lead the American people, by their example, to understand the enormity of what their government is doing . . . that the government cannot be allowed to continue with its daily crimes. . . .

There are many ways to avoid the draft, to stay clear of the war. Most of us now have deferments . . . but all these individual outs can have no effect on the draft, the war, or the consciousness of this country. To cooperate with conscription is to perpetuate its existence, without which, the government could not wage war. We have chosen to openly defy the draft and confront the government and its war directly. . . .

IV. THE RESISTANCE

Since the United States is engaged in criminal activity in Vietnam.

Since the major instrument of that criminal activity is the American military establishment.

Since the machinery of the military cannot effectively function without the acquiescence of the people it is supposed to represent.

Since we are young Americans who still believe in the ideals our country once stood for.

The RESISTANCE has been formed to organize and encourage resistance to, disruption of, and noncooperation with all the war-making machinery of the United States.

The RESISTANCE is a nationwide movement with organizations in New York, Illinois, Massachusetts, Iowa, Ohio, Wisconsin, Michigan, Oregon, and California.

ON OCTOBER 16, 1967, WE WILL PUBLICLY AND COLLECTIVELY RETURN OUR DRAFT CARDS TO THE SELECTIVE SERVICE SYSTEM IN MAJOR CITIES THROUGHOUT THE COUNTRY. We will clearly challenge the government's right to use any young lives for its own nefarious purposes. Our challenge will continue, and we will openly confront the Selective Service System, until the government is forced to deal with our collective action. After October 16, we will organize campuses and communities for similar waves of resistance in December, March, etc. We have gone beyond the "We Won't Go" statements in that we are renouncing all deferments, joining the forces of those who can and those who cannot afford deferments, and forcing an immediate confrontation by practicing total noncooperation with the military establishment. By turning in rather than burning our draft cards, we will be proudly giving our names to the public at large, and to the powers that be. Our hope is that upon our example every young man impelled to pursue his skill rather than embark upon some less important enterprise and is encouraged to apply his skill in an essential activity in the national interest. The loss of deferred status is the consequence for the individual who has acquired the skill and either does not use it or uses it in a nonessential activity.

The psychology of granting wide choice under pressure to take action is the American or indirect way of achieving what is done by direction in foreign countries where choice is not permitted. Here, choice is limited but not denied, and it is fundamental that an individual generally applies himself better to something he had decided to do rather than something he has been told to do.

Source: Alexander Bloom and Wini Breines, eds., *"Takin' It to the Streets": A Sixties Reader* (New York: Oxford University Press, 1995), 240–41.

COUNTERCULTURE

Document 6
YIPPIE MANIFESTO

The Youth International party, founded by Jerry Rubin and Abbie Hoffman in January 1968, was an absurd spoof of the more legitimate activist groups, such as Students for a Democratic Society and the National Mobilization Committee to End the War in Vietnam. The Yippies, as the party was popularly called, relied on a combination of confrontation, guerrilla theater, and generally outrageous behavior to attract media attention and shock mainstream America. The Yippie Manifesto that follows outlines the Yippie "revolution."

Come into the streets on Nov. 5, election day. Vote with your feet. Rise up and abandon the creeping meatball! Demand the bars be open. Make music and dance at every red light. A festival of life in the streets and parks throughout the world. The American election represents death, and we are alive.

Come all you rebels, youth spirits, rock minstrels, bomb throwers, bank robbers, peacock freaks, toe worshippers, poets, street folk, liberated women, professors and body snatchers: it is election day and we are everywhere.

Don't vote in a jackass-elephant-cracker circus. Let's vote for ourselves. Me for President. We are the revolution. We will strike and boycott the election and create our own reality.

Can you dig it: in every metropolis and hamlet of America boycotts, strikes, sit-ins, pickets, lie-ins, pray-ins, feel-ins, piss-ins at the polling places.

Nobody goes to work. Nobody goes to school. Nobody votes. Everyone becomes a life actor of the street doing his thing, making the revolution by freeing himself and fucking up the system.

Ministers dragged away from polling places. Free chicken and ice cream in the streets. Thousands of kazoos, drums, tambourines, triangles, pots and pans, trumpets, street fairs, firecrackers—a symphony of life on a day of death. LSD in the drinking water.

Let's parade in the thousands to the places where the votes are counted and let murderous racists feel our power.

Force the National Guard to protect every polling place in the country. Brush your teeth in the streets. Organize a sack race. Join the rifle club of your choice. Freak out the pigs with exhibitions of snake dancing and karate at the nearest pig pen.

Release a Black Panther in the Justice Department. Hold motorcycle races a hundred yards from the polling places. Fly an American flag out of every house so confused voters can't find the polling places. Wear costumes. Take a burning draft card to Spiro Agnew.

Stall for hours in the polling places trying to decide between Nixon and Humphrey and Wallace. Take your clothes off. Put wall posters up all over the city. Hold block parties. Release hundreds of greased pigs in pig uniforms downtown.

Check it out in Europe and throughout the world thousands of students will march on the USA embassies demanding to vote in the election cause Uncle Pig controls the world. No domination without representation.

Let's make 2-300 Chicago's on election day.

On election day let's pay tribute to rioters, anarchists, Commies, runaways, draft dodgers, acid freaks, snipers, beatniks, deserters, Chinese spies. Let's exorcise all politicians, generals, publishers, businessmen, Popes, American Legion, AMA, FBI, narcos, informers.

And then on Inauguration Day Jan. 20 we will bring our revolutionary theater to Washington to inaugurate Pigasus, our pig, the only honest candidate, and turn the White House into a crash pad. They will have to put Nixon's hand on the bible in a glass cage.

Begin now: resist oppression as you feel it. Organize and begin the word of mouth communication that is the basis of all conspiracies. . . .

Every man a revolution! Every small group a revolutionary center! We will be together on election day. Yippie!!!

Source: Alexander Bloom and Wini Breines, ed., *"Takin' It to the Streets": A Sixties Reader* (New York: Oxford University Press, 1995), 323–24.

Document 7
REVOLUTION FOR THE HELL OF IT
Abbie Hoffman

Abbie Hoffman, with cofounder Jerry Rubin, organized the Youth International party in early 1968 to promote their Festival of Life at the Democratic National Convention in Chicago in August 1968. On February 16 that year, he wrote a mock, satirical self-interview explaining the meaning of Yippies and their plans for the upcoming convention. Charged with rioting in Chicago, Hoffman was one of the Chicago Seven defendants convicted in 1969.

TALKING IN MY SLEEP—AN EXERCISE IN SELF-CRITICISM

A mythical interview of questions that are asked and answers that are given. Interviews are always going on. Here's one with myself.

You're planning to drop out?

Well, dropping out is a continual process. I don't see anything really definite in the future. I just don't want to get boxed-in to playing a predetermined role. Let's say, so much of what we do is theater—in life I just don't want to get caught in a Broadway show that lasts five years, even if it is a success. The celebrity bag is another form of careerism. But you see, celebrity status is very helpful in working with media. It's my problem and I'll deal with it just like any other problem. I'll do the best I can.

Is that why the Yippies were created? To manipulate the media?

Exactly. You see, we are faced with this task of getting huge numbers of people to come to Chicago along with hundreds of performers, artists, theater groups, engineers. Essentially, people involved in trying to work out a new society. How do you do this starting from scratch, with no organization, no money, nothing? Well, the answer is that you create a myth. Something that people can play a role in, can relate to. This is especially true of media people. I'll give you an example. A reporter was interviewing us once and he liked what we were doing. He said, "I'm going to tell what good ideas you guys really have. I'm going to tell the truth about the Yippies." We said, "That won't help a bit. Lie about us." It doesn't matter as long as he gets Yippie! and Chicago linked together in a magical way. The myth is about LIFE vs. DEATH. That's why we are headed for a powerful clash.

You don't want the truth told?

Well, I don't want to get philosophical but there is really no such animal. Especially when one talks of creating a myth. How can you have a true myth? When newspapers distort a story they become participants in the creation of the myth. We love distortions. Those papers that claim to be accurate, i.e., the *New York Times*, *Village Voice*, *Ramparts*, *The Nation*, *Commentary*, that whole academic word scene is a total bore. In the end they probably distort things more than the *Daily News*. The *New York Times* is the American Establishment, not the *Daily News*. The *Daily News* creates a living style. You know: "Pot-smoking, dirty, beatnik, pinko, sex-crazy, Vietnik, so-called Yippies." Compare that to the *New York Times*: "Members of the newly formed Youth International Party (YIP)." The *New York Times* is death. The *Daily News* is the closest thing to TV. Look at its front page, always a big picture. It looks like a TV set. I could go on and on about this. It's a very important point. Distortion is essential to myth-making.

That's some fantasy.

Of course. It'll come true, though. Fantasy is the only truth. Once we had a demonstration at the *Daily News* Building. About three-hundred people smoked pot, danced, sprayed the reporters with body deodorant, burned money, handed out leaflets to all the employees that began: "Dear fellow member of the Communist conspiracy . . ." We called it an "Alternative Fantasy." It worked great.

What do you mean, it worked great?

Nobody understood it. That is, nobody could explain what it all meant yet everyone was fascinated. It was pure information, pure imagery, which in the end is truth. You see, the *New York Times* can get into very theoretical discussions on the critical level of what we are doing. The *Daily News* responds on a gut level. That's it. The *New York Times* has no guts.

Then being understood is not your goal?

Of course not. The only way you can understand is to join, to become involved. Our goal is to remain a mystery. Pure theater. Free, with no boundaries except your own. Throwing money onto the floor of the Stock Exchange is pure information. It needs no explanation. It says more than thousands of anticapitalist tracts and essays. It's so obvious that I hesitate to discuss it, since everyone reading this already has an image of what happened there. I respect their images. Anything I said would come on like expertise. "Now, this is what *really* happened." In point of fact nothing happened. Neither we nor the Stock Exchange exist. We are both rumors. That's it. That's what happened that day. Two different rumors collided. . . .

THE YIPPIES ARE GOING TO CHICAGO

Last December a group of us in New York conceived the Yippie! idea. We had four main objectives:

1. The blending of pot and politics into a political grass leaves movement—a cross-fertilization of the hippie and New Left philosophies.
2. A connecting link that would tie together as much of the underground as was willing into some gigantic national get-together.
3. The development of a model for an alternative society.
4. The need to make some statement, especially in revolutionary action-theater terms, about LBJ, the Democratic Party, electoral politics, and the state of the nation.

To accomplish these tasks required the construction of a vast myth, for through the notion of myth large numbers of people could get turned on and, in that process of getting turned on, begin to participate in Yippie! and start to focus on Chicago. *Precision was sacrificed for a greater degree of suggestion.* People took off in all directions in the most sensational manner possible:

"We will burn Chicago to the ground!"

"We will fuck on the beaches!"

"We demand the Politics of Ecstasy!"

"Acid for all!"

"Abandon the Creeping Meatball!"

And, all the time: "Yippie! Chicago—August 25–30." . . .

Let's return to history. Remember a guy named Lyndon Johnson? He was so predictable when Yippie! began. And then *pow!* He really fucked us. He did the one thing no one had counted on. He dropped out. "My God," we exclaimed. "Lyndon is out-flanking us on our hippie side."

Then "Go-Clean-for-Gene [Eugene McCarthy]" and "Hollywood-Bobby [Robert Kennedy]." Well, Gene wasn't much. One could secretly cheer for him the way you cheer for the Mets. It's easy, knowing he can never win. But Bobby, there was the real threat. A direct challenge to our theater-in-the-streets, a challenge to the charisma of Yippie!

Remember Bobby's Christmas card: psychedelic blank space with a big question mark—"Santa in '68?" Remember Bobby on television stuttering at certain questions, leaving room for the audience to jump in and help him agonize, to battle the cold interviewer who knew all the questions and never made a mistake.

Come on, Bobby said, *join the mystery battle against the television machine*. Participation mystique. Theater-in-the-streets. He played it to the hilt. And what was worse, Bobby had the money and power to build the stage. We had to steal ours. It was no contest.

Yippie stock went down quicker than the money we had dumped on the Stock Exchange floor. Every night we would turn on the TV set and there was the young knight with long hair, holding out his hand (a gesture he learned from the Pope): "Give me your hand—it is a long road ahead."

When young longhairs told you how they'd heard that Bobby turned on, you knew Yippie! was *really* in trouble.

We took to drinking and praying for LBJ to strike back, but he kept melting. Then Hubert [Humphrey] came along exclaiming the "Politics of Joy" and Yippie! passed into a state of catatonia which resulted in near permanent brain damage.

Yippie! grew irrelevant.

National action seemed meaningless.

Everybody began the tough task of developing new battlegrounds. Columbia, the Lower East Side, Free City in San Francisco. Local action became the focus and by the end of May we had decided to disband Yippie! and cancel the Chicago festival.

It took two full weeks of debate to arrive at a method of dropping-out which would not further demoralize the troops. The statement was all ready when up stepped Sirhan Sirhan [Bobby Kennedy's assassin], and in ten second he made it a whole new ball game.

We postponed calling off Chicago and tried to make some sense out of what the hell had just happened. It was not easy to think clearly. Yippie!, still in a state of critical shock because of LBJ's pullout, hovered close to death somewhere between the 50/50 state of Andy Warhol and the 0/0 state of Bobby Kennedy.

The United States political system was proving more insane than Yippie! Reality and unreality has in six months switched sides.

It was *America* that was on a trip; we were just standing still.

How could we pull our pants down? America was already naked.

What could we disrupt? America was falling apart at the seams.

Yet Chicago seemed more relevant than ever. Hubert had a lock on the convention; it was more closed than ever. Even the squares who vote in primaries had expressed a mandate for change. Hubert canned the "Politics of Joy" and instituted the "Politics of Hope"—some switch—but none of the slogans mattered. We were back to power politics, the politics of big-city machines and back-room deals.

The Democrats had finally got their thing together by hook or crook and there it was for all to see—fat, ugly, and full of shit. The calls began pouring into our office. They wanted to know only one thing: "When do we leave for Chicago?"

What we need now, however, is the direct opposite approach from the one we began with. We must sacrifice suggestion for a greater degree of precision. We need a reality in the face of the American political myth. We have to kill Yippie! and still bring huge numbers to Chicago.

If you have any Yippie! buttons, posters, stickers or sweatshirts, bring them to Chicago. We will end Yippie! in a huge orgasm of destruction atop a giant medial altar. We will in Chicago begin the task of building Free America on the ashes of the old and from the inside out.

A Constitutional Convention is being planned. A convention of visionary mind-benders who will for five long days and nights address themselves to the task of formulating the goals and means of the New Society.

It will be a blend of technologists and poets, of artists and community organizers, of anyone who has a vision. We will try to develop a Community of Consciousness.

There will be a huge rock-folk festival for free. Contrary to rumor, no groups originally committed to Chicago have dropped out. In fact, additional ones have agreed to participate. In all about thirty groups and performers will be there.

Theater groups from all over the country are pledged to come. They are an integral part of the activities, and a large amount of funds raised from here on in will go for the transportation of street theater groups.

Workshops in a variety of subjects such as draft resistance, drugs, commune development, guerrilla theater and underground media will be set up. The workshops will be oriented around problem-solving while the Constitutional Convention works to developing the overall philosophical framework.

There will probably be a huge march across town to haunt the Democrats.

People coming to Chicago should begin preparations for five days of energy-exchange. Do not come prepared to sit and watch and be fed and cared for. It just won't happen that way. It is time to become a life-actor. The days of the audience died with the old America. If you don't have a thing to do, stay home, you'll only get in the way.

All of these plans are contingent on our getting a permit, and it is toward that goal that we have been working. A permit is a definite contradiction in philosophy since we do not recognize the authority of the old order, but tactically it is a necessity.

We are negotiating, with the Chicago city government, a six-day treaty. All of the Chicago newspapers as well as various pressure groups have urged the city of Chicago to grant the permit. They recognize full well the huge social problem they face if we are forced to use the streets of Chicago for our action.

They have tentatively offered us use of Soldiers' Field Stadium or Navy Pier (we would have to re-name either, of course) for our convention. We have had several meetings, principally with David Stahl, Deputy Mayor of Chicago, and there remains but to iron out the terms of the treaty—suspension of curfew laws, regulations pertaining to sleeping on the beach, etc.—for us to have a bona fide permit in our hands.

The possibility of violence will be greatly reduced. There is no guarantee that it will be entirely eliminated.

This is the United States, 1968, remember. If you are afraid of violence you shouldn't have crossed the border.

This matter of a permit is a cat-and-mouse game. The Chicago authorities do not wish to grant it too early, knowing this would increase the number of people that descend on the city. They can ill afford to wait too late, for that will inhibit planning on our part and create more chaos.

It is not our wish to take on superior armed troops who outnumber us on unfamiliar enemy territory. It is not their wish to have a Democrat nominated amidst a major bloodbath. The treaty will work for both sides.

There is a further complicating factor: the possibility of the Convention being moved out of Chicago. Presently there are two major strikes taking place by bus drivers and telephone and electrical repairmen in addition to a taxi strike scheduled to begin on the eve of the Convention.

If the Convention is moved out of Chicago we will have to adjust our plans. The best we can say is, keep your powder dry and start preparing. A good idea is to begin raising money to outfit a used bus that you can buy for about $300, and use locally before and after Chicago.

Prepare a street theater skit or bring something to distribute, such as food, poems, or music. Get sleeping bags and other camping equipment. We will sleep on the beaches. If you have any free money we can channel this into energy groups already committed. We are fantastically broke and in need of funds. . . .

The point is, you can use Chicago as a means of pulling your local community together. It can serve to open up a dialogue between political radicals and those who might be considered hippies. The radical will say to the hippie: "Get together and fight, you are getting the shit kicked out of you." The hippie will say to the radical: "Your protest is so narrow, your rhetoric is so boring, your ideological power plays so old-fashioned."

Each can help the other, and Chicago—like the Pentagon demonstration before it—might well offer the medium to put forth the message.

Source: Judith Clavir Albert and Stewart Edward Albert, eds., *The Sixties Papers: Documents of a Rebellious Decade* (New York: Praeger, 1984), 417–27.

Document 8
TUNING IN, TURNING ON, DROPPING OUT
Jane DeGennaro

> After working as a farm caretaker, bartender, and for Head Start, Jane DeGennaro is now an account executive for a graphic media firm. Divorced from her second husband, she lives in Bound Brook, New Jersey, with her daughter, Elissa. During an interview in the mid-1980s, she recounted how her world changed when she made the transition from high school. While other baby boomers shared similar experiences, only a small minority of the generation became part of the drug culture or participated in group sex.

After I graduated from high school in 1967, I wanted to have all the experience and pleasure and inspiration that I could possibly accumulate. I wanted to explore the new world. So I went to Ohio State University in Columbus.

There was a clash of cultures between the sororities and fraternities and the hippies and the freaks. I was being courted by the established sororities, but that didn't inspire me. I had no interest in beer and necking and humiliating initiations, like men in go-go outfits and women in togas. Right away I wanted to learn more about the freaks. During high school, I had been initiated into the drug culture—marijuana and hashish—and I wanted to see more.

Especially I wanted to see some LSD. The media was advertising it, saying things like "heightening your perception," "seeing things like you've never seen them before," "getting to the roots of religion and ritual," "playing with madness." All that was just fascinating to me. I thought, Wow! Give me some.

One day I met this guy Dan in my theater class. He was attractive and I just sensed an affinity. We had a lot to talk about. His major area of interest in school was psychology, and mine was too. That was my minor. He had smoked pot, and we were interested in the same music and the avant-garde. And we were also interested in making love.

Dan and I had a very nice relationship, and we decided that we wanted to move in together. A bunch of students had this apartment together, and we rented a room there. And we were all exploring the universe: Carl Jung and synchronicity and anthropology and religion, be it the religion of the American Indians or the Zen Buddhists. We were looking for whatever transcended barriers, for freedom, and drugs were part of it.

The first time we did LSD, Dan told me that he had done it before. So he was going to be the guide. We had a mattress on the floor, posters on the walls, incense. We dropped the LSD—little orange barrel-shaped things— and we waited and waited, and nothing seemed to be happening. Then we just started feeling silly, which wasn't unlike us. We started chasing each other around the room, and at one point he admitted that he had never done LSD before. It was about that time that we realized that we were off.

It was so funny. We had been studying the *Tibetan Book of the Dead* and books by Alan Watts and others about Zen Buddhism, and there seemed to be a theme running through a lot of them about the death of the ego. Leary also talked about breaking out of the restrictions of your concepts of yourself into a greater self—a greater awareness that transcends the temporary, including the body, perhaps. At one level we were scared of it, and on another level we were fascinated by what, we had read in the literature, was the possibility of ego death and expansion of awareness beyond the limited ego. So we were trying to prime ourselves to go through a psychic death experience while we were tripping: "Okay, now I'm going to die. Now I'm going to know what it's like."

A friend came visiting, and she had her flute. She played for us, and it was just miraculous, just gorgeous. I cried, it moved me so much. There was so much soul in the music. It was just so touching. We ended up going out in a Volkswagen, out into the streets, driving around, and I had a strong sense of myself as a cell in a bloodstream. . . .

One day I was tripping at a party with Dan. I was in the living room, and the music *And Thus Spake Zarathustra* by Strauss was playing. Unconsciously, automatically, Dan and I and another fellow, who later became a friend of ours, came together. People were walking in and out of the room and sitting on couches and chairs, and we were *drawn*, without thought, onto the floor on the center of that room. It may have been where the acoustic vibration was the strongest, I don't know, but we just sat there in a little circle. I closed my eyes and what I saw was a spiraling tunnel. At the end of the tunnel there was an eye, and I knew, somehow, that I had the choice of whether or not I wanted to move down that tunnel. And I decided to go.

I started traveling down the tunnel, and the eye became, you know, an eye and a nose, then another eye, and a mouth and a beard, and dark hair, and laughing eyes, and it was the most magnificent man I ever saw in my whole life. I don't know who it was—I've hypothesized—but I experienced religious ecstasy. I got a communication from that man. Basically without words he said to me, "We made it. You're here. We did it. Here we are. We're together." And there was no greater goal. That was it. I was absolutely, completely, one hundred percent satisfied. If I had died right then, I wouldn't look back. Not at all. That was it. That was what life was about. I cannot express how fulfilled I was, how absolutely, totally happy. . . .

Dan and I had an open relationship. As soon as I had got to college and counseling was a service at the health center, I decided that I might as well take advantage of it and construct my own personality. So I went to this psychologist, and when Dan and I got together, he joined me.

The psychologist seemed like a very conservative figure, but by today's standards he was radical. Dan and I expressed to him that being so young, we found ourselves attracted to other people and didn't know what to do with our sexual impulses. Both of us had a hunger for more experience, and we didn't know how to handle it. So the psychologist suggested that one option was that we have an open relationship, meaning we allow each other the freedom to explore other partners. He even gave us some literature. So we did.

And I had my first and only experience with group sex. I know there's all that kind of stuff going on today, but when it happened to me there was an innocence about it—a purity—that I think was unique to the time.

We were at a birthday party with old friends, something like fifteen people. We were doing a variety of different drugs, Quaaludes, marijuana—and all of a sudden this one woman took off her clothes, and everybody just followed suit, or unsuit. Everybody started dancing together, and then some people went to bed and some people took baths together, and they were just doing everything they always wanted to do—together. At one point there were a lot of people lying on a bed, and it was just *undulating*.

Dan was doing fine. He jumped right in. He had a good time. But at one point he got jealous. When he didn't have anybody with him, he came into the bathroom and found me with another man in the bathtub, and he wanted to drag me home by the hair. He asked me to come, and I was ready. We said goodbye to our friends, put on our clothes, and went home.

Actually I learned from that experience that I don't really like orgies as much as I do one-to-one experience. I didn't get that much satisfaction out of it. But I was hungry for experience, and I got it.

In 1968, we ended up getting married, but we didn't want to imprison each other. Our feeling was that all through time people have been *cheating* on each other. Everybody wants to do this, but why do they have to *lie* about it? We should be able to be honest with one another, and not destroy what we have by sharing ourselves with other people as well.

But it was difficult for us to accept. It was an adjustment every time you knew the other person was with somebody, and little by little we started getting more and more discreet, you know, to spare the other person's feelings.

Everyone knew we had an open relationship. I remember there was a girl who was after Dan. She would ask me, "What's he like?" and they would sometimes talk on the phone. Once we had a party, and I turned around, there she was kissing Dan passionately in the doorway of our bedroom. Right then and there I put my foot down, and I said, "That'll be enough of that." She said, "But you told me you guys both have this open relationship." And I said, "I don't care what I said. Don't you kiss my husband now, in front of me, no. That's it."

Ultimately, I guess, the open relationship broke up our marriage. It was just too easy to look elsewhere for intimacy.

... Today I'm learning that my happiness and satisfaction are to be found within myself. I'm just grateful that I'm here and now. I don't have the financial security that I'm working toward. I don't have the abundance that I'm working toward. I don't have a family, and it is not easy being a single parent. But Elissa's a gift, and I'm grateful for being able to take care of her. I'm aware of what I have as opposed to what I don't have. It's a balancing act, and I'm learning.

Source: Joan Morrison and Robert K. Morrison, *From Camelot to Kent State: The Sixties Experience in the Words of Those Who Lived it* (New York: Times Books, 1987), 205–9.

GENERAL

Document 9
IMPUDENCE IN THE STREETS
Spiro T. Agnew

In 1968, Republican presidential candidate Richard M. Nixon chose
Maryland governor Spiro T. Agnew as his vice-presidential running
mate. During the campaign and until he was forced to resign in 1973 after an investigation of income tax evasion charges, Agnew frequently
employed invective and contempt when he criticized counterculture
types, student movement leaders, most political activists, and especially antiwar protesters. In the speech that follows, delivered before a
Republican dinner during Nixon's first term, Agnew scored points
with the "silent majority" as he denounced demonstrators for undermining the Democratic process.

A little over a week ago, I took a rather unusual step for a Vice President. I
said something. Particularly, I said something that was predictably unpopu-
lar with the people who would like to run the country without the inconven-
ience of seeking public office. I said I did not like some of the things I saw
happening in this country. I criticized those who encouraged government by
street carnival and suggested it was time to stop the carousel.

It appears that by slaughtering a sacred cow I triggered a holy war. I have
no regrets. I do not intend to repudiate my beliefs, recant my words, or run
and hide.

What I said before, I will say agin. It is time for the preponderant majority, the responsible citizens of this country, to assert *their* rights. It is time to
stop dignifying the immature actions of arrogant, reckless, inexperienced
elements within our society. The reason is compelling. It is simply that their
tantrums are insidiously destroying the fabric of American democracy.

By accepting unbridled protest as a way of life, we have tacitly suggested
that the great issues of our times are best decided by posturing and shouting
matches in the streets. America today is drifting toward Plato's classic definition of a degenerating democracy—a democracy that permits the voice of
the mob to dominate the affairs of government.

Last week I was lambasted for my lack of "mental and moral sensitivity."
I say that any leader who does not perceive where persistent street struggles
are going to lead this nation lacks mental acuity. And any leader who does
not caution this nation on the danger of this direction lacks moral strength.

I believe in constitutional dissent. I believe in the people registering their
views with their elected representatives, and I commend those people who

care enough about their country to involve themselves in its great issues. I believe in legal protests within the constitutional limits of free speech, including peaceful assembly and the right of petition. But I do not believe that demonstrations, lawful or lawful, merit my approval or even my silence where the purpose is fundamentally unsound. In the case of the Vietnam Moratorium [a demonstration against the war], the objects announced by the leaders—immediate unilateral withdrawal of all our forces from Vietnam—was not only unsound but idiotic. . . .

So great is the latitude of our liberty that only a subtle line divides use from abuse. I am convinced that our preoccupation with emotional demonstration, frequently crossing the line to civil disruption and even violence could inexorably lead us across that line forever.

Ironically, it is neither the greedy nor the malicious but the self-righteous who are guilty of history's worse atrocities. Society understands greed and malice and erects barriers of law to defend itself from these vices. But evil cloaked in emotional causes is well disguised and often undiscovered until it is too late.

We have just such a group of self-proclaimed saviors of the American soul at work today. Relentless in their criticism of intolerance in America, they themselves are intolerant of those who differ with their views. In the name of academic freedom, they destroy academic freedom. Denouncing violence, they seize and vandalize buildings of great universities. Fiercely expressing their respect for truth, they disavow the logic and discipline necessary to pursue truth.

They would have us believe that they alone know what is good for America—what is true and right and beautiful. They would have us believe that their reflexive action is superior to our reflective action; that their reveled righteousness is more effective than our reason and experience.

Think about it. Small bands of students are allowed to shut down great universities. Small groups of dissidents are allowed to shout down political candidates. Small cadres of professional protestors are allowed to jeopardize the peace efforts of the President of the United States.

It is time to question the credentials of their leaders. And, if in questioning we disturb a few people, I say it is time for them to be disturbed. If, in challenging, we polarize the American people, I say it is time for a positive polarization.

It is time for a healthy in-depth examination of policies and constructive realignment in this country. It is time to rip away the rhetoric and to divide on authentic lines. It is time to discard the fiction that in a country of 200 million people, everyone is qualified to quarterback the government. . . .

Now, we have among us a glib, activist element who would tell us our values are lies, and I call them impudent. Because anyone who impugns a legacy of liberty and dignity that reaches back to Moses, is impudent.

I call them snobs for most of them disdain to mingle with the masses who work for a living. They mock the common man's pride in his work, his family and his country. It has also been said that I called them intellectuals. I did not. I said that they characterized themselves as intellectuals. No true intellectual, no truly knowledgeable person, would so despise democratic institutions. . . .

Finally—and most important—regardless of the issue, it is time to stop demonstrating in the streets and start doing something constructive about our institutions. America must recognize the dangers of constant carnival. Americans must reckon with irresponsible leadership and reckless words. The mature and sensitive people of this country must realize that their freedom of protest is being exploited by avowed anarchists and communists who detest everything about this country and want to destroy it.

This is a fact. These are the few; these are not necessarily leaders. But they prey upon the good intentions of gullible men everywhere. They pervert honest concern to something sick and rancid. They are vultures who sit in trees and watch lions battle, knowing that win, lose or draw, they will be fed.

Abetting the merchants of hate are the parasites of passion. These are the men who value a cause purely for its political mileage. These are the politicians who temporize with the truth by playing both sides to their own advantage. They ooze sympathy for "the cause" but balance each sentence with equally reasoned reservations. Their interest is personal, not moral. They are ideological eunuchs whose most comfortable position is straddling the philosophical fence, soliciting votes from both sides. . . .

This is what is happening in this nation. We *are* an effete society if we let it happen here. . . .

Will Congress settle down to the issues of the nation and reform the institutions of America as our President asks? Can the press ignore the pipers who lead the parades? Will the heads of great universities protect the rights of all their students? Will parents have the courage to say no to their children? Will people have the intelligence to boycott pornography and violence? Will citizens refuse to be led by a series of Judas goats down tortuous paths of delusion and self-destruction?

Will we defend fifty centuries of accumulated wisdom? For that is our heritage. Will we make the effort to preserve America's bold, successful experiment in truly representative government? Or do we care so little that we will cast it all aside?

Because on the eve of our nation's 200th birthday, we have reached the crossroads. Because at this moment totalitarianism's threat does not necessarily have a foreign accent. Because we have a home-grown menace, made and manufactured in the U.S.A. Because if we are lazy or foolish, this nation could forfeit its integrity, never to be free again.

Source: Alexander Bloom and Wini Breines, eds., *"Takin' It to the Streets": A Sixties Reader* (New York: Oxford University Press, 1995), 355–58.

Document 10
FREEDOM VS. ANARCHY ON CAMPUS
Ronald Reagan

In 1966, just two years after the Free Speech Movement erupted at the University of California–Berkeley campus and precipitated student activism on college campuses, Ronald Reagan was elected governor of California. In 1976 he was an unsuccessful Republican presidential candidate, losing to Gerald R. Ford, but he won election to the White House in 1980 and again in 1984. In this excerpt from a 1968 radio address, Reagan defended the traditional role of the university and declared his hard-line position against students who threatened state and university authority.

The people of California founded and generously support what has become the finest system of public higher education in the land.

Within this system there are now nine university campuses, nineteen state college campuses and 81 community colleges, plus many fine independent colleges and universities which are also supported, for the most part, by the people of California.

The system has worked well.

Yes—on these campuses, generations of Californians have pursued knowledge within the widest range of disciplines. They have sampled widely of man's knowledge of man, of the history of his ideas and what he knows of the world around him.

This is the role of higher education in California. At least this has been the case up until recently.

Within the past five or six years, something new has been added—a violent strident something that has disturbed all of us; a something whose admitted purpose is to destroy or to capture and use society's institutions for its own purpose. I say "whose admitted purpose" because the leadership minces no words. It is boastful, arrogant and threatening.

Consider these words from a campus teacher: "I think we agree that the revolution is necessary and that you don't conduct a revolution by attacking the strongest enemy first. You take care of your business at home first, then you move abroad. Thus we must make the university the home of the revolution."

From the capture of a police car and negotiations conducted in an atmosphere of intimidation, threats and fear, we went from free speech to filthy speech.

The movement spread to other campuses. There has been general incitement against properly constituted law enforcement authorities and general trampling of the will, the rights and freedom of movement of the majority by the organized, militant, and highly vocal minority.

Though the causes were cloaked in the dignity of academic and other freedoms, they are—in fact—a lusting for power. Some protesters even marched under banners that ranged from the black flag of anarchy, the red flag of revolution, to the flags of enemies engaged in killing young Americans—the North Vietnamese and the Viet Cong.

Academic freedom is one of the important freedoms to go in the new order envisioned by the New Left. There was no academic freedom in Hitler's Germany. There is no academic freedom in Mao's China or Castro's Cuba. And there is no academic freedom in the philosophies or the actions of the George Murrays, the Eldridge Cleavers or the Jerry Rubins.

It is therefore most imperative that we—the great and thoughtful majority of citizens of all races—keep our perspective. We must recognize the manipulations being carried out to frustrate our common interest in living together with dignity in one American society. And we must also recognize that those who exercise violence must be held accountable for their actions—and held equally accountable regardless of their color.

Nationwide, experience has shown that prompt dealing with disturbances leads to peace, that hesitation, vacillation, and appeasement leads to greater disorder.

Isn't it logical, in view of past experience to ask that no campus official negotiate or hold conferences with any individual or group while such individual or group is disturbing or disrupting campus activities, violating any rule or regulation of the campus or its governing board, or committing any criminal offense? And, likewise, to insist that there shall be no consideration of the demands or requests of any such individual or group while their disruptive or disorderly conduct continues?

And finally, isn't it time to demand that when individuals have been arrested as a result of their participation in the disturbances and disorders, the chief campus officer—or such other person designated by him—shall sign a criminal complaint against such persons and shall co-operate in the prosecution of those individuals and shall immediately suspend them from the university? . . .

From which group will we—and, really, from which group will you young people now going to college—elect your future leaders? Will it be from the few, but militant, anarchists and others now trying to control and run our campuses? Or will we elect our future leaders from the majority of fine young men and women dedicated to justice, order, and the full development of the true individual?

Source: Alexander Bloom and Wini Breines, eds., *"Takin' It to the Streets": A Sixties Reader* (New York: Oxford University Press, 1995), 345–47.

Document 11
THE GREEN BERETS AND HAIR

Strom J. Thurmond, from South Carolina, was a Democratic states' rights presidential candidate who ran against Harry S Truman in 1948. In 1954 he was appointed to a seat in the U.S. Senate, which he continues to hold in 2000. Changing his allegiance to the Republican party in 1964, Thurmond has been a conservative voice in the party since. At age ninety-seven, he is the oldest member of Congress. In 1968, amid the growing and increasingly emotional issue of American involvement in Vietnam and the public's general concern about eroding standards of morality and decency, Senator Thurmond introduced into the *Congressional Record* reviews of the patriotic Hollywood film, *The Green Berets*, and the counterculture play, *Hair.*

Mr. THURMOND. Mr. President, this afternoon the Town Theater will present the Washington premiere of a new film called *The Green Berets*, starring John Wayne and codirected by John Wayne. I have not yet had the opportunity to see this movie, but I am extremely anxious to do so. This is not only the first major studio movie about the Vietnam war, but it also portrays our American heroes in action. But if my admiration for John Wayne were not enough to make me want to see the movie, I became convinced that this must be one of the finest and most admirable movies of our generation, after reading the review which appeared last week in the *New York Times* when the movie opened there. The first paragraph of this review was enough to convince anyone that this was a good movie. Please listen carefully to what the *New York Times* reviewer had to say:

The Green Berets is a film so unspeakable, so stupid, so rotten and false in every detail that it passes through being fun, through being funny, through being camp, through being everything and becomes an invitation to grieve not for our soldiers or for Vietnam . . . but for what has happened to the fantasy-making apparatus in this country. Simplicity of the right, simplicity of the left, but this one is beyond the possible. It is vile and insane. On top of that, it is dull.

That last sentence is the tip-off, since I find it hard to believe that John Wayne could ever be dull. But it set me to wondering what on earth the standards of criticism are that are current in the *New York Times* that a film which is patriotic and pro-American should receive such treatment.

I got a small clue about the *New York Times* standards when looking back over recent reviews on the entertainment page in the *New York Times*. I came across a review that begins in ecstatic terms of admiration. This is the review of the recent Broadway musical entitled *Hair.* The reviewer says:

What is so likeable about *Hair,* that tribal rock musical that Monday completed its trek from downtown, via a discotheque, and landed, positively panting with love and smelling of sweat flowers, at the Biltmore Theatre? I think it is simply that it is so likeable. So new, so fresh, and so unassuming, even in its pretensions.

So here we have a review that starts out just the opposite of the review of *The Green Berets.* Whereas *The Green Berets* is unspeakable, stupid, rotten, false, vile, and insane, *Hair* is likable, new, fresh, unassuming.

Now what is *Hair* all about? Well, the reviewer goes on to explain why it is so likable and fresh. He says that he cannot spell out what happens on stage because the *Times* is a "family newspaper." However, he does go on with the following description:

A great many four-letter words, such as "love," are used freely. At one point—in what is later affectionately referred to as "the nude scene"—a number of men and women (I should have counted) are seen totally nude and full, as it were, face. Frequently references—frequent approving references—are made to the expanding benefits of drugs. Homosexuality is not frowned upon—one boy announces that he is in love with Mike Jagger [*sic,* lead singer of the Rolling Stones], in terms unusually frank. The American flag is not desecrated—that would be a Federal offense, wouldn't it?—but it is used in a manner that not everyone would call respectful. Christian ritual also comes in for a bad time, the authors approve enthusiastically of miscegenation, and one enterprising lyric catalogues somewhat arcane sexual practices more familiar to the pages of the "Kama Sutra" than The *New York Times.* So there—you have been warned. Oh yes, they also hand out flowers.

So there we have the story of *Hair,* at least insofar as it is fit to print. This is what is fresh and frank and likable. But a movie about honor and glory and courage and loyalty and duty and country is a film that is unspeakable, stupid, rotten, false, vile, and insane. I think now we have a clear picture of the standards of criticism used by the *New York Times* reviewers. If the *New York* Times says that a film in unspeakable, and so forth, it must be pretty good. And if the *New York Times* says a film about depravity is fresh and likable, we know well enough to avoid it.

Mr. President, there is something utterly perverted with our society's standards of art and entertainment if these examples from the *New York Times* in any way actually reflect the temper of our time. We have come to the point described by [George] Orwell in *1984*, where he talks about newspeak. In newspeak, words are used to mean the opposite of the commonly accepted meaning. Love means hate, peace means war, and so forth. We are now at the point where depravity is fresh and likable, whereas virtue is apparently false and insane. Despite the ecstatic review of *Hair* by the *Times*, I confess that I have no desire whatsoever to see it. Despite the incredible blast by the *Times* at *The Green Berets*, I am eager to see the film. I trust John Wayne's judgement more than I would trust that of the *Times* movie critic.

John Wayne is one of the great actors of our time. He is a true and loyal patriot and a great American. It is men of his caliber and stripe who have built America and made it what it is today—the greatest country in the world.

Source: Strom Thurmond, "Remarks on John Wayne, *The Green Berets*, and *Hair*," *Congressional Record*, 90th Cong., 2nd sess., 114, Pt. 14 (June 26, 1968): 18856–57.

Glossary of Selected Terms

Acid: A counterculture term for LSD.

Acid rock: A new genre of popular music originating in San Francisco in the 1960s referring to psychedelic rock and lyrics making references to drugs. The most popular acid rock bands were the Grateful Dead, Jefferson Airplane, and Iron Butterfly.

Antiwar movement: Refers collectively to marches, demonstrations, and protests against the war in Vietnam.

Bell-bottoms: A hippie style of pants that were tight at the waist, then flared out from the knee to the ankle.

Days of Rage: Part of the Weathermen's "revolution" of the working class when six hundred radicals fought with Chicago police in October 1969.

Doves, hawks: Figurative labels for people who opposed and supported the Vietnam War, respectively.

Draft card: A card issued by the Selective Service System designating one's status for military duty; every American male citizen over age eighteen was required to carry one; the most frequently used classifications were 1-A (eligible for the draft), 2-S (student deferment), and 1-Y (temporary deferment).

Earth Day: First observed on April 22, 1970, as a day to show nationwide concern for the environment.

The establishment: A counterculture term referring to people over thirty years old who exerted power and authority.

Freak: A young hippie who wore long hair and used hallucinogenic drugs.

Free Speech Movement (FSM): Started in 1964 at the University of California–Berkeley, when students protested university policy restricting students' exercise of free speech.

Grass: A slang term for marijuana.

Hard rock: Also sometimes the same as "acid" rock or psychedelic music. Artists used electric guitars to play drug-inspired music frequently enhanced with strobe lights.

Hashbury: A hippie neighborhood in San Francisco where Haight and Ashbury streets intersect.

Hawks. *See doves, hawks.*

Head: A young person who is a heavy drug user; also referred to as a *freak*.

Hippies: Usually people under age thirty who dropped out of "straight," or mainstream, society and rejected its values, including work, religion, monogamy, attire, and disdain of hallucinogenic drugs.

Hog Farm: One of the more popular hippie communes in the 1960s, whose best-known member was Wavy Gravy.

Love-ins: Any gathering of counterculture types to celebrate peace and love; similar to a "be-in."

LSD: Lysergic acid diethylamide, a potent psychedelic drug that was a favorite of hippies.

Make love, not war: Popular antiwar slogan in the 1960s.

Marijuana: The most widely used illicit drug of the 1960s; also known as "grass," "weed," "pot," and "MaryJane."

MOBE: Acronym for national Mobilization Committee to End the War in Vietnam which coordinated antiwar protests.

Mod: Abbreviated form of "modernist," which probably originated in Britain, referring to modern-style clothing.

The Movement: A nebulous term for political protests, sometimes referring to the counterculture's efforts to reshape society.

New Left: The political manifestation of the counterculture.

Peace symbol: Displayed either with the two forefingers forming the letter V, or on posters, clothes, and placards as an inverted V with a vertical line through it in a circle.

"Pigs": Derisive term for police.

The Pill: Common reference to the birth control pill.

Psychedelic: Coined in 1957 and used in the 1960s to describe drugs, music, art, or anything else that resembled a drug-induced experience.

SDS: Students for a Democratic Society, an activist group that emerged in 1960 as a revolutionary group committed to civil rights, students' rights, and eventually antiwar causes.

Silent majority: The American middle class, usually considered as part of the establishment.

Teach-ins: Held on college campuses when professors met with students to educate them about American military escalation in Vietnam.

Woodstock Generation: A term coined by Abbie Hoffman to describe the baby boomers who attended and/or were contemporaries of the Woodstock Music Festival in 1969.

Yippies: The Youth International party, created as a joke in 1967, intended to parody the absurdities of mainstream society.

Annotated Bibliography

GENERAL

Anderson, Terry H. *The Movement and the Sixties: Protest in America from Greensboro to Wounded Knee*. New York: Oxford University Press, 1995. An excellent, detailed study of sixties' activism loaded with names, events, and quotations that make for a lively chronological narrative.

Archer, Jules. *The Incredible Sixties: The Stormy Years That Changed America*. New York: Harcourt Brace Jovanovich, 1986. A broadly focused history of the 1960s that emphasizes the social chaos.

Brown, Joe David, ed. *Sex in the '60s*. New York: Time-Life Books, 1968. An anthology of articles from *Time* magazine that provides a contemporary chronicle of how marriage, sexual permissiveness, and morality in general changed during the 1960s.

Burner, David, *Making Peace with the 60s*. Princeton, NJ: Princeton University Press, 1996. A comprehensive history of the sixties that discusses numerous subjects, including music, drugs, student unrest, the counterculture, and politics.

Chafe, William H. *The Unfinished Journey: America Since World War II*. New York: Oxford University Press, 1995. Although the focus is not on the 1960s, this book provides a solid background of the events and people who shaped the decade.

Conlin, Joseph R. *Troubles: A Jaundiced Glance Back at the Movement of the Sixties*. New York: Franklin Watts, 1982. In a reflective look at the 1960s, the author views the decade as more popularly significant than it really was.

Dickstein, Morris. *Gates of Eden: American Culture in the Sixties*. New York: Basic Books, 1977. A cultural history of the sixties with chapters discussing the cold war as a prologue to the decade. A good intellectual overview of the decade.

Farber, David. *The Age of Great Dreams: America in the 1960s*. New York: Hill & Wang, 1994. A very readable, balanced overview of the 1960s, though survey-level instructors might find William L. O'Neill's *Coming Apart* or Terry H. Anderson's *The Movement* more evocative.

Gitlin, Todd. *The Sixties: Years of Hope, Days of Rage*. New York: Bantam Books, 1987. A former president of the Students for a Democratic Society emphasizes cultural influences and provides an insightful and intelligent account of the sixties social upheaval.

Gottlieb, Annie. *Do You Believe in Magic? The Second Coming of the Sixties Generation*. New York: Times Books, 1987. A first-person look back at the sixties generation through interviews with baby boomers who were there.

Hodgson, Geoffrey. *America in Our Time: From World War II to Nixon—What Happened and Why*. New York: Vintage Books, 1978. A good overview history of the 1960s.

Jones, Landon Y. *Great Expectations: America and the Baby Boom Generation*. New York: Coward, McCann, 1980. An examination of the impact of the baby boomer generation on American society.

Manchester, William. *The Glory and the Dream: A Narrative History of America, 1930–1972*. New York: Bantam Books, 1974. A massive, solidly researched, four-decade sociopolitical history. Part IV of this best-seller covers 1961–1968.

Matusow, Allen J. *The Unraveling of America: A History of Liberalism in the 1960s*. New York: Harper & Row, 1984. After evaluating the success of liberal domestic programs in the Kennedy and Johnson administrations, the author concludes that they fell short of expectations.

Morgan, Edward P. *The 60s Experience: Hard Lessons About Modern America*. Philadelphia: Temple University Press, 1991. A useful overview of the 1960s.

Morrison, Joan, and Morrison, Robert K. *From Camelot to Kent State: The Sixties Experience in the Words of Those Who Lived It*. New York: Times Books, 1987. Interviews with "survivors" of the sixties, grouped in twelve categories including civil rights, Vietnam veterans, antiwar protestors, and the women's movement.

O'Neill, William O. *Coming Apart: An Informal History of America in the 1960s*. New York: Quadrangle Books, 1977. A good detailed social history of the decade. Short profiles of influential individuals, groups, or issues preceding each chapter serve as anecdotal introductions.

Sann, Paul. *The Angry Decade: The Sixties*. New York: Crown Publishers, 1979. A year-by-year pictorial and narrative chronicle of the sixties.

Schaller, Michael, Virginia Scharff, and Robert D. Schulzinger. *Present Tense: The United States Since 1945*. Boston: Houghton Mifflin, 1996. A useful and engaging overview of the postwar era, with four chapters devoted to the 1960s.

Steigerwald, David. *The Sixties and the End of Modern America*. New York: St. Martin's Press, 1995. A good source for acquiring an understanding of the sixties. The first half of the book outlines the failures of liberal politics; the latter half is a sociological assessment of the era.

Stern, Jane, and Michael Stern. *Sixties People*. New York: Knopf, 1990. A socio-cultural look at groups that shaped the sixties, including hippies, rebels, women, youth, and "folkniks."

Tipton, Steven M. *Getting Saved from the Sixties: Moral Meaning in Conversion and Cultural Change*. Berkeley, CA: University of California Press, 1982. A sociological examination of moral, religious, and political issues as they influenced the transformation of the sixties youth.

Unger, Irwin, and Debi Unger. *Turning Point: 1968*. New York: Charles Scribner's Sons, 1988. Authors focus on the New Left and other political movements to demonstrate how, in just twelve months, the nation changed ideological direction.

Viorst, Milton. *Fire in the Streets: America in the 1960s*. New York: Simon & Schuster, 1979. A superb history of the 1960s, focusing on social disorder, from the Greensboro sit-ins in 1960 to the shootings at Kent State University in 1970.

REFERENCE BOOKS

Albert, Judith Clavir, and Stewart Edward Albert. *The Sixties Papers: Documents of a Rebellious Decade*. New York: Praeger, 1984. Anthology combining narrative history with primary sources. Includes the writings of such figures as Norman Mailer, Martin Luther King, Jr., C. Wright Mills, Kate Millett, and Carl Olgesby, and has sections on civil rights, the SDS, the counterculture, and women's rebellion.

Bloom, Alexander, and Wini Breines, eds. *"Takin' It to the Streets": A Sixties Reader*. New York: Oxford University Press, 1995. An excellent, comprehensive, topically organized anthology of primary documents from periodicals, pamphlets, and speeches relative to the social, political, and cultural aspects of the 1960s.

Bronson, Fred. *Billboard's Hottest Hot 100 Hits: Facts and Figures About Rock's Top Songs and Song Makers*. New York: Billboard Publications, 1995. A year-by-year listing of rock 'n' roll's most popular songs and anecdotal, behind-the-scenes glimpses of the performers.

Buhle, Mari Jo, Paul Buhle, and Dan Georgakas, eds. *Encyclopedia of the American Left*. New York: Garland Publishing, 1990. An alphabetical listing of people and events associated with leftist radicalism in the United States.

DeLeon, David, ed. *Leaders from the 1960s: A Biographical Sourcebook of American Activism*. Westport, CT: Greenwood Press, 1994. Biographical profiles of activist leaders in the sixties.

Editors of Time-Life Books. *The Turbulent Years: The 60s*. Alexandria, VA: Time-Life Books, 1998. A pictorial history.

Hamilton, Neil A. *The 1960s Counterculture in America*. Santa Barbara, CA: ABC-CLIO, 1997. An encyclopedia of "who's who" and "what's what" in the counterculture. Each entry includes a brief bibliography.

Jackson, Rebecca. *The 1960s: An Annotated Bibliography of Social and Political Movements in the United States*. Westport, CT: Greenwood Press, 1992. A comprehensive compilation of sources organized according to subject. Topics include youth, protest, the counterculture, radicalism, Vietnam, and the year 1968.

Kleinfelder, Rita Lang. *When We Were Young: A Baby-Boomer Yearbook*. New York: Prentice-Hall, 1993. A wonderful year-by-year chronology of events, fads, fashions, music, movies, obituaries, and more.

McNeil, Alex. *Total Television: A Comprehensive Guide to Programming from 1948 to the Present*. New York: Penguin Books, 1980. Lists virtually every show since television began to appear in people's homes.

Miller, Albert, J. *Confrontation, Conflict, and Dissent: A Bibliography of A Decade of Controversy*. Metuchen, NJ: Scarecrow Press, 1972. The author organizes 1960s conflict-related material into the gender gap, student dissent, civil disobedience, and several other topics.

O'Neil, Doris C., ed. *Life: The 60s*. Boston: Little, Brown, 1989. Comprehensive pictorial narrative of the sixties. Includes photos of well-known political figures and vignettes from the civil rights movement, Vietnam, space program, counterculture, and antiwar demonstrations. Also includes such famous photographs as LBJ being sworn in after Kennedy's assassination, the Kent State coed kneeling over the body of a fellow student, and Gen. Loan executing a Vietcong terrorist.

Szatmary, David P. *Rockin' in Time: A Social History of Rock and Roll*. London: Schirmer Books, 1996. A reflective study of the evolution of rock 'n' roll.

FURTHER READINGS

The New Left

Bone, Christopher. *The Disinherited Children: A Study of the New Left and the Generation Gap*. New York: Schenkman Publishing Company, 1977. The author's premise is that the 1960s youth generation never felt the pride of having overcome an international depression and a world war. Rebellion in the sixties occurred, in part, because of a "spirited disinheritance" among young people.

Boskin, Joseph, and Robert A. Rosenstone, eds. "Protest in the Sixties." *Annals of the American Academy of Political and Social Science* 382 (March 1969). A collection of essays by noted scholars who discuss various aspects of the sixties protest movement, including the generation gap, antiwar movement, hippies, music, and the role of the federal government.

Breines, Winifred. *The Great Refusal: Community and Organization in the New Left, 1962–1968.* New York: Praeger, 1982. A member of the New Left at the University of Wisconsin provides a from-the-bottom-up history of the New Left's organizational structure, focusing on the activities of local chapters.

Burns, Stewart. *Social Movements of the 1960s: Searching for Democracy.* Boston: Twayne Publishers, 1990. A good narrative of activism in the sixties that examines the underlying currents of intellectual dissent, while considering the practical problems of trying to implement the popular concepts of an informed democracy.

Farber, David. *Chicago '68.* Chicago: University of Chicago Press, 1988. An examination of the chaotic Democratic National Convention told from the perspective of the Yippies, the National Mobilization Committee to End the War, and the police.

Flacks, Dick. "What Happened to the New Left?" *Berkeley Journal of Sociology* 33 (1988): 91–110. Scholarly analysis by a sociologist and political activist, who concludes that the collapse of the New Left was due largely to a conflict between the youth in the counterculture and the New Left.

Harrington, Michael. *The Other America: Poverty in the United States.* New York: Macmillan, 1962. A leading member of the radical League for Industrial Democracy and former social worker argues that the government largely ignored poor people and that poor people stay poor because they are poor.

Hayden, Tom. *Reunion: A Memoir.* New York: Random House, 1988. The primary author of *The Port Huron Statement* and the most famous of the sixties radicals recalls his involvement in the New Left.

Isserman, Maurice. *If I Had a Hammer . . . The Death of the Old Left and the Birth of the New Left.* New York: Basic Books, 1987. A historical treatment focusing on the late 1950s and early 1960s to trace the origins of the New Left, which, the author argues, emerged in the collapse of the Old Left.

Jacobs, Paul, and Saul Landau. *The New Radicals: A Report with Documents.* New York: Random House, 1966. A contemporary account of radicalism in the 1960s examining the origins of the New Left, the Student Non-Violent Coordinating Committee, and other groups. The documents section is especially useful.

Levitt, Cyril. *Children of Privilege: Student Revolt in the Sixties.* Toronto: University of Toronto Press, 1964. A conservative perspective by a sociologist on the New Left.

Miller, James. *Democracy is in the Streets: From Port Huron to the Siege of Chicago*. New York: Simon and Schuster, 1987. A former Students for a Democratic Society member analyzes the intellectual evolution of early SDS activists and traces how the SDS failed to deliver on the concept of "participatory democracy."

Rorabaugh, William J. *Berkeley at War: The 1960s*. New York: Oxford University Press, 1989. Draws on firsthand accounts of activists to examine the direct action tactics of the protest movement on the University of California–Berkeley campus.

Sale, Kirkpatrick. *SDS*. New York: Random House, 1993. Sale was the first historian to cull the SDS archives at the Wisconsin State Historical Society. Based on those files and interviews with SDS members, he discusses the influence of the civil rights movement, escalation of the Vietnam War, and liberalism on SDS.

Whalen, Jack, and Richard Flacks. *Beyond the Barricades: The Sixties Generation Grows Up*. Philadelphia: Temple University Press, 1989. A chronological study of student political activism based primarily on interviews with the participants.

The Antiwar Movement

Baritz, Loren. *Backfire: A History of How American Culture Led Us into Vietnam and Made Us Fight the Way We Did*. New York: Morrow, 1985. A very readable and provocative history of the cultural influences on American involvement in Vietnam and the opposition to the war at home.

Baskir, Lawrence M., and William A. Strauss, *Chance and Circumstance: The Draft, the War, and the Vietnam Generation*. New York: Alfred A. Knopf, 1978. Discusses the draft and the experiences of men who were not drafted, managed to escape the draft, left the country, or deserted.

Carper, Jean. *Bitter Greetings: The Scandal of the Military Draft*. New York: Grossman Publishers, 1967. A critical examination of how the Selective Service System operated the draft during the Vietnam War.

DeBenedetti, Charles. *An American Ordeal: The Antiwar Movement of the Vietnam Era*. Syracuse, NY: Syracuse University Press, 1990. An interpretative history of the antiwar movement assessing the Vietnam War's divisive effect on college campuses, churches, political elections, and families.

Garfinkle, Adam. *Telltale Hearts: The Origins and Impact of the Vietnam Antiwar Movement*. New York: St. Martin's Press, 1995. A good descriptive account of the protests against the Vietnam War and analysis of how they influenced policymakers.

Issacs, Arnold R. *Vietnam Shadows: The War, Its Ghosts, and Its Legacy*. Baltimore: Johns Hopkins University Press, 1997. A scholarly study of what Americans left behind in Vietnam. Topics discussed include the war's legacy, the controversy over the Vietnam Veterans' Memorial in Washington, D.C., and the class disparity between Americans who were killed in Vietnam and those who were not.

Lynd, Alice. *We Won't Go: Personal Accounts of War Objectors*. Boston: Beacon Press, 1968. An oral history of two dozen people who share their antiwar experiences.

Powers, Thomas. *The War at Home: Vietnam and the American People*. New York: Grossman Publishers, 1973. A historical treatment of opposition to the war, which, the author argues, forced President Lyndon B. Johnson to abandon his policy in Vietnam.

Zaroulis, Nancy, and Gerald Sullivan. *Who Spoke Up? American Protest Against the War in Vietnam, 1963–1975*. Garden City, NY: Doubleday, 1984. Examines the antiwar movement, arguing that it was unique in history because so many citizens protested against their government in a time of war, and suggests the protest movement was more successful than its leaders had anticipated.

The Counterculture

Brown, Joe David. *The Hippies*. New York: Time, 1967. A collection of essays addressing cultural disaffection in the 1960s by focusing on drugs, communes, music, and alternative lifestyles as part of the counterculture.

Feigelson, Naomi. *The Underground Revolution: Hippies, Yippies, and Others*. New York: Funk & Wagnalls, 1970. A useful examination of various counterculture elements who were part of the crisis in the nation's social and cultural order. The "others" include "drug prophets" such as Timothy Leary.

Goodman, Paul. *Growing Up Absurd: Problems of Youth in the Organized System*. New York: Random House, 1960. Examines disaffected youth on the eve of the sixties. Claims an inefficient capitalistic system paid more attention to prestige and profit than to people's needs. Goodman contends that education was a superficial concern during the cold war, and that youth needed a more worthwhile world to grow up in.

Kaiser, Charles. *1968 in America: Music, Politics, Chaos, Counterculture, and the Shaping of a Generation*. New York: Weidenfeld & Nicolson, 1988. A lively treatment and social history of arguably the most tumultuous year of the 1960s.

Lee, Martin A., and Bruce Shlain. *Acid Dreams: The CIA, LSD, and the Sixties Rebellion*. New York: Grove Press, 1985. The subtitle pretty much says it all. Chapters 6 and 7 are devoted to drugs and the counterculture.

Sorrell, Richard, and Carl Francese. *From Tupelo to Woodstock: Youth, Race, and Rock and Roll in America, 1954–1969*. Dubuque, IA: Kendall/Hunt Publishing Company, 1993. A social history of the youth movement in the 1950s and 1960s as viewed through rock 'n' roll. The authors illustrate how popular music reflected the chaos and political turmoil of the era.

Stevens, Jay. *Storming Heaven: LSD and the American Dream*. New York: Atlantic Monthly Press, 1987. A good account of how Timothy Leary helped to popularize LSD. Chapter 22 focuses on the counterculture.

Witmer, Peter O. *Aquarius Revisited: Seven Who Created the Sixties Counterculture That Changed America*. New York: Macmillan, 1987. Minibiographies of William Burroughs, Allen Ginsberg, Ken Kesey, Timothy Leary, Norman Mailer, Tom Robbins, and Hunter S. Thompson.

VIDEOS

General

America, Love It or Leave It. Really Good Stuff, Botchford, CT, 60 minutes, 1990. A look at the impact of draft dodgers, deserters, and political exiles during the Vietnam era.

Berkeley in the '60s. California Newsreel, 118 minutes, 1990. Chronicles student participation in the protest movements at Berkeley from the 1960 House Un-American Activities Committee in San Francisco to the 1969 People's Park confrontation. Fifteen former Berkeley radicals relate their experiences.

Bob & Carol & Ted & Alice. Columbia, 1969. A contemporary feature-length film in the comedy genre that depicts changing attitudes in the sixties about drug use and sexual permissiveness.

The Graduate. Avco, 1967. Anne Bancroft's seduction of Dustin Hoffman, who is trying to "find himself," symbolizes the generational gap and the alienation of the baby boomers.

Making Sense of the Sixties. PBS, six parts, 60 minutes each, 1991. A documentary series describing the tumultuous and confusing decade by using archival footage to examine the significance of the largest youth rebellion in American history.

1968: America Is Hard to See. Really Good Stuff, Botchford, CT, 88 minutes, 1991. Presents 1968 as a year that symbolizes the depth of changes that occurred in the sixties.

1968: The Year That Shaped a Generation. PBS, 60 minutes, 1998. A provocative documentary examination of the social and political shifts that occurred in the United States because of the youth rebellion.

Our World: It's About Time. ABC, 1986–1987. Focuses on a part of a year, using original footage and interviews with many of the subjects. The years 1961, 1963, 1968, 1969, and 1970 are particularly useful.

A Walk Through the 20th Century with Bill Moyers: Change, Change. PBS Video, 56 minutes, 1984. Journalist Moyers focuses on the impact of television, the Vietnam War, social unrest, and assassinations in presenting the 1960s as an era of rapid change.

Counterculture

Easy Rider. Columbia, 1969. In the cinematic anthem of the counterculture, a cult favorite in the 1990s, Dennis Hopper and Peter Fonda are drug-dealing hippies riding Harley-Davidson motorcycles in search of America.

Woodstock. Warner Brothers. 184 minutes, 1970. A documentary of the music festival that defined a generation.

Antiwar

Alice's Restaurant. Fox, 1969. Folk-rock singer Arlo Guthrie's re-creation of his experience spoofs the draft board, which disqualified him after he had been arrested for illegally dropping trash.

M*A*S*H. Fox, 1970. Donald Sutherland and Elliot Gould are doctors drafted during the Korean War in this thinly disguised and popular antiwar film released about the same time as the Kent State shootings. Neither the army nor the air force permitted the movie to be shown on their military installations.

WEB SITES

General

"Links to 1960s Sites." <http://vi.uh.edu/pages/buzzmat/60slinks.htm> Features documents and material on the Diggers, the Free Speech Movement, Woodstock, the Summer of Love, rock groups, and hippies.

"Welcome to the New Sixties." <http://www.sixties.net/> Offers links to numerous sixties events, including the space program, Woodstock, the Vietnam War, and fashions.

Counterculture

"Digger Archives." <http://www.diggers.org/> An on-going web project to preserve and present the history of guerrilla street theater.

"Old Hip's Groovy Hippie Links." <http://members.ayenet/-hippie/hippie/real-hip.htm> Has links to several hippie-related sites, including the Monterey Pop Festival, the Summer of Love, and Woodstock.

"The Psychedelic '60s." <http://www.lib.virginia.edu/exhibits/sixties/> Offers links to Ken Kesey, Timothy Leary, rock music, social protest, drugs, hippies, Woodstock, and several other sixties social-related topics.

"Woodstock: The Music Festival Home Page."<http://www.geocities. com.SunsetStrip/3869/woodstock.htm> Contains links to numerous articles dealing with almost every facet of 1969's "three days of love and peace."

Index

About the Author

JOHN C. McWILLIAMS is associate professor of history at Penn State University-DuBois. His special area of interest is American social-political history since World War II. He is author of *The Protectors: Harry J. Anslinger and the Federal Bureau of Narcotics, 1930–1962* (1990) and is currently working on a history of corrections in Pennsylvania.